SCOTT FORESMAN
Everyday Spelling

Authors

James Beers

Ronald L. Cramer

W. DorSey Hammond

PEARSON

Scott
Foresman

Editorial Offices: Glenview, Illinois • Parsippany, New Jersey
New York, New York
Sales Offices: Boston, Massachusetts • Duluth, Georgia
Glenview, Illinois • Coppell, Texas • Sacramento, California
Mesa, Arizona

ACKNOWLEDGMENTS

TEXT

p. 225: Illustration from *Peterson First Guide to Birds* by Roger Tory Peterson. Copyright © 1986 by Roger Tory Peterson. Reprinted by permission of Houghton Mifflin Company. All rights reserved. **p. 228:** Joke from *Puns, Gags, Quips, and Riddles* by Roy Doty. **p. 229:** "Knock-Knock" joke adapted by permission of Sterling Publishing Co., Inc., 387 Park Avenue South, New York, NY 10016 from *Knock Knock! Who's There?* by Joseph Rosenbloom. Copyright © 1984 by Joseph Rosenbloom.

ILLUSTRATIONS

Cover: Pablo Bernasconi; **pp. 12, 38, 64C, 90, 116:** Jared D. Lee; **pp. 12, 13, 15–17, 19, 20, 23, 24, 27–29B, 31, 32:** Maria Stroster; **pp. 14, 18, 21, 22, 25, 26, 29C, 30, 33, 34T:** Janinne Cabossel; **pp. 34B, 63C,BL,BR, 88TL, 139T, 140B, 167T, 171B, 212, 223B, 225, 226B, 227B:** Three Communication Design; **pp. 36T, 89T, 141B, 202, 203, 220B, 221B:** John Sanford; **pp. 37B, 174, 175, 194B, 195B, 202, 203:** Chris Sheban; **pp. 38–54, 57, 58, 60, 198B, 199T:** Brian Karas; **pp. 55, 56, 59:** Shelly Dietrichs; **pp. 63T,TL, 198, 199:** Leslie Cober; **pp. 64–86:** Susan Swan; **pp. 89B, 114TL,TR, 140T:** Paul Dolan; **pp. 90–112, 140T:** Steve Henry; **pp. 113T, 210LC, 211RC, 228C,B, 229T:** Lee Lee Brazeal; **p. 115BL:** Linda Kelen; **pp. 116–120, 122–124, 126–138:** Mary O'Keefe Young; **pp. 121, 125:** Joe Rogers; **p. 138B:** Susan Spellman; **pp. 142–164:** Mary Jones; **pp. 166B, 167B, 204C, 205T, 205C:** Scott McKowen; **p. 172R:** Ruta Daugaveitis; **pp. 178–179C:** Tom Bookwalter; **pp. 184LB, 196LC,LB, 197T:** Ka Botzis; **pp. 192T, 193:** John Burgoyne; **pp. 216C,B, 217T,C:** Steven Mach; **pp. 218, 219:** Lisa Adams; **pp. 222LC,LB, 223TR:** Harry Roolaart; **p. 223B:** Harvey House, Publishers; **p. 225:** Illustration from *Peterson First Guide to Birds* by Roger Tory Peterson, Copyright © 1986 by Roger Tory Peterson. Reprinted by permission of Houghton Mifflin Company. All rights reserved. **pp. 226CR, 227TR:** Joel Spector; **p. 297:** Dick Meier/Courtesy Los Angeles County Museum of Natural History; **p. 300:** Lance Paladino; **p. 303:** Evan Schwarze; **p. 305:** Cristine Mortensen; **p. 306:** Patricia Barbee; **p. 308:** *Carnival Athlete* by Camille Bombois/ Musee National d'Art Modern, Paris; **p. 309:** Don Dudley; **p. 310:** Carolyn Ewing

PHOTOGRAPHS

Every effort has been made to secure permission and provide appropriate credit for photographic material. The publisher deeply regrets any omission and pledges to correct errors called to its attention in subsequent editions.

Unless otherwise acknowledged, all photographs are the property of Scott Foresman, a division of Pearson Education.

Photo locators denoted as follows: Top (T), Center (C), Bottom (B), Left (L), Right (R), Background (Bkgd).

35 ©Gary Milburn/Tom Stack & Associates, Inc.; **62** ©Studio Tony Generico, LTD.; **112** ©Thomas D. W. Friedman/Photo Researchers, Inc.; **113** ©William McKinney/Photo Researchers, Inc.; **141** ©Alfred B. Thomas/Animals Animals/Earth Scenes; **165 (CL)** ©Alan Odie/PhotoEdit, **(BR)** ©Vic Bider/PhotoEdit; **166** ©Don & Pat Valenti Photography; **170** ©Mapping Specialists; **172** ©Woody Woodworth/ SuperStock; **173** ©Don & Pat Valenti Photography;

174 Adler Planetarium and Astronomy Museum; **181 (BR)** ©Katherine Wetzel/Museum of the Confederacy, Richmond, VA, **(TR)** Library of Congress; **186** ©David Fitzgerald/Getty Images; **188 (B)** ©Milt & Joan Mann/Cameramann International, Ltd., **(CL)** ©Wernher Krutein/Photovault; **189** ©Michael Krasowitz/Getty Images; **197** Hedrich Blessing; **206** Courtesy of 20th Century Fox; **208** ©Milt & Joan Mann/Cameramann International, Ltd.; **209 (B)** ©Comstock Inc., **(T)** ©Lori Adamski Pekk/Getty Images; **223** Advertisement for 'Ritter Road Skates', The Road Skate Company, London (color litho), English School (20th century)/Barbara Singer, Private Collection/Bridgeman Art Library; **229** ©Hulton Archive/Getty Images; **248** ©Radius Images/Jupiter Images; **249 (T)** ©Milt & Joan Mann/Cameramann International, Ltd., **(B)** United States Department of the Interior; **250** Daemmrich Photography; **252 (T)** ©Don & Pat Valenti Photography, **(B)** Library of Congress; **253 (T, B)** Daemmrich Photography; **255 (T)** Daemmrich Photography, **(B)** ©Phyllis Picardi/Stock Boston; **256 (T)** ©Bob Daemmrich/Daemmrich Photography, **(B)** ©John Elk III/Stock Boston; **259** Jupiter Images; **260** ©Ellis Herwig/Stock Boston; **261 (T)** ©Milt & Joan Mann/Cameramann International, Ltd., **(B)** ©Tim Barnwell/Stock Boston; **262 (B)** ©J. Patrick Forden Photography, **(T)** ©Roger Ressmeyer/Corbis; **263** ©Tom McHugh/Photo Researchers, Inc.; **264** Jupiter Images; **265** ©Aaron Haupt/Stock Boston; **266 (B)** Daemmrich Photography, **(T)** ©Chris Johns/National Geographic Image Collection; **268** Daemmrich Photography; **269** ©David Hiser/Getty Images; **270 (B)** ©Don & Pat Valenti Photography, **(T)** ©Dawson Jones/Stock Boston; **271 (T)** Gemmedia, **(B)** ©Charles Gupton/Getty Images; **272** ©Bruce Wellman/Stock Boston; **273** ©Bob Wallace/Stock Boston; **274** ©Charles Thatcher/Getty Images; **275** ©Owen Franken/Stock Boston; **276 (T)** ©Charles Feil/Stock Boston, **(B)** ©D. H. Hessell/Stock Boston; **277 (T)** ©Peter Menzell/Stock Boston, **(B)** Courtesy of WTTW, Chicago IL; **278** ©Raoul Hackel/Stock Boston; **280** ©Milt & Joan Mann/Cameramann International, Ltd.; **281** ©Paul Chesley; **282 (T)** ©Susan van Etten/ Index Stock Imagery, **(B)** ©Martin Rogers/Stock Boston; **283 (T)** ©Milt & Joan Mann/Cameramann International, Ltd., **(B)** ©John Elk III/Stock Boston; **284** ©Lawrence Migdale/Stock Boston; **285** ©Milt & Joan Mann/Cameramann International, Ltd.; **287 (B)** Los Alamos National Laboratory Imaging Services, **(T)** ©William Johnson/Stock Boston; **288** Corbis; **290** Official U.S. Naval Photograph; **291 (B)** ©Tim Barnwell/Stock Boston, ©Leo Ainsworth/ National Oceanic and Atmospheric Administration; **293** ©David Joel Photography, Inc.; **294** Grant Heilman Photography; **299** ©Tom & Pat Leeson/ Photo Researchers, Inc.

■ CONTENTS

UNIT 3

UNIT 5

■ CONTENTS

Cross-Curricular Lessons

■ CONTENTS

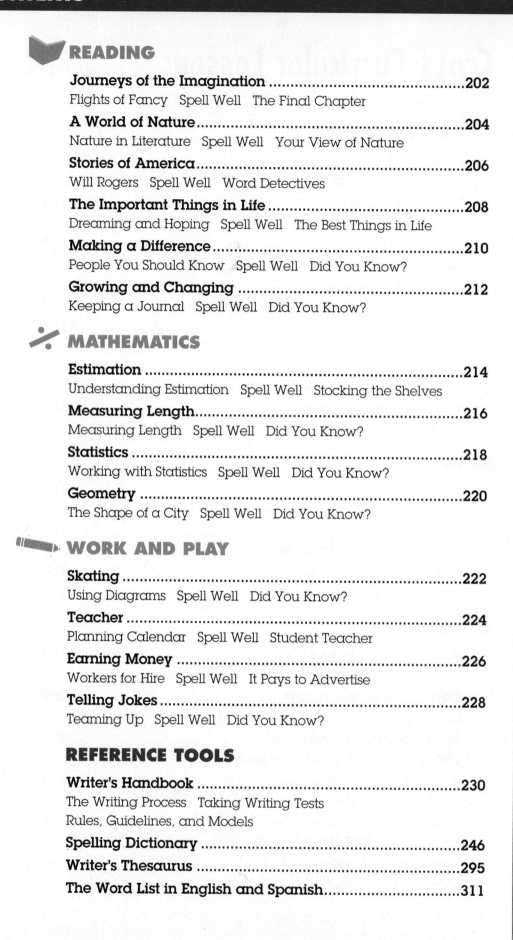

📗 READING

➗ MATHEMATICS

✏️ WORK AND PLAY

REFERENCE TOOLS

✳ FREQUENTLY MISSPELLED WORDS!

Lots of words on your spelling lists are marked with green asterisks ✳ These are the words that are misspelled the most by students your age.*

Pay special attention to these frequently misspelled words as you read, write, and practice your spelling words.

a lot	friend	we're	maybe	buy
too	they	everybody	said	Dad's
their	you're	Mom	there's	doesn't
there	friends	everyone	thought	everything
because	through	one	upon	except
favorite	were	went	usually	tried
that's	believe	decided	knew	and
finally	know	especially	sometimes	another
our	something	getting	want	clothes
they're	probably	Halloween	which	don't
it's	Christmas	off	caught	excited
really	to	always	let's	outside
different	when	whole	stopped	piece
where	didn't	happened	TV	school
again	heard	I'm	beautiful	
until	then	into	before	

* Research in Action is a research project conducted in 1990–1993. This list of frequently misspelled words is one result of an analysis of 18,599 unedited compositions. Words are listed in the order of their frequency of misspelling.

STRATEGY WORKSHOP

Steps for Spelling Problem Parts

REVIEW THE STEPS FOR SPELLING Review this step-by-step strategy for studying all spelling words.

1. **Look** at the word. **Say** it and listen to the sounds.
2. **Spell** the word aloud.
3. **Think** about the spelling. Look for anything special that you need to remember.
4. **Picture** the word with your eyes shut.
5. **Look** at the word and **write** it.
6. **Cover** the word and picture it. **Write** the word again and **check** its spelling.

DISCOVER THE PROBLEM PARTS STRATEGY If some words are still hard for you to spell, try the Problem Parts Strategy.

Think about the word.

Which part gives me problems?

Mark your problem part.

knot glasses

Picture the word. Focus on the problem part.

knot glasses

TRY IT OUT Practice the Problem Parts Strategy with words that gave another writer problems. Follow the directions on the next page.

Work with a partner or group. Find the four misspelled words in the paragraph below and write them correctly. Underline the part of each word that gave the writer problems. Use a dictionary if you need help.

I love action-packed mysterys. One I read was about a train reck near a mining camp in Colorado. The year was 1872. The train had jumped the tract and plunged off a brige.

Now practice the Problem Parts Strategy with your own personal words.

List four words you sometimes misspell. Be sure to spell them right. Underline the part of each word that gives you a problem. Picture the words. Focus on the problem parts.

Have your partner or group quiz you on your words. Then check the results. How did you do?

LOOK AHEAD Look through the list words in the next five lessons. Pick out four list words that look hard to spell. Write them and underline the part of each word that might give you a problem.

Words with sk, sp, st

SPELLING FOCUS

Some words have **blends** with two consonant sounds blended together: **ri<u>sk</u>**, **<u>sp</u>ider**, **<u>st</u>opped**.

✳
WATCH OUT FOR FREQUENTLY MISSPELLED WORDS!

■ **STUDY** Say each word and read the sentence.

1. *skinny* The **skinny** cat looked for milk.
2. *task* Your **task** is to make the bed.
3. *risk* She took a **risk** when she skydived.
4. *spider* A **spider** traps insects in a web.
5. *wasp* He was stung by a **wasp**.
6. *crisp* I like **crisp** crackers.
7. *stopped* ✳ A car **stopped** at the crossing.
8. *style* That is a new **style** of haircut.
9. *arrest* Police officers **arrest** criminals.
10. *suggest* An editor may **suggest** changes.

11. *skeleton* The adult **skeleton** has 206 bones.
12. *skunk* The **skunk** released a strong odor.
13. *brisk* A **brisk** wind turned the sailboat.
14. *spilled* Water **spilled** out of the bucket.
15. *spinach* The chef made a **spinach** salad.
16. *grasp* Please **grasp** the handlebars firmly.
17. *stumble* Young toddlers often **stumble**.
18. *statue* The sculptor molded a clay **statue**.
19. *boast* Undefeated teams often **boast**.
20. *adjust* I must **adjust** my bicycle seat.

CHALLENGE!

snakeskin
inspire
respect
frostbite
obstacle

■ **PRACTICE** Sort the list words by writing
- six words with **sk**
- eight words with **st**
- six words with **sp**

■ **WRITE** Choose ten words to write in sentences.

MEANING CLUES   Write the list word that answers each question.

1. Which word names a figure carved out of stone?
2. What is another word for *a chance of danger?*
3. Which word names an insect that flies and stings?
4. Which word describes crunchy food?
5. What is another word for *trip?*
6. What is one way to hold an object?
7. Which word describes a sharp wind?
8. Which word names a tiny animal that spins a web?
9. Which word names a framework of bones?
10. What is another word for *brag?*
11. Which word is a way to propose an idea?
12. Which word names a black-and-white animal?

HIDDEN WORDS   Each word below is hidden in a list word. Write the list word.

13. stop
14. just
15. ask
16. rest

17. sty
18. skin
19. spin
20. ill

FREQUENTLY MISSPELLED WORDS ✳ FREQUENTLY MISSPELLED WORDS ✳ FREQUENTLY MISSPELLED WORDS

Stopped is a frequently misspelled word because students often misspell it with one **p**. Spell *stopped* with two **p**'s like *hopped* and *popped*.

STRATEGIC SPELLING

Using the Problem Parts Strategy

21–24. Study the problem parts of words. Write four list words that are hard for you. Mark the part of each word that gives you problems and study it extra hard.

≡	Make a capital.
/	Make a small letter.
∧	Add something.
℮	Take out something.
⊙	Add a period.
¶	New paragraph

PROOFREAD AN OPINION Find four misspelled words in this opinion. Write them correctly. Fix two sentence errors.

My vote for best costume: *spiter*

Barney used to *baost* that he would win the Halloween costume contest. Today I saw his outfit. I just *stoped* and stared it's so original. He made it himself. He painted his face well, the legs must have been a tough *taske*. I think Barney ought to win.

PROOFREADING TIP

This voter wrote so many things about Barney that he forgot to stop at the end of a sentence. You can fix a run-on sentence with a period and a capital letter.

WRITE AN OPINION Vote for something you think is terrific. It can be a vehicle, dance, sport, or other item. Name it and explain your opinion. Try to use four list words.

My vote for best ___: ___

Word List

spider	skeleton	task	crisp
suggest	statue	spinach	adjust
boast	wasp	arrest	style
brisk	stopped	skunk	grasp
spilled	skinny	stumble	risk

Personal Words 1. ___ 2. ___

Review

CROSSWORD PUZZLE Complete the crossword puzzle by writing the word from the box that matches each definition.

| skinny |
| task |
| risk |
| spider |
| wasp |
| crisp |
| stopped |
| style |
| arrest |
| suggest |

Across

1. an insect with a powerful sting
4. thin, bony, slender
5. to take to jail
6. a chance of danger
7. a small, eight-legged animal
8. fashion

Down

2. offer an idea or thought
3. hard and thin, breaking easily with a snap
7. not moving, paused
9. a job

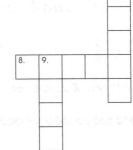

Word *Study*

SIMILES   At times, people use plain talk. At other times, people use word pictures such as similes. A **simile** compares two unlike things using the word *like* or *as.* Read the sentences below.

Plain Talk	Simile
That horse is thin.	That horse is as skinny as a snake.
The clouds have funny shapes.	The clouds look like dinosaurs.

Create your own similes for the sentences below. Don't forget to use *like* or *as.*

Plain Talk	Simile
1. The sand is hot.	____
2. The hills have many pine trees.	____

Words with ng, nk, th

SPELLING FOCUS

Some words have two consonants together that are pronounced as one sound: **strong**, **blank**, **north**.

■ **STUDY** Read each word and sentence.

**WATCH OUT FOR
FREQUENTLY
MISSPELLED
WORDS!**

1.	*strong*	Soccer players have **strong** legs.
2.	*nothing*	There is **nothing** in the jar but air.
3.	*everything* ✳	Put **everything** in the cabinet.
4.	*blank*	Use a sheet of **blank** paper.
5.	*trunk*	Don't overload the car **trunk.**
6.	*Thanksgiving*	We ate turkey on **Thanksgiving.**
7.	*they* ✳	The friends talk as **they** walk.
8.	*then* ✳	Write one, and **then** another.
9.	*north*	A compass needle points **north.**
10.	*there* ✳	He ran **there** and back just now.

11.	*clothing*	I wear warm **clothing** in winter.
12.	*among*	A flower grew **among** the weeds.
13.	*sting*	A bee **sting** can be painful.
14.	*hanger*	Put the ironed shirt on a **hanger.**
15.	*lightning*	The tree was struck by **lightning.**
16.	*chipmunk*	A **chipmunk** scurried up a tree.
17.	*shrink*	The sweater will **shrink** if washed.
18.	*without*	A car cannot run **without** fuel.
19.	*though*	We ran, **though** we were tired.
20.	*thought* ✳	I just **thought** of another answer.

CHALLENGE!

misunderstanding
strengthen
bankrupt
although
rhythm

■ **PRACTICE** Write four words that contain two or more of these pairs: **nk, th,** or **ng.** Then write
- four other words with **nk**
- seven other words with **th**
- five other words with **ng**

■ **WRITE** Choose two sentences to use in a paragraph.

CLASSIFYING Write the list word that belongs in each group below.

1. I, we, ___
2. mighty, powerful, ___
3. hook, rack, ___
4. Fourth of July, New Year's Day, ___
5. costume, dress, ___
6. bite, pinch, ___
7. here, where, ___
8. west, south, ___
9. squirrel, field mouse, ___
10. now, when, ___
11. hood, fender, ___

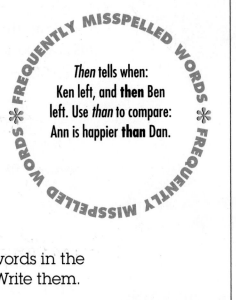

Then tells when:
Ken left, and **then** Ben
left. Use *than* to compare:
Ann is happier **than** Dan.

WORD SEARCH 12–19. Find the eight list words in the puzzle. They may be printed across or down. Write them.

```
t b e s h r i n k t
o l u t t h b o b h
o w i t h o u t l o
c o t o t w s h a u
e v e r y t h i n g
n t h o u g h n k h
o c s a m o n g r t
```

STRATEGIC SPELLING

Seeing Meaning Connections

Complete each phrase with a word from the box.

20. struck by ___
21. ran ___ up the stairs
22. batteries for a ___

Words with *light*
lightly
flashlight
lightning

≡	Make a capital.
/	Make a small letter.
∧	Add something.
℮	Take out something.
⊙	Add a period.
⁋	New paragraph

PROOFREAD DIRECTIONS The custodian at a school wrote these directions. Find the four misspelled words and write them correctly. Add three missing punctuation marks.

Red light! Read this now! Do not take books paper pencils, or folders out of this storage room with out a permission slip. Put the slip in the red box and than find a blannk form in the blue box. Fill it out. Write your name your teacher's name, and what you are taking. Keep everthing in order. Got it? Green light!

PROOFREADING TIP

Words or phrases in a series should be separated with commas. A series is a list such as *two books, lined paper, and some pencils.*

WRITE DIRECTIONS Think of a chore or job you might do at home or at school. Write directions so that someone else could do it. Use three list words and a personal word.

Word List

clothing	everything	nothing	among
sting	hanger	there	north
they	chipmunk	without	shrink
blank	then	Thanksgiving	though
lightning	trunk	thought	strong

Personal Words 1. ___ 2. ___

Review

PARAGRAPH COMPLETION Some words are missing in the paragraph below. Write the words from the box that complete the paragraph.

> strong
> nothing
> everything
> blank
> trunk
> Thanksgiving
> they
> then
> north
> there

Every November, during the week of (1), Wagner's Supermarket has a drawing for a twenty-pound turkey. Mom filled out the entry form by writing her name on the (2) line. She dropped it in a fish bowl located near the (3) east exit of the store. I bet (4) were at least 100 entries in the bowl. She smiled and (5) said, "We have (6) to lose." Just as we were putting (7) in the (8) of our car, Mr. and Mrs. Wagner came running out of the store. Together, (9) yelled, "Ms. Martinez, you've won this year's turkey drawing!" I had a (10) feeling we would win.

Using a Dictionary

PRONUNCIATION KEY Whenever you aren't sure how to pronounce a word, do these two quick checks in your dictionary.

Quick Check #1 Look at the pronunciation in the parentheses following the entry word.

Quick Check #2 Look at the pronunciation key. It tells you what sounds the symbols in the pronunciation stand for. The key is on most pages of a dictionary.

Pronunciation Key

a	hat	u̇	put
ā	age	ü	rule
ä	far, calm	ch	child
âr	care	ng	long
e	let	sh	she
ē	equal	th	thin
ėr	term	ᵺ	then
i	it	zh	measure
ī	ice		
o	hot	**ə stands for**	
ō	open	a	in about
ȯ	saw	e	in taken
ô	order	i	in pencil
oi	oil	o	in lemon
ou	out	u	in circus
u	cup		

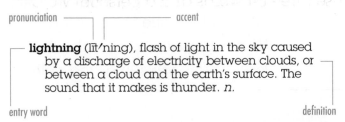

pronunciation ———— ———— accent

lightning (līt′ning), flash of light in the sky caused by a discharge of electricity between clouds, or between a cloud and the earth's surface. The sound that it makes is thunder. *n.*

entry word ———— definition

Use the dictionary entry and the pronunciation key to answer these questions.

1. What word in the key shows the sound /ī/?
2. How many syllables are in *lightning*?
3. Write the syllable that you say with more force.

Words with kn, mb, gh, st

SPELLING FOCUS

Sometimes two consonants together stand for only one sound: **kn**ew, nu**mb**, fas**t**en.

■ **STUDY**   As you say each word and sentence, study the spelling.

1.	knowledge	Her **knowledge** of chess is great.
2.	know ✳	I **know** how to add fractions.
3.	knew ✳	The actor **knew** all of his lines.
4.	numb	My toes were **numb** from the cold.
5.	bomb	The **bomb** exploded loudly.
6.	ghost	A **ghost** town is deserted.
7.	spaghetti	Taste my **spaghetti** and meatballs.
8.	Christmas ✳	December 25 is **Christmas** Day.
9.	listening	I was **listening** to the radio.
10.	fasten	Always **fasten** your seat belts.

11.	knead	Use your hands to **knead** dough.
12.	knitting	She is **knitting** woolen mittens.
13.	knapsack	The hiker carried a **knapsack.**
14.	tomb	The king is buried in a **tomb.**
15.	climber	A mountain **climber** must be fit.
16.	plumbing	Fix the kitchen sink's **plumbing.**
17.	aghast	I was **aghast** when I saw the fire.
18.	hustle	She had to **hustle** to get ready.
19.	mistletoe	We hung **mistletoe** over the door.
20.	whistling	People were **whistling** and yelling.

✳

WATCH OUT FOR FREQUENTLY MISSPELLED WORDS!

CHALLENGE!

- knickknacks
- ghetto
- glistened
- chestnut
- wrestling

■ **PRACTICE**   Sort the list by writing
- three words with **gh**
- six words with **kn**
- five words with **mb**
- six words with **st** in which the **t** is silent

■ **WRITE**   Choose two words to use in an advertisement.

RHYMES   Write the list word that rhymes with each word below. Underline each list word in which the rhyming part is spelled differently from the word it rhymes with.

1. plum
2. bead
3. zoom
4. sitting

5. most
6. timer
7. bustle
8. humming

DEFINITIONS   Write the list word that fits the definition.

9. bag, worn on the back, to carry things
10. slender sticks made of flour and water
11. tie, lock, or fix in place
12. trying to hear
13. making a shrill sound by using the teeth and lips
14. struck with surprise
15. plant with small, white berries
16. holiday on December 25
17. container filled with an explosive

STRATEGIC SPELLING

Seeing Meaning Connections

know
knew
knowledge

Use the related words from the box to complete the sentences.

Meg didn't (18) who lost the old, broken china doll, but she (19) it could be fixed. She had picked up this (20) from her Aunt Delia, whose hobby is restoring antique dolls.

Did You Know?
The word *spaghetti* comes from the Italian word meaning "cord." Can you see how spaghetti could remind someone of a cord?

☰	Make a capital.
/	Make a small letter.
∧	Add something.
ℯ	Take out something.
⊙	Add a period.
ℊ	New paragraph

PROOFREAD A SIGN When people put up a sign, they want the message to stand out, not a spelling mistake. Find the misspelled word. Write it correctly.

PROOFREADING TIP

Signs may be short, but they're not always easy to write. People often leave out letters and whole words on signs. Proofread before you post one.

CREATE A SIGN Create a new sign that advertises a special item at a different kind of restaurant. Don't use more than thirteen words.

Word List

knead	knew	hustle	ghost
numb	fasten	know	spaghetti
Christmas	aghast	mistletoe	whistling
knitting	listening	knowledge	knapsack
tomb	climber	bomb	plumbing

Personal Words 1. ___ 2. ___

Review

CONTEXT CLUES Use the context in each sentence to help you write the word. The word in the box answers the riddle: What are thousands of "meeters" that don't know anybody?

knowledge
know
knew
numb
bomb
ghost
spaghetti
Christmas
listening
fasten

1. Julie didn't ___ about the surprise party.
2. My dad enjoys ___ to sports on the radio.
3. The ___ of our team's loss caused sadness.
4. A ___ demolished the abandoned building.
5. The dentist had to ___ my gums.
6. You should always ___ your seat belt.
7. Al dressed up as a ___ for the costume party.
8. Our class ___ we were going to have a fire drill.
9. Monica's birthday is the same day as ___.
10. The twins loved ___ with meatballs.

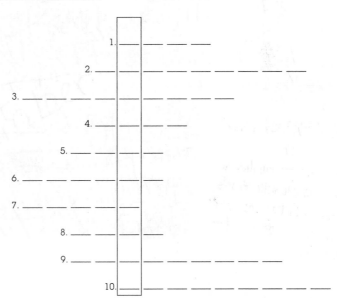

Using a *Thesaurus*

OVERUSED WORDS The following paragraph overuses the word *know*. Use the synonyms below from your Writer's Thesaurus to choose more exact words for *know*.

recognize
realize
understand

Tyrell and his older brother have to make his mother (1) <u>know</u> that they are old enough to take the city bus alone. This Saturday, kids ride for free. Their mother does not (2) <u>know</u> why the boys want to ride the city bus. She thinks they will get lost. Many of their friends take the city bus. Janet and Pete even (3) <u>know</u> some of the bus drivers.

Adding -s and -es

SPELLING FOCUS

Add **-s** to most words, but add **-es** to words that end with **sh, ch, s, ss,** or **x: bushes.** Change **y** to **i** and add **-es** to words ending with **consonant** and **y: companies.**

■ **STUDY** Notice whether **-s** or **-es** is added to each base word.

*

WATCH OUT FOR FREQUENTLY MISSPELLED WORDS!

month	1. *months*
friend	2. *friends* ✱
grade	3. *grades*
cowboy	4. *cowboys*
valley	5. *valleys*
match	6. *matches*
bush	7. *bushes*
pass	8. *passes*
battery	9. *batteries*
company	10. *companies*

donkey	11. *donkeys*
missile	12. *missiles*
costume	13. *costumes*
picture	14. *pictures*
morning	15. *mornings*
kiss	16. *kisses*
dress	17. *dresses*
bench	18. *benches*
speech	19. *speeches*
century	20. *centuries*

CHALLENGE!

eyebrows
ambulances
toothbrushes
trophies
secretaries

■ **PRACTICE** Sort the list words by writing
- three words in which **y** changed to **i**
- seven words to which just **-es** was added
- ten words to which just **-s** was added

■ **WRITE** Choose ten words to write in sentences.

WORD MATH Answer each problem with a list word.

1. lips + puckers + smacks = ___
2. hoofs + long ears + short manes = ___
3. skirts + sleeves + bodices = ___
4. sunrises + dawns + alarm clocks = ___
5. months + years + decades = ___
6. rockets + explosives + launchers = ___
7. seats + wood + legs = ___
8. leaves + berries + branches = ___
9. cells + electricity + currents = ___
10. masks + clothes + styles = ___

Did you finish with *ends* when you spelled *friends?*

WORD FORMS Write the plural forms of the words in parentheses.

11. Use (match) to light a fire.
12. Most (valley) have rivers running through them.
13. Men who herd cattle are called (cowboy).
14. Tracy caught three (pass) in today's game.
15. My parents work for different trucking (company).
16. Marks on a report card are (grade).
17. People we know and like are our (friend).
18. The governor and the mayor gave (speech).
19. Every year has twelve (month).
20. Photographs are (picture) taken with a camera.

STRATEGIC SPELLING

Building New Words

Use the rules you learned to add **-s** or **-es** to each word.

21. business
22. Christmas

23. risk
24. lady

≡	Make a capital.
/	Make a small letter.
∧	Add something.
ℓ	Take out something.
⊙	Add a period.
℀	New paragraph

PROOFREAD AN ADVERTISEMENT

Find the four misspelled words in the ad below and write them correctly. Fix three capitalization errors.

PROOFREADING TIP

Someone should have proofread this ad! Don't forget to capitalize all the important words in titles.

Join the fun!

The Old West festival of Rock creek

July 3, 4, and 5

See cow boys and cowgirls rope calves and ride broncos at the rodeo. Enjoy rides and games on the Grand midway. Get ther before 10 A.M. and you'll receive two free pases to the wrestling maches!

WRITE AN ADVERTISEMENT Ads are short, but they are packed with information. Write an ad for a festival, party, or parade in your town, church, or school. Use at least two list words and a personal word.

Word List

friends	costumes	bushes	cowboys
mornings	missiles	dresses	valleys
months	speeches	kisses	batteries
pictures	matches	passes	centuries
grades	benches	donkeys	companies

Personal Words   1. ___   2. ___

Review

TONGUE TWISTERS Write the word from the box that would best complete each tongue twister. Here's a clue: the answer will start with the same letter as the first word in each sentence.

months
friends
grades
cowboys
valleys
matches
bushes
passes
batteries
companies

1. Villains vacation in ___.
2. Calvin called the ___ collect.
3. Fred's ___ frown.
4. Molly's marathon is many ___ away.
5. Balls bounce in the ___.
6. Pat put the ___ in the pocket.
7. Calling ___ count the cattle.
8. Ben bargained for the ___.
9. Grandpa grinned because of my ___.
10. Misuse of ___ causes mishaps.

Multicultural *Connection*

ART The tribal costumes of each group of Native Americans have different styles and decorations. The Blackfeet, whose tribal homes were in Montana and Canada, used these designs on leggings and robes.

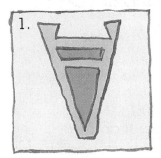

Read about the types of designs at the right. Which type fits each picture? Write the number of each picture and the type of design it represents.

Types of Designs

floral
resembling flowers

geometric
straight lines, circles, triangles

realistic
lifelike

Adding *-ed* and *-ing*, *-er* and *-est*

SPELLING FOCUS

Here are five things to remember when adding **-ed**, **-ing**, **-er**, and **-est**:

- Some base words do not change: **follow<u>ed</u>, follow<u>ing</u>**.
- If the base word ends with **e**, drop the **e**: **cut<u>er</u>, cut<u>est</u>**.
- In one-syllable words that end with **consonant-vowel-consonant**, double the final consonant: **big<u>ger</u>, big<u>gest</u>**.
- In words that end with **y**, the **y** is changed to **i** before adding **-ed**, **-er**, or **-est**: **tr<u>ied</u>, earl<u>ier</u>, earl<u>iest</u>**.
- In words that end in **y**, keep the **y** when adding **-ing**: **try<u>ing</u>**.

■ **STUDY** Look at the words in each column. Notice if the base word changes when different endings are added.

follow	1. *followed*	2. *following*
try	3. *tried* ✳	4. *trying*
cute	5. *cuter*	6. *cutest*
big	7. *bigger*	8. *biggest*
early	9. *earlier*	10. *earliest*

excite	11. *excited* ✳	12. *exciting*
wrap	13. *wrapped*	14. *wrapping*
amuse	15. *amused*	16. *amusing*
light	17. *lighter*	18. *lightest*
easy	19. *easier*	20. *easiest*

✳
WATCH OUT FOR FREQUENTLY MISSPELLED WORDS!

■ **PRACTICE** Sort the list words by writing
- five words in which the base word does not change when **-ed**, **-ing**, **-er**, or **-est** is added
- five words in which the **y** was changed to **i**
- four words in which the final consonant doubled
- six words in which the **e** was dropped

■ **WRITE** Choose five words to write in a paragraph.

CHALLENGE!

continued
wealthier
magnified
continuing
wealthiest
magnifying

OPPOSITES Write the words that complete the phrases.

1. not the darkest, but the ___
2. not leading, but ___
3. not giving up, but ___
4. not later, but ___
5. not smaller, but ___
6. not ugliest, but ___
7. not hardest, but ___
8. not uncovered, but ___

Take a Hint
Remember that *big* doesn't become *bigger* until it has two *g*'s.

WORD EXPANDING Write list words by adding the ending in parentheses to each word.

9. wrap (ing)
10. cute (er)
11. early (est)
12. amuse (ed)

13. light (er)
14. easy (er)
15. big (est)
16. excite (ing)

17. try (ed)
18. follow (ed)
19. amuse (ing)
20. excite (ed)

STRATEGIC SPELLING

Building New Words

Write the words that complete the chart. Remember what you learned.

Base word	-ed ending	-ing ending
21. chop	—	—
22. arrest	—	—
23. stumble	—	—

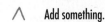
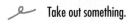

☰	Make a capital.
/	Make a small letter.
∧	Add something.
ℓ	Take out something.
⊙	Add a period.
¶	New paragraph

PROOFREAD A DESCRIPTION Kim's description has five misspellings. Correct them. Then fix three places where he used the wrong verb form.

PROOFREADING TIP

Kim used *gone* instead of *went*. Read the paragraph again to catch where he used the wrong forms of *be* and *see*.

> I thout we had plenty of pets, but now we have more. Madam had five kittens on an old quilt in the basement! I gone downstairs and watched the new family. The babies been tumbling all over Madam tring to feed. I seen one dozing under her chin. Madam is dark gray with stripes, but four kittens have liter fur. The dark one is the cutist and bigest.

WRITE A DESCRIPTION Close your eyes and think of a scene that you have experienced, or look around and think about what you see right now. Then write a description. Use at least four list words.

Word List

followed	lighter	following	lightest
amused	cuter	amusing	cutest
excited	bigger	exciting	biggest
wrapped	earlier	wrapping	earliest
tried	easier	trying	easiest

Personal Words 1. ___ 2. ___

Review

ANALOGIES   Write the word from the box that completes each analogy.

1. Pulling is to pushing as leading is to ___.
2. Last is to first as latest is to ___.
3. Shortest is to tallest as smallest is to ___.
4. Dirtiest is to cleanest as ugliest is to ___.
5. Dropping out is to joining as quitting is to ___.

CONTEXT   Write the list word that completes each sentence.

6. The mother goose led, the goslings ___.
7. Meg's little sister did not taste the stew. Meg ___ it.
8. The kittens were adorable, but the puppies were ___.
9. Jake wanted the smaller size, not the ___ one.
10. The sooner you leave, the ___ you will arrive.

followed
tried
cuter
bigger
earlier
following
trying
cutest
biggest
earliest

Word *Study*

WORDS FOR COMPARISONS   How are you at comparing things that are different sizes? Read the words. Under which head would you write each word? After you write your answers, discuss your choices with a partner.

house   slide   tepee   skyscraper   glider airplane
log   bear   spacesuit   flagpole   watermelon
hot-air balloon   ladder   elevator   rubber raft   pig

big   bigger   biggest

Review

Lesson 1: Words with sk, sp, st
Lesson 2: Words with ng, nk, th
Lesson 3: Words with kn, mb, gh, st

Lesson 4: Adding -s and -es
Lesson 5: Adding -ed and -ing, -er and -est

REVIEW WORD LIST

1. crisp
2. risk
3. skunk
4. spider
5. spinach
6. stopped
7. stumble
8. suggest
9. task
10. among
11. chipmunk
12. everything
13. lightning
14. nothing
15. strong
16. then
17. there
18. they
19. though
20. trunk
21. without
22. aghast
23. bomb
24. Christmas
25. climber
26. fasten
27. hustle
28. knew
29. know
30. mistletoe
31. numb
32. batteries
33. centuries
34. costumes
35. friends
36. kisses
37. missiles
38. months
39. mornings
40. passes
41. pictures
42. amused
43. biggest
44. earlier
45. earliest
46. exciting
47. lighter
48. thought
49. tried
50. wrapping

spider
chipmunk
strong
exciting
friends

STAMPS

**Ed designed stamps with messages.
Write the missing list words.**

USA 29¢

A (1) is one of our many animal (2).

In the (3) world of nature a silky (4) web is surprisingly (5). USA 19¢

Making Labels

passes
crisp
wrapping
costumes
without
spinach
suggest
mornings

Erin found lots of uses for the computer labels she makes. Write the missing words.

NATURE WORLD SHOW
This coupon is worth two free __(1)__ .

Don't complain about the rules; __(2)__ some new ideas!

THE LAKELAND HIKERS CLUB
meets on Thursday __(3)__ from 8-8:30.

Members of the
Hilltop Chorus
are selling __(4)__
paper for holiday
and birthday gifts.
Buy some today.

This bag contains __(5)__ that was picked on June 10 from the garden.

Put this box in the Drama Room. Contents: Pirate __(6)__ and swords.

We like the cereal to stay __(7)__ ! Don't put it away __(8)__ closing the box first.

Visitor at Camp

Write the missing list words in the poem.
trunk stopped skunk tried knew everything task

I did my __(1)__ at seven last night—

I loaded __(2)__ into the car.

I __(3)__ to do the job just right

But I left the __(4)__ ajar.

Well, I __(5)__ I was in trouble when

We were ready to drive to Lamar.

A nasty odor __(6)__ us then.

A __(7)__ had gotten inside the car!

Write the missing words to these weather fun facts.

there
lightning
biggest
fasten
lighter
batteries

There is enough **electricity** in one (1) flash to light up your house for a whole year.

The driest place in the world is the Atacama Desert in Chile. It didn't rain (2) for **400** years!

The (3) hailstone ever measured weighed **1.67** pounds.

To prepare for a hurricane, people often (4) boards over their windows. They buy extra food and (5) .

Warm, damp air is (6) than cold, dry air.

ANCIENT WEAPONS

Arthur wrote in his journal after a field trip.

Use the list words to complete the entry.

Before I went to the museum, I (1) that (2) were used only in modern times. To me a missile is a rocket or (3). Now I (4) that missiles have been used for (5). Some of the (6) ones were sticks, stones, arrows, and boomerangs. Even (7) the early missiles didn't use explosives, (8) could go a long way to hit a target.

know
they
centuries
earliest
missiles
though
thought
bomb

Mountain Adventure

Write the list words that complete this conversation.

Grant: What would you like to be?

Shelly: I want to be a rock __(1)__. I've been taking classes for two __(2)__. You should come to a class with me.

Grant: No, thanks. I am not __(3)__ by that sport, and I don't want to __(4)__ my life.

Shelly: Don't worry! Kids always go with adult climbers. There's __(5)__ to be afraid of. Give it a try.

Grant: No! I know I'd __(6)__ and fall. Besides, heights make me __(7)__ with terror.

Shelly: Ropes protect us. We don't hurry or __(8)__. Now, how about it?

Grant: OK! I'll go. I won't climb, but I will take __(9)__ !

stumble
pictures
nothing
numb
risk
months
climber
hustle
amused

Holiday Legend

Write the list words that complete this tag.

then
kisses
Christmas
earlier
among
mistletoe
aghast

The plant you have just bought to hang in your home is __(1)__. Did you think this was only a __(2)__ custom?

A Norse legend tells us that the custom started __(3)__. In the story, a boy was killed by an arrow made from mistletoe. His mother, a goddess, was __(4)__ at his death. The gods talked __(5)__ themselves and decided to bring the boy back to life. The happy goddess __(6)__ decreed that mistletoe should be a plant of peace, and people who meet under it should exchange __(7)__.

STRATEGY WORKSHOP

Divide and Conquer

DISCOVER THE STRATEGY You can conquer long words by dividing them into short parts. Study the words part by part and then put them back together. Here are three different ways to divide and conquer words.

Divide long words into syllables.	Divide them into prefixes, suffixes, and base words.	Divide compounds into their base words.

TRY IT OUT Now practice the strategy.

1. Divide into Syllables You often can hear the syllables when you say a word. A syllable is a word or part of a word that you say as a unit. You can divide most long words into syllables.

Write *spaghetti, excellent, knowledge,* and *Christmas.* Say each word and listen for the syllables. Then divide each word into syllables. Use a dictionary to check words you're not sure of.

2. Separate Prefixes and Suffixes Separate the base word from its prefix or suffix. You'll notice if the base word's spelling was changed.

Work with a partner. Write *disagree, happiness, beautiful,* and *invisible.* Draw lines between each base word and any prefixes or suffixes. Look at the words. Notice that the spelling of two base words changed when the suffix was added. Underline those words.

3. Split Compounds If the word is a compound, divide it where the two words were joined. You will see that neither word was changed.

Write these compounds: *without, everything, Thanksgiving,* and *earrings.* Draw a line between the two base words that make up each compound.

Write *everyone, happily, mornings,* and *eyelashes.* Say the words to yourself. Divide each into smaller pieces. For each word, choose the way that works best for you. Compare your words with a partner's. Did your partner divide some words differently?

LOOK AHEAD Look ahead at the next five lessons. Write four list words that are long and look hard to spell. Then divide each word into parts.

Using Just Enough Letters

SPELLING FOCUS

Pronouncing a word correctly and picturing how it looks can help you avoid writing too many letters.

■ **STUDY** Read each word. Notice how it looks and sounds and how many letters it has.

WATCH OUT FOR FREQUENTLY MISSPELLED WORDS!

1.	*until* ✽	I waited **until** you were ready.
2.	*went* ✽	Yesterday we **went** bowling.
3.	*enough*	Two cookies are **enough** for me.
4.	*TV* ✽	We watched a news report on **TV.**
5.	*one* ✽	Only **one** student was absent.
6.	*didn't* ✽	The puppy **didn't** like its food.
7.	*a lot* ✽	The job needed **a lot** of workers.
8.	*want* ✽	I **want** to give you my new address.
9.	*doesn't* ✽	It **doesn't** matter if you stay or go.
10.	*always* ✽	Clowns **always** make me laugh.

11.	*necklace*	The gold **necklace** sparkled.
12.	*exact*	He measured the **exact** length.
13.	*burglar*	The **burglar** stole a stereo.
14.	*equipment*	Skydivers use safety **equipment.**
15.	*chimney*	Smoke went up the **chimney.**
16.	*exist*	Animals need food to **exist.**
17.	*rumbling*	We heard the **rumbling** of thunder.
18.	*upon* ✽	Divers depend **upon** each other.
19.	*athlete*	The **athlete** trained for the race.
20.	*examine*	I'll **examine** the X ray carefully.

CHALLENGE!

sherbet
icicles
pajamas
explode
chlorine

■ **PRACTICE** First, write the words that are easiest for you to spell correctly. Then write the words that are most difficult for you to spell correctly.

■ **WRITE** Choose ten words to write in sentences.

DEFINITIONS Write the list word that matches the clue. The word in the box answers the riddle "What kind of tale will never be a best seller?"

1. does not
2. accurate
3. up to the time when
4. have life; live
5. much or many
6. a single person or thing
7. did not
8. at all times; every time
9. string of jewels or beads
10. supplies

1. _ _ _ _ _ _
2. _ _ _ _ _
3. _ _ _ _ _
4. _ _ _ _ _
5. _ _ _ _
6. _ _ _
7. _ _ _ _
8. _ _ _ _ _
9. _ _ _ _ _ _ _ _
10. _ _ _ _ _ _ _ _

TONGUE TWISTERS Write the list word that would best complete each tongue twister. Here's a clue: the answer will start with the same letter as the first word in each sentence.

11. Enormous elephants eat ___.
12. Wiggly worms ___ westward.
13. Rolling rocks made a ___ roar.
14. Where would Wanda ___ to wander?
15. Terry turned on the ___ twenty times.
16. Ursa is unwilling to ride ___ a unicorn.

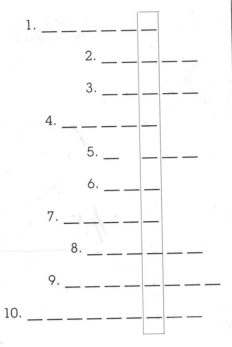

FREQUENTLY MISSPELLED WORDS

If you shorten *did not* and *does not* to *didn't* and *doesn't*, you must use apostrophes. You must also pronounce the new words differently.

STRATEGIC SPELLING
The Divide and Conquer Strategy

17–20. Spell long words part by part. Write *examine*, *burglar*, *athlete*, and *chimney*. Draw lines to break them into smaller parts. Study the parts.

≡	Make a capital.
/	Make a small letter.
∧	Add something.
ℰ	Take out something.
⊙	Add a period.
¶	New paragraph

PROOFREAD INSTRUCTIONS Find the five misspelled words in the instructions below and write them correctly. Fix three punctuation errors.

PROOFREADING TIP

Oops! There's an exclamation mark at the end of a question. Check that periods, question marks, and exclamation marks end the correct kinds of sentences.

Do you whant to make your dog a coat! It's easy. It dosen't cost alot? Use this equiptment:

iron-on tape	needle
large snap	thread
scissors	pins

You also need enought thick fabric to cover the dog's back and sides?

WRITE INSTRUCTIONS Write instructions for a project. It might involve building, drawing, sewing, painting, or something else. Start by telling what your project is and what supplies are needed. Use three list words.

Word List

a lot	always	doesn't	upon
until	exact	enough	rumbling
necklace	burglar	didn't	chimney
athlete	went	TV	examine
exist	one	want	equipment

Personal Words   1. ___ 2. ___

Review

POEM Write the word from the box that completes the poem.

Ian (1) like to play outside, read joke books, or take a ride.
What he really enjoyed was watching (2).
Home from school, there he would be, in front of the television, staring endlessly.
It was (3) turned on, if Ian was there. He even sat in the very same chair.
Day after day, Ian turned into a bore. (4) (5) day his parents said, "(6), no more!
We (7) you to play and make (8) of friends.
Invent silly games and set new trends.
(9) this sound great? Please, turn it off before it's too late!"
To his parents' amazement, off the TV (10).

until
went
enough
TV
one
didn't
a lot
want
doesn't
always

Word *Study*

EXACT WORDS The meaning of equipment is "supplies" or "outfit," but many specific things can be called *equipment*. Look at some of the equipment that a construction worker uses. Then list five pieces of equipment that a cook uses.

Backhoe

Hard hat

Drill

Gloves

Construction Worker

Short e and Long e

Short **e** can be spelled **ea** and **ai**: h<u>ea</u>vy, s<u>ai</u>d.
Long **e** can be spelled **ee** and **ie**: degr<u>ee</u>, p<u>ie</u>ce.

■ **STUDY** Say each word. Find the letters that stand for the vowel sound you hear in **said** or **thief.**

**WATCH OUT FOR
FREQUENTLY
MISSPELLED
WORDS!**

1.	*heavy*	The crate was too **heavy** to lift.
2.	*ahead*	Our group leader walked **ahead.**
3.	*measure*	I'll **measure** the width of the room.
4.	*already*	We **already** walked on this path.
5.	*said* ✳	The student **said** the answer aloud.
6.	*again* ✳	He looked at the directions **again.**
7.	*degree*	She earned a college **degree.**
8.	*cheese*	We served **cheese** and crackers.
9.	*goalie*	He is the **goalie** on a soccer team.
10.	*piece* ✳	One **piece** of the puzzle is lost.

11.	*jealous*	I was **jealous** of his new car.
12.	*meadow*	Flowers bloomed in the **meadow.**
13.	*weapon*	A rifle is one kind of **weapon.**
14.	*against*	He pushed **against** the heavy door.
15.	*succeed*	Hard work helped her **succeed.**
16.	*Halloween* ✳	His **Halloween** costume is a dragon.
17.	*breeze*	The cool **breeze** felt good.
18.	*believe* ✳	I **believe** you are telling the truth.
19.	*thief*	He stopped the **thief** from stealing.
20.	*chief*	The police **chief** praised her officers.

CHALLENGE!

treasurer
breaststroke
dungarees
speedometer
windshield

■ **PRACTICE** Sort the list by writing
- five words with **long e** spelled **ee**
- five words with **long e** spelled **ie**
- three words with **short e** spelled **ai**
- seven words with **short e** spelled **ea**

■ **WRITE** Choose two sentences to use in a paragraph.

ANALOGIES   Write the list word that completes each analogy.

1. Baseball is to catcher as soccer is to ___ .
2. Sand is to desert as grass is to ___ .
3. Vegetable is to carrot as dairy product is to ___ .
4. Ruler is to inch as thermometer is to___ .
5. Flag is to Fourth of July as costume is to ___ .

WORD FORMS   Write the list words that are the base words for the following.

6. believer
7. apiece
8. heavier
9. succeeding
10. jealousness
11. weaponry
12. measurement
13. chieftain

BEFORE AND AFTER   Write the list word that begins and ends with the same letters as each word below.

14. alley ___
15. agreement ___
16. adorn ___
17. tiff ___
18. salad ___
19. brave ___

STRATEGIC SPELLING

Seeing Meaning Connections

Write the words from the box that fit the clues below.

Words with *head*
headache
forehead
ahead

20. When you frown, you give me wrinkles.
21. When you ride your bike, you should look my way.
22. I give people a pain.

=	Make a capital.
/	Make a small letter.
∧	Add something.
℮	Take out something.
⊙	Add a period.
⁋	New paragraph

PROOFREAD AN ANNOUNCEMENT

Nate wrote this announcement to read to the class. Find the five misspelled words and write them correctly. Fix three careless errors.

PROOFREADING TIP

Reading a draft aloud is an easy way to find careless mistakes. Proofread this announcement by reading it softly aloud. You'll hear the problems.

Yesterday, the Hulks played aginst the Stars in soccer. The final score 2–1. Rita Ori scored two goals in the first quarter, and the Hulks stayed a head for the rest the game. The Stars' captain siad, "Our regular goaly was out. It was just the first game of season. When we pay the Hulks again, we'll win."

WRITE AN ANNOUNCEMENT

Write an announcement telling about a game, activity, or project that you saw or participated in. Use three spelling words.

Word List

goalie	breeze	heavy	meadow
believe	chief	measure	again
succeed	degree	already	jealous
thief	piece	said	weapon
Halloween	cheese	ahead	against

Personal Words   1. ___   2. ___

Review

MAKING INFERENCES Write the word from the box
that fits each clue.

1. To repeat something is to do it this way.
2. There was only one of these left in the pie tin.
3. If something is not light in weight, it is this.
4. Most pizzas come with this ingredient on them.
5. My sister is away at college, earning one of these.
6. The person who plays this position blocks the goals.
7. They had to do this to make sure the piano would fit.
8. Jim couldn't hear what was this.
9. The score was six to one; we were this in the game.
10. If something is done beforehand, it's done this way.

heavy
ahead
measure
already
said
again
cheese
degree
goalie
piece

Using a *Dictionary*

FINDING THE RIGHT MEANING An entry word
in a dictionary can have more than one meaning. Read
the meanings of *piece* below.

> **piece** (pēs), **1** portion, limited part; small quantity:
> *a piece of bread.* **2** a single thing of a set or class.
> **3** single composition in art or music. **4** join the
> pieces of 1—3, *n.,* 4, *v.*

One entry word may be used as a noun, verb, or other part
of speech. Notice the abbreviations at the end of the entry.
They tell you which definitions are nouns or verbs.

Write the number that answers each question.

1. Which definition of *piece* is Alicia using? ___

2. Which definition of *piece* is
   Khanh using? ___

3. Which definition of
   piece is Jim using? ___

Short Vowels a, i, o, u

SPELLING FOCUS

Short **a** is usually spelled **a: <u>a</u>nd**. Short **i** can be spelled **e: b<u>e</u>fore**. Short **o** is usually spelled **o: pr<u>o</u>blem**. Short **u** can be spelled **u** and **oo: sw<u>u</u>ng, bl<u>oo</u>d.**

■ **STUDY** Say each word and study its spelling.

WATCH OUT FOR FREQUENTLY MISSPELLED WORDS!

1.	*past*	She likes to remember the **past.**
2.	*and* ✳	Please pass the salt **and** pepper.
3.	*perhaps*	**Perhaps** we can meet tomorrow.
4.	*before* ✳	Check the water **before** you dive.
5.	*possible*	It's **possible** to cure the disease.
6.	*solve*	We used clues to **solve** the mystery.
7.	*problem*	This math **problem** is difficult.
8.	*swung*	The monkey **swung** on a rope.
9.	*because* ✳	Practice ended **because** of rain.
10.	*blood*	The injured man lost a lot of **blood.**

11.	*accident*	Breaking the glass was an **accident.**
12.	*adventure*	She told a great **adventure** story.
13.	*decided* ✳	I **decided** on wallpaper, not paint.
14.	*pretend*	Let's **pretend** to be astronauts.
15.	*belong*	We **belong** to the math club.
16.	*lobster*	A **lobster** has claws and a shell.
17.	*python*	The **python** squeezed its prey.
18.	*jungle*	It was hot and humid in the **jungle.**
19.	*shuttle*	We rode a **shuttle** to the airport.
20.	*flood*	Heavy rains caused the **flood.**

CHALLENGE!

asphalt
avalanche
betray
monopoly
umbrella

■ **PRACTICE** Sort the words by writing
- five words with the **short a** sound spelled **a**
- five words with the **short o** sound spelled **o**
- five words with the **short u** sound spelled **u** or **oo**
- five words with the **short i** sound spelled **e**

■ **WRITE** Choose a sentence to write a slogan.

WORD MATH Complete each equation to make a list word.

1. besides – sides + fore = ___
2. decimal – mal + ded = ___
3. belief – ief + ong = ___
4. possum – um + ible = ___
5. pretty – ty + end = ___
6. became – me + use = ___
7. ape – pe + nd = ___
8. perfume – fume + haps = ___
9. sweep – eep + ung = ___

Take a Hint
Past means "time gone by" in this sentence: "In the *past,* people used horses instead of cars." Since *past* has a **t,** link it in your mind with *time* and don't write *passed* by mistake.

CLASSIFYING Write the list word or words that belong in the categories below.

vehicle	traffic problem	woodland
van	*crash*	*forest*
10. ___	13. ___	16. ___

animal	math	history
		ago
11. ___	14. ___	17. ___
12. ___	15. ___	

STRATEGIC SPELLING

Seeing Meaning Connections

Write the list word that completes each sentence. The underlined word is a clue. Circle the letters that are the same in both words.

18. People are going in the <u>bloodmobile</u> to donate ___.
19. <u>Adventurous</u> people enjoy risk and ___.
20. <u>Floodwater</u> covered the field after the ___.

☰	Make a capital.
/	Make a small letter.
∧	Add something.
℮	Take out something.
⊙	Add a period.
¶	New paragraph

PROOFREAD A BLURB A blurb tells a little about a story to make you want to read more. Correct the five misspellings in Lee's blurb. Fix three punctuation errors.

Pati, a playful young monkey, has a grown-up problem. He must find fruit in the jungul treetops for his injured mother. Pati is a good climer, but he is afraid of the pithon and the anaconda. As he hides near his mother, a parrot lands on a limb nearby. It is posible to save your mother," she squawks. Listen to me!

PROOFREADING TIP

Lee wrote the parrot's exact words, but he didn't mark them right. Mark the beginnings and endings of quotations in your writing.

WRITE A BLURB Either write a blurb about a story you liked or tell about a time when you were afraid. Tell only a little of the story—enough to make the reader want more. Use four list words and a personal word.

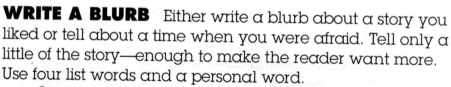

Word List

adventure	problem	shuttle	belong
past	lobster	flood	because
accident	solve	swung	before
perhaps	python	blood	pretend
and	possible	jungle	decided

Personal Words 1. ___ 2. ___

Review

SYNONYMS IN CONTEXT   Write a word from the box that means about the same as the underlined word or phrase in each sentence.

past
and
perhaps
before
possible
solve
problem
swung
because
blood

1. The nurse drew <u>red liquid</u> from the patient's vein.
2. Mitch arrived <u>earlier than</u> the rest of us.
3. The tire tied to the tree <u>moved back and forth</u>.
4. Darvin bought pens <u>in addition to</u> pencils.
5. Belinda had to <u>find the answers to</u> the puzzle.
6. If we try, anything is <u>within our reach</u>.
7. History is the study of the <u>time gone by</u>.
8. The timing had created <u>a difficulty</u>.
9. <u>It may be that</u> you had the wrong number.
10. <u>Since</u> the weather was nice, we didn't wear jackets.

Word *Study*

WORDS AT WORK   Words are the tools that can be used for different jobs. Read this traveler's words. Notice that the person uses *shuttle* to do the job of both a noun and a verb.

Change the job that these nouns do by using them as verbs in sentences. The first one is done for you.

1. bus   We're busing downtown to see a movie.

2. rocket

3. ship

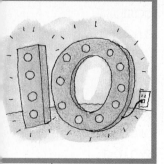

Long Vowels a, i, o

SPELLING FOCUS

Long **a** can be spelled **ai** and **a**: **brain**, **favorite**. Long **i** is often spelled **i-consonant-e**: **slide**. Long **o** can be spelled **ow** and **o-consonant-e**: **owner**, **whole**.

■ **STUDY** Say each word and listen for the **long a, i,** or **o** sound. Read the sentence.

❋
WATCH OUT FOR FREQUENTLY MISSPELLED WORDS!

1. brain — The hard skull protects the **brain.**
2. main — I knew the **main** idea of the story.
3. favorite ❋ — Cherry pie is my **favorite** dessert.
4. stranger — We didn't know the **stranger.**
5. sidewalk — Please don't skate on the **sidewalk.**
6. slide — Our car began to **slide** on the ice.
7. bowling — She went to the **bowling** alley.
8. owner — He returned the cat to its **owner.**
9. whole ❋ — I cleaned my **whole** room today.
10. globe — We found the equator on the **globe.**

11. claim — Did anyone **claim** the lost dog?
12. complain — Don't **complain** about the weather.
13. aliens — The story is about **aliens** from Mars.
14. vacation — We planned a summer **vacation.**
15. survive — People need water to **survive.**
16. crime — Stealing is a serious **crime.**
17. arrow — They hunted with bow and **arrow.**
18. snowball — I threw a **snowball** at the tree.
19. antelope — An **antelope** looks like a deer.
20. slope — The ski **slope** was icy and steep.

CHALLENGE!

campaign
radiation
requirement
postpone
casserole

■ **PRACTICE** Sort the list words by writing
- eight words with **long a** spelled **a** or **ai**
- four words with **long i** spelled **i-consonant-e**
- eight words with **long o** spelled **ow** or **o-consonant-e**

■ **WRITE** Choose ten words to write in sentences.

ANALOGIES Write the list word that completes each sentence.

1. Ribs protect the lungs. The skull protects the ___.
2. You play tennis on a court. You go ___ in an alley.
3. Drivers use the street. Walkers use the ___.
4. You row along a river bend. You climb a mountain ___.
5. A clock hand shows the time. An ___ shows direction.
6. To obey the law is right. To commit a ___ is wrong.
7. A rectangle has square corners. A ___ of the Earth is round.
8. An ostrich has two legs. An ___ has four legs.

Take a Hint
Don't confuse *main* and *mane*. Remember *main* this way: The m**ai**n door is **in** the front. *Mane* with **ne** is the hair on a horse's **neck**.

WORDS IN CONTEXT Write the list word that is missing from each person's statement.

9. Explorer: "I carry supplies so I can ___ in any climate."
10. Minister: "Let's welcome this ___ to our church."
11. Columbus: "I ___ that the land I found belongs to Spain."
12. Animal Lover: "I want to be the ___ of some gerbils."
13. Newcomer: "Where is the ___ street of this town?"
14. Diner: "I can't believe I ate that ___ pie!"
15. Author: "I write about ___ from other planets."
16. Mother: "Don't throw an icy ___ at anyone."
17. Artist: "My ___ things to paint are flowers."

Building New Words

Write the base words *vacation, slide,* and *complain.* Add the suffix **-er** to make a new word. **Remember:** When **-er** is added to a word ending in **e,** drop the **e.**

Base word	-er ending
18. ___	___
19. ___	___
20. ___	___

≡	Make a capital.
/	Make a small letter.
∧	Add something.
ℓ	Take out something.
⊙	Add a period.
¶	New paragraph

PROOFREAD A LETTER Emily wrote to complain about a toy. Find five misspelled words and three handwriting errors. Write the words correctly.

I am returning this water slid to your company. It broke the first time I used it! I folod the instructions. I didn't use it on the sidewalk. Please send me a new one befor vaction ends.

Emily Cisneros
844 Oak Street
Paso Robles, CA 93446

PROOFREADING TIP

If Emily wants the company to understand the problem, she needs to form her letters clearly. Did you notice why *your* and other words are hard to read?

WRITE A LETTER Write a letter to the manufacturer of something you bought. You can compliment the company or complain. Use two spelling words and a personal word.

Word List

slide	aliens	main	bowling
snowball	favorite	slope	brain
vacation	antelope	owner	claim
stranger	complain	crime	survive
whole	globe	sidewalk	arrow

Personal Words 1. ___ 2. ___

Review

CROSSWORD PUZZLE Use the clues to help you fill in the puzzle with the words from the box.

brain
main
favorite
stranger
sidewalk
slide
bowling
owner
whole
globe

Across

4. to move smoothly
5. the mind
6. an unknown person
8. the entire thing
9. a sphere with a map of the Earth

Down

1. liked better than the others
2. most important
3. where pedestrians walk
5. a game with a ball and pins
7. the one who owns

Multicultural *Connection*

SHELTERS People build different kinds of shelters in order to survive.

Write a sentence telling how you would solve each problem about shelters. Use the words at the right.

Problem: You live in a farmhouse in South Africa. How do you protect your home from the hot sun and still let in the breezes?

1. **Solution:** ___

Problem: You live in Indonesia. You need to protect your home from the heavy rains that flood the ground during certain seasons.

2. **Solution:** ___

insulation packing material that keeps heat, sound, or electricity from escaping

stilts long poles that raise a house above the ground

veranda a large porch, with open sides and a roof

55

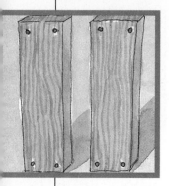

Vowel Sounds in rule, use, off

■ **STUDY**   Read each word and sentence.

WATCH OUT FOR FREQUENTLY MISSPELLED WORDS!

1.	*choose*	Please **choose** soup or salad.
2.	*school* ✳	I now attend middle **school.**
3.	*threw*	The catcher **threw** the baseball.
4.	*crew*	The ship's **crew** went ashore.
5.	*drew*	He **drew** a picture in art class.
6.	*future*	No one can predict the **future.**
7.	*music*	Soft **music** can be very soothing.
8.	*usually* ✳	I **usually** read one hour each day.
9.	*taught*	The dancer **taught** us a new step.
10.	*laundry*	My dirty **laundry** must be washed.

11.	*broom*	He used a **broom** to sweep the floor.
12.	*scoop*	Use a shovel to **scoop** out the dirt.
13.	*booth*	We waited at the ticket **booth.**
14.	*jewel*	The large **jewel** sparkled.
15.	*humor*	Her sense of **humor** made us laugh.
16.	*Utah*	We hiked in the mountains of **Utah.**
17.	*naughty*	The **naughty** child broke a window.
18.	*daughter*	He has one **daughter** and no sons.
19.	*sausage*	I like **sausage** with my eggs.
20.	*launch*	They will **launch** a rocket at noon.

CHALLENGE!

igloo
mildew
accumulate
slaughter
applause

■ **PRACTICE**   Sort the list words by writing
- nine words which have a vowel sound spelled **oo** or **ew**
- five words which have a vowel sound spelled **u**
- six words which have a vowel sound spelled **au** or **augh**

■ **WRITE**   Choose two sentences to use in a paragraph.

DRAWING CONCLUSIONS Write the list word that fits each clue.

1. A hot dog is one type of this food.
2. If you behave well, no one will call you this.
3. You would find the Great Salt Lake in this state.
4. You can do this to a missile, a ship, or a satellite.
5. This place has books, desks, and a playground.
6. Passengers on a ship or airplane have to trust this.
7. This piece of cleaning equipment is in most houses.
8. A man can use this word to describe his son's sister.
9. If you are good at predicting, you will be able to tell about this period of time.

SYNONYMS Write a list word that means the same as each word or phrase below.

10. pick out
11. tossed
12. made a picture
13. regularly
14. instructed
15. small shovel
16. stall
17. dirty clothes

Take a Hint
Think of this sentence when you want to check your spelling of *threw* and *through*: Hank **threw** the ball **through** the window.

STRATEGIC SPELLING

Seeing Meaning Connections

Write the list word that completes each sentence. The underlined word is a clue. Circle the letters in the answer that are the same in both words.

18. A <u>humorous</u> friend is often in good ___.
19. The expert <u>jeweler</u> examined the ___.
20. The <u>musician</u> composed his own ___.

	Make a capital.
/	Make a small letter.
∧	Add something.
ℯ	Take out something.
⊙	Add a period.
¶	New paragraph

PROOFREAD RULES These sisters made up rules for sharing a bedroom. Correct five misspelled words in the rules and fix four punctuation errors.

The Kraft Sisters Rules

1. Ask before using another persons things, especially her faverite things.

2. Take turns carrying the landry downstairs.

3. Don't play Carlas radio or Brendas tape player after 9:30 P.M. during the shcool year.

4. Keep a sense of humer so we can surrvive.

PROOFREADING TIP

The sisters forgot to use apostrophes to show who owns what. Some of their words should look like these: Emmy's pen, the brothers' skates.

WRITE RULES Think of something that you must share with others such as the bathroom, the telephone, or the TV. Make up rules for using it. Try to use three list words.

Word List

daughter	naughty	Utah	launch
music	crew	laundry	jewel
taught	choose	booth	future
school	sausage	usually	humor
threw	drew	scoop	broom

Personal Words 1. ___ 2. ___

Review

WORDS IN CONTEXT Write the word from the box that is missing from each person's statement.

choose
school
threw
crew
drew
future
music
usually
taught
laundry

1. Principal: "I am looking forward to a great ___ year."
2. Pitcher: "I ___ the baseball to the catcher."
3. Game show host: "It's your turn to ___ a category."
4. Teacher: "I've ___ at this school for ten years."
5. Stock boy: "The ___ detergent is in aisle four."
6. Deejay: "We play the ___ you want to hear."
7. Sailor: "The ship can't sail without the ___."
8. Parent: "My daughter ___ plays soccer after school."
9. Architect: "I ___ the plan for the building."
10. Scientist: "In the ___, Halley's comet will appear."

Word *Study*

OLD WORDS, NEW MEANINGS Many ordinary words that you use every day were borrowed from other languages. Over time their meanings changed. The chart below shows the old and modern meanings of three words.

	Long Ago	Now
naughty	very wicked, evil	misbehaving a little
school	free time, time off from work	place for teaching and learning
poison	something to drink	anything dangerous or deadly

Read each sentence and decide if the underlined word has the meaning of long ago or the meaning we use now. Then write "long ago" or "now" for each sentence.

1. During <u>school</u>, Alex went to town with his friends.
2. Lindy uses a computer at the <u>school</u> on Fourth Street.
3. The king was thirsty and wanted some <u>poison</u>.
4. A three-year-old girl had to go to the hospital after swallowing <u>poison</u>.
5. That <u>naughty</u> child won't wash his hands.
6. The murderer was a <u>naughty</u> person.

Review

Lesson 7: Using Just Enough Letters
Lesson 8: Short e and Long e
Lesson 9: Short Vowels a, i, o, u

Lesson 10: Long Vowels a, i, o
Lesson 11: Vowel Sounds in rule, use, off

REVIEW WORD LIST

1. a lot
2. athlete
3. burglar
4. enough
5. equipment
6. examine
7. necklace
8. TV
9. want
10. went
11. again
12. against
13. cheese
14. goalie
15. Halloween
16. heavy
17. said
18. succeed
19. thief
20. weapon
21. adventure
22. because
23. before
24. jungle
25. perhaps
26. possible
27. pretend
28. problem
29. python
30. aliens
31. antelope
32. arrow
33. bowling
34. crime
35. favorite
36. globe
37. owner
38. sidewalk
39. slope
40. vacation
41. whole
42. booth
43. broom
44. future
45. sausage
46. school
47. scoop
48. taught
49. usually
50. Utah

Shopping

Write the names of the items in the bag. Use the word list.

scoop
cheese
broom
sausage

SPECIAL FEATURE

Wildlife Photographer

Write the list words that complete the interview.

went	possible	jungle
globe	python	weapon
want	adventure	

Why did you become a wildlife photographer?
I love wildlife and _(1)_ . I wanted to shoot animals with my camera, not with a _(2)_ .

Where do you go on your assignments?
I travel to different countries around the _(3)_ . Last month, I _(4)_ to a tropical _(5)_ in New Guinea.

What did you photograph there?
I took photos of snakes—especially the _(6)_ .

What can I do now if I _(7)_ to become an animal photographer?
Plenty! Get to know animals and learn as much as _(8)_ about science.

Use the list words to complete the poster.

because succeed sidewalk
before school future
booth

Project Taffy Apple
Fifth-grade students will set up a _(1)_ to sell taffy apples at _(2)_ . The money they earn will be donated to the Animal Shelter _(3)_ it needs a new wing for injured animals.

Help the project to _(4)_ ! Help a puppy or kitten have a happy _(5)_ .

What to do: Buy a taffy apple.
When: Wednesday _(6)_ 3 P.M.
Where: At the front of school, on the _(7)_ near the flagpole.

Costumes & Characters

Rick is planning ahead. Use the list words to complete his journal entry.

**Halloween perhaps pretend aliens
burglar enough again TV**

It's only September and my friends are thinking about

(1) costumes. Last year, Josh and Arch were (2) from

another planet, and they want to be them (3) . Two other

guys will be Batman and a (4) he is trying to catch. I know!

I could (5) to be one of those silly dinosaurs from the (6) show.

If I give myself (7) time, (8) I could make the costume myself.

Favorite Sports

What sports do you like to play? Use the list words to complete the sentences.
arrow usually goalie athlete a lot bowling taught problem

Alice: I'm good at **(3)** . My brother **(4)** me. Now I beat him!

Latrice: I want to be a **(1)** on a soccer team, but the practices are far away. I need help to solve this **(2)** !

Tanya: I like archery **(7)** . Once I made an **(8)** out of cedar wood.

Ginny: I compete in basketball and tennis, and **(5)** I win. I want to be an all-around **(6)** .

62

Going Places

Debbie used a map to talk about a place. Write the missing list words.

Utah   equipment   vacation   favorite   whole   antelope   owner   slope

My __(1)__ place in the __(2)__ world is the state of __(3)__.

I travel here on __(4)__ to visit my grandfather and go sightseeing.

My aunt is the __(5)__ of a store near a snowy mountain __(6)__. She rents ski __(7)__ to tourists.

Utes and other American Indians hunted deer and __(8)__ in this region.

Detective Story

Marlene began to write a story. Use the list words to complete her ideas.

The Inside Job

said   crime   necklace   examine   heavy   against   thief

Detective Guy Clever rushed to a museum where a **1. ?** had been committed.

▶ He wanted to be the first to **2. ?** the evidence.

▶ He saw a **3. ?** antique chair leaning **4. ?** a shattered display case.

▶ The museum guides **5. ?** that the lights had gone out at noon.

▶ He learned that a **6. ?** had stolen a valuable **7. ?** that day.

63

STRATEGY WORKSHOP

Pronouncing for Spelling

DISCOVER THE STRATEGY 1   The answer to Randy's question is easy. The word is missing an **r.** If he had carefully pronounced the sounds of the two **r**'s when he said **library,** he would have spelled it correctly. Use this strategy so you won't misspell a word because you say it wrong:

1. Read the word aloud carefully and correctly. Listen to the sound of each letter.
2. Pronounce the word again as you write it.

TRY IT OUT   Now practice the strategy.

Pronounce each word in dark type. Pay special attention to the sounds of the underlined letters. Pronounce each word again as you write it.

1. Say **didn't** (not "dint") ___
2. Say **sandwich** (not "samwich") ___
3. Say **February** (not "Febuary") ___
4. Say **fifth** (not "fith") ___
5. Say **empty** (not "emty") ___

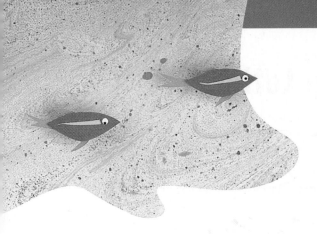

DISCOVER THE STRATEGY 2   Some spellers make up secret pronunciations to help them spell difficult words.

- If a word has silent letters, pronounce them. Don't worry if the word sounds funny. For example, say the **k** at the beginning of knot: "**k**-not."

- Exaggerate or change a sound in the word. For example, look at *clothes*. Do you see the word *the* in the middle? To remember the spelling, say "clo-**the**-s" to yourself.

TRY IT OUT   Now practice this strategy.

Look at the underlined letters in the words below. Make up secret pronunciations for the words. Write each word correctly as you say its secret pronunciation to yourself.

   1. ev<u>e</u>ning   2. fav<u>o</u>rite   3. <u>k</u>nown

Make up secret pronunciations for these words. Decide which letters you will exaggerate. Write each word and circle the part that you are exaggerating.

   4. usually   5. nation   6. island

LOOK AHEAD   Look ahead at the next five lessons. Write four list words you could use these strategies with. Mark the part of each word that you'll pay special attention to when you pronounce it.

Including All the Letters

Some words have more letters than you might expect. To spell these words, pronounce each syllable carefully.

■ **STUDY** Say each word. Notice how it looks and sounds and how many letters it has. Then read the sentence.

WATCH OUT FOR FREQUENTLY MISSPELLED WORDS!

1.	answer	My first **answer** was correct.
2.	minute	I was only one **minute** late.
3.	happened ✳	The storm **happened** yesterday.
4.	library	She got a book from the **library.**
5.	opened	He **opened** a window for fresh air.
6.	length	She swam the **length** of the pool.
7.	getting ✳	I am **getting** a puppy as a gift.
8.	when ✳	Let me know **when** you arrive.
9.	finished	We **finished** cleaning our rooms.
10.	maybe ✳	If it rains, **maybe** we'll stay in.

11.	mystery	The **mystery** puzzled the detective.
12.	dentist	The **dentist** examined my teeth.
13.	actually	Is today **actually** your birthday?
14.	width	I measured the **width** of the box.
15.	caramel	He ordered a **caramel** sundae.
16.	pumpkin	I carved a huge orange **pumpkin.**
17.	quarter	It costs a **quarter** to play the game.
18.	sandwich	I made myself a tuna **sandwich.**
19.	grabbed	She **grabbed** the cat before it ran.
20.	frightening	We watched a **frightening** movie.

CHALLENGE!

necessary
environment
adopted
embarrassed
ambulance

■ **PRACTICE** Which **ten** list words are you more likely to misspell in writing? Write these ten words first. Then write the remaining **ten** words in any order you choose.

■ **WRITE** Choose two sentences to use in a paragraph.

POEMS   Write the list words that complete the poems.

In the Chair
I (1) my mouth wide;
The (2) peered inside.
She saw a cavity, or perhaps two,
Some mints and (3) candy too!

Impatient Fan at the Race
Has Sam (4) ahead of the pack?
Did he run the (5) of the track?
What (6)? Did he win it?
Oh, tell me the (7) this (8)!

LINKING IDEAS   Write the list word that is associated
with each item below.

9. perhaps
10. captured
11. jack-o'-lantern
12. books
13. coin

14. peanut butter
15. at the time
16. receiving
17. side-to-side measurement

STRATEGIC SPELLING
Pronouncing for Spelling

Some words are not spelled the way they're pronounced.
Making up a secret pronunciation can help you spell them.
Pronounce or exaggerate the sounds of the underlined
letters. Then write each word as you say its secret
pronunciation.

18. act<u>ua</u>lly
19. fright<u>en</u>ing

20. m<u>y</u>stery

≡	Make a capital.
/	Make a small letter.
∧	Add something.
ℓ	Take out something.
⊙	Add a period.
¶	New paragraph

PROOFREAD A RECIPE Find the five misspelled words in this recipe and write them correctly. Fix three careless errors.

PROOFREADING TIP

This sandwich is unusual, but the mistakes aren't. Most writers repeat a word or skip a word now and then. That's why they proofread for careless mistakes.

My Mystery Sandwich

My freinds ask what is actully between the two slices bread that I eat every day. They're curious when they see the colors. Here's the anser. The green stuff is is avocado. The yellow is shredded cheese. The white meat tuna. Sometimes I add a slice of tomato. My sandwitch is no mysery. It's good!

WRITE A RECIPE Is your favorite sandwich plain, fancy, or from a fast-food restaurant? Write a simple recipe that tells how you like it made. Use at least two list words.

Word List

library	actually	minute	pumpkin
getting	mystery	length	quarter
happened	answer	finished	sandwich
maybe	dentist	width	grabbed
when	opened	caramel	frightening

Personal Words 1. ___ 2. ___

Review

ANTONYMS   Write the word from the box that means the opposite of the underlined word in each sentence.

1. Sue really enjoyed <u>giving</u> presents.
2. Pilar <u>started</u> the art project before Ben.
3. Neither the height nor the <u>width</u> will change.
4. I would be surprised if the store <u>closed</u> before noon.
5. Tom's <u>question</u> made the class laugh.

MAKING INFERENCES   Write the word from the box that fits each clue.

6. This is between a second and an hour.
7. This is where you would find a collection of books.
8. Tina's mom didn't say yes or no, she said this.
9. The accident must have done this during the storm.
10. I knew where the party was, but I didn't know this.

> answer
> minute
> happened
> library
> opened
> length
> getting
> when
> finished
> maybe

Using a *Dictionary*

FINDING THE RIGHT MEANING   When words are spelled the same, but have different meanings and histories, they are **homographs.**

Look at the separate entries for *minute.* Each has a raised number. If the first word is not the one you want, the number reminds you to look at the next one. Read the entries. Notice that the words are pronounced differently. Then write *minute*¹ or *minute*² to answer the questions.

pronunciation ———┐ ┌——— accent

┌——**minute**¹ (min′it), **1** one of the 60 equal periods of time that
make up an hour; sixty seconds. **2** a short time; instant:
I'll be there in a minute. n.

entry word   **minute**² (mī nüt′ or mī nyüt′), very small; tiny:
a minute speck of dust. adj.

1. Which homograph could describe a grain of sand?
2. Which do you use when you talk about time?
3. Which has the accent on the first syllable?

Consonant Sounds /j/ and /k/

SPELLING FOCUS

The consonant sound /j/ can be spelled **j**, **dge**, and **g**: <u>j</u>u<u>dge</u>, **general**. The consonant sound /k/ can be spelled **ch**, **c**, and **cc**: **cha<u>ra</u>cter**, **o<u>cc</u>ur**.

■ **STUDY**   Say each word and read the sentence. Notice the letters that spell the sounds /j/ and /k/.

1.	*judge*	A **judge** must be fair in court.
2.	*major*	We saw the **major** sights of the city.
3.	*subject*	My favorite **subject** is science.
4.	*legend*	She told a **legend** about a monster.
5.	*general*	He explained the **general** idea.
6.	*character*	One **character** in the play sings.
7.	*chorus*	The **chorus** sang at the concert.
8.	*occur*	Tornadoes **occur** on land.
9.	*accurate*	My watch is **accurate** to the second.
10.	*occasion*	New Year's is a special **occasion.**

11.	*junior*	The **junior** division is for children.
12.	*lodge*	We rested at the ski **lodge.**
13.	*ridge*	The mountain **ridge** was narrow.
14.	*ledge*	He put a pot on the window **ledge.**
15.	*Georgia*	We bought peaches in **Georgia.**
16.	*orchestra*	The **orchestra** played a symphony.
17.	*mechanic*	The **mechanic** repaired our car.
18.	*chord*	A loud piano **chord** began the song.
19.	*accuse*	Don't **accuse** me without proof.
20.	*raccoon*	A **raccoon** has a ringed tail.

CHALLENGE!

prejudice
partridge
allergic
headache
accompany

■ **PRACTICE** ▪ Write five words with /k/ spelled **cc**
▪ Write five words with /k/ spelled **ch**
▪ Write seven words with /j/ spelled **j** and **dge**
▪ Write three words with /j/ spelled only **g**

■ **WRITE**   Choose ten words to write in sentences.

RIDDLES   Write list words to answer the riddle.

How's business?

1. A ___ league baseball player: "It has its ins and outs."
2. An auto ___: "It started up again."
3. A fruit grower from ___ : "It's just peachy."
4. A singer in a ___: "Well, it has its highs and lows."
5. A ___ in high school: "Mine is a learning experience."
6. A ___ in the woods: "The night shift is doing fine."
7. A ___ in a play: "Mine is acting funny lately."
8. A drummer in an ___: "It's booming."

MEANING MATCH   Write the list word that means the same as the underlined word or words.

9. The builder took <u>exact</u> measurements.
10. The storyteller told an old <u>tale</u> about a flood.
11. She put the jar on the window <u>shelf</u>.
12. The guitarist strummed a <u>combination</u> of notes.
13. What <u>course</u> will you study after geography?
14. Safety rules should help the <u>common</u> public.
15. We climbed over the <u>long, high part</u> of the hill.
16. A birthday is a good <u>time</u> for a party.

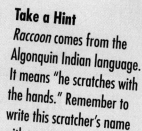

Take a Hint
Raccoon comes from the Algonquin Indian language. It means "he scratches with the hands." Remember to write this scratcher's name with two **c**'s.

STRATEGIC SPELLING
Building New Words

Write *occur, accuse, judge,* and *lodge.* Then write the forms of these words that complete the chart. Remember to make spelling changes where they're needed.

	Base word	Add -ed
17.	___	___
18.	___	___
19.	___	___
20.	___	___

 71

☰	Make a capital.
/	Make a small letter.
∧	Add something.
ℓ	Take out something.
⊙	Add a period.
¶	New paragraph

PROOFREAD A SIGN Signs may have just a few words, but they are tricky to write. Find the misspelled word in the sign below. Write it correctly.

PROOFREADING TIP

After you've made a sign, it's hard to notice your own mistakes. Before you hang a sign in public, ask someone to read it. If you've goofed, you'll find out fast.

WRITE A SIGN Make a sign advertising the play *The Legend of the Raccoon and the Turtle.* Invent the date, place, time, and ticket price. Proofread the sign.

Word List

junior	major	accuse	occur
ledge	ridge	chord	mechanic
legend	general	raccoon	chorus
judge	lodge	orchestra	character
Georgia	subject	occasion	accurate

Personal Words   1. ___ 2. ___

judge
major
subject
legend
general
character
chorus
occur
accurate
occasion

Review

ASSOCIATIONS Write the word from the box that is associated with each item below.

1. courtroom, jury, law
2. topic, issue, theme
3. exact, correct, precise
4. story, tale, myth
5. singers, songs, performance

MAKING CONNECTIONS Write the word from the box that answers each question.

6. What information is given without the specifics?
7. What word means "happen" or "take place"?
8. What is a special reason to celebrate?
9. What is a person in a play, story, or movie called?
10. What kind of event is not minor?

Multicultural *Connection*

LANGUAGE In many Korean legends, the turtle and the tiger are important characters. These two animals usually have these traits:

turtle	tiger
thinks things through	is fun loving
is not in a hurry	is kind
has a healthy way of life	is helpful

The fox is another character in Korean legends. It often has evil traits or those that are opposite of the turtle's and the tiger's. List three traits that the fox might have. Then choose an animal that is popular in legends of the United States, such as the wolf, the rabbit, or the bear, and list three traits.

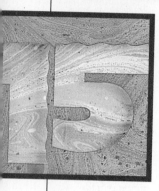

Contractions

In contractions an apostrophe takes the place of letters that are left out, so **let us** becomes **let's.**

■ **STUDY** Say each pair of words. Then say the contraction. Notice which letters are left out.

✳
WATCH OUT FOR FREQUENTLY MISSPELLED WORDS!

can + not	=	1. can't
would + not	=	2. wouldn't
I + am	=	3. I'm ✳
you + are	=	4. you're ✳
I + will	=	5. I'll
let + us	=	6. let's ✳
that + is	=	7. that's ✳
do + not	=	8. don't ✳
there + is	=	9. there's ✳
I + have	=	10. I've

were + not	=	11. weren't
what + is	=	12. what's
she + is	=	13. she's
they + are	=	14. they're ✳
who + is	=	15. who's
we + are	=	16. we're ✳
you + have	=	17. you've
should + have	=	18. should've
could + have	=	19. could've
we + have	=	20. we've

CHALLENGE!

there've
who'd
mightn't
who've
what'll

■ **PRACTICE** Sort the list by writing
- ten contractions that you use most often in your writing
- ten other contractions

■ **WRITE** Choose ten words to write in sentences.

HOMOPHONES   Write the contraction that has the same sound as each word below.

1. aisle
2. lets
3. theirs
4. there

5. weave
6. whose
7. your

SNAPPY ANSWERS   Pretend someone is asking you these questions. Write the contraction that completes each answer.

8. Have you found any shells? Yes, ___ found some.
9. Have I made you sad? No, ___ made me happy.
10. Were the kids at the beach? No, they ___ .
11. Are you from an island? No, ___ from the mainland.
12. Are we ready to go fishing? Yes, ___ ready!

CONTRACTIONS   Write the contraction that contains each word below.

13. do
14. would
15. she
16. that

17. should
18. can
19. what
20. could

Building New Words

Add the contraction for *is* to the base words. Remember what you learned.

21. here
22. how
23. where

Take a Hint
Do not write *of* after *could, should,* or *would*. Use *could've, should've,* or *would've.*

≡	Make a capital.
/	Make a small letter.
∧	Add something.
ℓ	Take out something.
⊙	Add a period.
⁋	New paragraph

PROOFREAD A NOTE Find the five misspelled words in this note and write them correctly. Then fix four capitalization mistakes.

PROOFREADING TIP

Kyle was feeling small and writing small. He wrote a small letter for the pronoun that means "me." He also used small letters for people's names.

Dear Shawna,

I'm sure youre mad at me because i forgot to feed your fish while you were at dad's. I dont know what hapend. Maybe i was excited about being a caracter in the play. Anyway, I forgot. Luckily mom fed them in time. I'am sorry.

Your brother,

Kyle

WRITE A NOTE You read how Kyle feels. Pretend that you are Shawna and answer Kyle's note. Tell how *you* feel. Use at least three list words and a personal word.

Word List

don't	what's	they're	could've
can't	that's	we're	we've
weren't	there's	you're	I've
wouldn't	she's	you've	I'll
I'm	who's	should've	let's

Personal Words 1. ___ 2. ___

Review

PARAGRAPH COMPLETION Write the word from the box that completes each unfinished sentence in the letter.

can't
wouldn't
I'm
you're
I'll
let's
that's
don't
there's
I've

Dear Mom and Dad,

   Thank you for letting me come to Washington, D.C., on the class trip. I have only been here for one day and you (1) believe all of the stuff (2) learned. My teacher, Mr. Pearson, says (3) a good tourist, because I really listen to the tour guides. He's always saying, " (4) all be good listeners." I (5) believe how much history this city has. There are monuments to three American Presidents. (6) the Washington Monument, the Lincoln Memorial, and the Jefferson Memorial. I have taken so many pictures, (7) not going to believe it. (8) all for now. I will write again soon, and (9) also send a postcard to Grandma and Grandpa.

Love,
Yolonda

P.S. Please (10) forget to feed my fish.

Word *Study*

HYPERBOLE "My locker is so messy, it makes the city dump look neat!" Do you and your friends exaggerate for fun? When you exaggerate just for effect, you are using **hyperbole.** Often when you use hyperbole, someone tries to top you by exaggerating even more. Read this example:

Larry: I'm so thirsty, I could drink a gallon of water.
Cherilyn: I'm so thirsty, I could drink the Atlantic Ocean!

Write sentences that top these exaggerations.

1. I'm so hungry, I could eat five hamburgers.

2. I've got so many clothes on, I feel as big as a whale.

Compound Words 1

Compound words are usually made of two smaller words. Keep all the letters when spelling compounds:
some + times = sometimes.

■ **STUDY**   Say each compound word and look at the two words that formed it. Then read the sentence.

WATCH OUT FOR FREQUENTLY MISSPELLED WORDS!

1.	*mailbox*	I put the letter in the **mailbox.**
2.	*nearby*	We fished in a **nearby** lake.
3.	*into* ✳	The swimmer dived **into** the pool.
4.	*sometimes* ✳	I **sometimes** forget my lunch.
5.	*sunset*	After **sunset** comes darkness.
6.	*anything*	He didn't bring **anything** to eat.
7.	*daylight*	We traveled only in **daylight.**
8.	*something* ✳	I want **something** else for dinner.
9.	*haircut*	The stylist gave me a new **haircut.**
10.	*notebook*	I use a **notebook** for each class.

11.	*earthquake*	The **earthquake** destroyed a town.
12.	*hideout*	A cave can be used as a **hideout.**
13.	*textbook*	Look at your science **textbook.**
14.	*volleyball*	I hit the **volleyball** into the net.
15.	*horseback*	The cowboy rode on **horseback.**
16.	*handwriting*	Neat **handwriting** is easy to read.
17.	*kickstand*	I use a **kickstand** to park my bike.
18.	*rattlesnake*	We heard the **rattlesnake.**
19.	*fireplace*	A fire blazed in the **fireplace.**
20.	*housework*	Dusting is part of **housework.**

CHALLENGE!

throughout
silverware
thumbtack
clothesline
blueprint

■ **PRACTICE**   Write the words in alphabetical order.

■ **WRITE**   Choose ten words to write in sentences.

JOINING WORDS   Find two words in each sentence that can be joined to make a list word. Write the word.

1. Did you find any mail in the box?
2. Who wants their hair to be cut very short?
3. The pony in the pasture came to me.
4. The telephone is near the office by the bulletin board.
5. My hand is tired because I've been writing all day.
6. Get rid of old papers and any other useless thing.
7. That fielder made some errors and struck out two times.
8. This note says that the book is overdue.
9. When day begins, the light comes in my window.
10. I found some leaves, a feather, and one thing more.

DRAWING CONCLUSIONS   Write the list word that answers each question.

11. On what do ranchers often travel?
12. What kind of work is ironing and cooking?
13. In what can you burn wood?
14. In what sport do you use a net but not a racket?
15. What can you use to park your bicycle?
16. What animal makes a sound with its tail?
17. What may be happening when the ground shakes?
18. What kind of book do you often use for studying?
19. What place is supposed to be hard to find?

STRATEGIC SPELLING

Seeing Meaning Connections

Words with **sun**
*sun*flower
*sun*tan
*sun*set

Write the words from the box that fit the definitions.

20. reddish-brown skin caused by the sun
21. a tall plant
22. close of day

Did You Know?
The eastern diamondback **rattlesnake** can be over seven feet long and weigh over thirty pounds.

≡	Make a capital.
/	Make a small letter.
∧	Add something.
ℓ	Take out something.
⊙	Add a period.
¶	New paragraph

PROOFREAD A SHORT REPORT

Darrin wrote this report to go with a picture. Correct five misspelled words. Then fix two places where he used adjectives incorrectly.

PROOFREADING TIP

Darrin forgot this easy rule about using the adjectives more and most. "Don't use more and most with words that end in -er and -est."

<u>The Clermont</u> This steamboat was built by Robert Fulton in 1807. Other steamboats were built more earlier, but the <u>Clermont</u> was the most fastest and easyest to use. The people who came to see Fulton lunch it wanted to see some thing exiting ocur. They thought a steamboat would blow up. It didn't. It worked!

WRITE ABOUT A SHORT REPORT Comment on Darrin's short report. Tell why it was interesting to you or not. Use two list words and one personal word.

Word List

daylight	hideout	handwriting	fireplace
earthquake	textbook	kickstand	sunset
into	volleyball	nearby	horseback
sometimes	anything	rattlesnake	mailbox
something	haircut	housework	notebook

Personal Words   1. ___   2. ___

mailbox
nearby
into
sometimes
sunset
anything
daylight
something
haircut
notebook

Review

SYNONYMS IN CONTEXT   Write a word from the box that means about the same as the underlined word or words in each sentence.

1. Carmen and I will wake up to go fishing before <u>dawn</u>.
2. The bus driver asked, "Is there a gas station <u>around</u>?"
3. The campers went <u>inside of</u> the tent.
4. Mrs. Diaz <u>occasionally</u> gives homework on Fridays.
5. At <u>nightfall</u>, Huang returned home from the park.

MAKING INFERENCES   Write a word from the box that completes each sentence. Here's a clue: the answer will start with the same letter as the first word in each sentence.

6. Sam asked Kenji if he wanted to do ___ on Saturday.
7. Nora lost her assignment ___.
8. Haley needs to get a ___, because her bangs are too long.
9. My sister put the letter in the ___.
10. Aunt Luz said, "Order ___ you want."

Word *Study*

DESCRIPTIVE WORDS   When a parrot repeats words, it doesn't really understand them. To understand words that we hear or read, we often picture them in our minds.

Stop and think about the phrases below. Paint a picture of them in your mind.

a hideout

an earthquake

swimming underwater

Write a word picture of one scene that you pictured. Describe details that you imagined.

Irregular Plurals

Sometimes plurals are formed in ways that don't follow rules: **rad<u>ios</u>, hero<u>es</u>, belie<u>fs</u>, lea<u>ves</u>.**

■ **STUDY** Notice how each word becomes plural.

radio	1. *radios*
video	2. *videos*
piano	3. *pianos*
hero	4. *heroes*
potato	5. *potatoes*
cuff	6. *cuffs*
belief	7. *beliefs*
himself herself	8. *themselves*
life	9. *lives*
leaf	10. *leaves*

patio	11. *patios*
banjo	12. *banjos*
echo	13. *echoes*
tornado	14. *tornadoes*
tomato	15. *tomatoes*
cliff	16. *cliffs*
hoof	17. *hoofs*
roof	18. *roofs*
loaf	19. *loaves*
half	20. *halves*

CHALLENGE!

portfolios
embargoes
chefs
handkerchiefs
calves

■ **PRACTICE** Sort the words by writing
- ten words in which just **-s** was added
- five words in which **f** changed to **v**
- five words in which just **-es** was added

■ **WRITE** Choose ten words to write in sentences.

CLASSIFYING Write one or two list words that belong in each category below.

1–2. garden plants
3. weather disasters
4–5. entertainment machines
6. parts of a plant
7. land formations
8. feet of some animals
9–10. parts of houses

> **Take a Hint**
> Don't say *themself* or *theirselves*. Those words aren't even in the dictionary! Do say *themselves*. It's correct.

WORDS IN CONTEXT Complete each sentence with a list word. Here's a hint: The last three letters of the underlined word are the same as the last three letters in the word you will write.

11. Stephen always bakes two ___ of bread and <u>saves</u> one for us.
12. Two tiny <u>elves</u> divided an orange into ___.
13. Did you hear about ___ who fought the <u>foes</u> of justice?
14. The toddlers put the cans on the <u>shelves</u> all by ___.
15. The swimmers made the best <u>dives</u> of their ___.
16. Elly brushes the ___ of her pants and <u>buffs</u> her shoes each day.
17. The <u>chiefs</u> of the tribes explained their ___.

STRATEGIC SPELLING
Using the Problem Parts Strategy

18–23. Forming the plural of words ending in **-o** can be a spelling problem. Write *pianos, echoes, banjos, tomatoes, tornadoes,* and *videos.* Mark the **-s** or **-es** at the end of each word to help you remember it.

≡	Make a capital.
/	Make a small letter.
∧	Add something.
ℯ	Take out something.
⊙	Add a period.
⁋	New paragraph

PROOFREAD A LETTER Breann's letter to a naturalist has five misspelled words and four handwriting errors. Correct the mistakes.

PROOFREADING TIP

We humans can communicate in writing, but sometimes our writing is hard to read. Breann needs to add space between certain words to make her writing clearer.

Dear Ms. Herringa,

Thanks for explaining howanimals talk. I usally don't like speechs, but I likedyours. I never knew thatdolphins beam sounds an follow the echos to find fishto eat. When I'm hungry, all I hear is my stomach rumbeling!

Your friend,
Breann

WRITE A LETTER Write a letter to Ms. Herringa. Invite her to speak to your class. Tell her which animals you would like to learn about. Use at least one list word.

Word List

patios	echoes	hoofs	themselves
radios	tornadoes	beliefs	loaves
videos	heroes	roofs	lives
banjos	tomatoes	cuffs	halves
pianos	potatoes	cliffs	leaves

Personal Words   1. ___   2. ___

Review

TONGUE TWISTERS Write the word from the box that would best complete each tongue twister. Here's a hint: the answer will start with the same letter as the first word in each sentence.

radios
videos
pianos
heroes
potatoes
cuffs
beliefs
themselves
lives
leaves

1. Laurel ___ lay on the lawn.
2. Carlos's ___ curl.
3. Put the player ___ in the parlor.
4. Rain ruined the ___.
5. Bullfighters' ___ bother the bull.
6. The Thortons thump ___ thoughtlessly.
7. Penelope put pickles and ___ in the pie.
8. Lions' ___ are longer than lizards'.
9. Hand the ___ their handcuffs.
10. Volumes of ___ vanished.

Using a *Thesaurus*

USING EXACT WORDS Complete each sentence with the best synonym for *belief*. Use your Writer's Thesaurus if you need help.

Synonyms: trust   confidence   faith

1. Lee appreciated the student council's vote of ___.
2. Officer Cruz said, "I ___ that you are telling the truth."
3. We have ___ in our ability to win the final game.

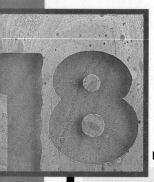

Review

REVIEW WORD LIST

1. actually
2. answer
3. caramel
4. dentist
5. frightening
6. happened
7. length
8. library
9. minute
10. mystery
11. pumpkin
12. quarter
13. sandwich

14. when
15. width
16. chorus
17. Georgia
18. judge
19. mechanic
20. occasion
21. orchestra
22. raccoon
23. ridge
24. can't
25. don't
26. there's

27. weren't
28. anything
29. daylight
30. earthquake
31. fireplace
32. haircut
33. horseback
34. into
35. nearby
36. sometimes
37. volleyball
38. banjos

39. cliffs
40. halves
41. heroes
42. hoofs
43. loaves
44. pianos
45. potatoes
46. radios
47. roofs
48. themselves
49. tomatoes
50. videos

Write the missing words.

| there's | minute | nearby | mystery | answer |

Can you solve this (1) in just a (2)? You throw a baseball hard. It doesn't hit anything, but it comes back to you. No one is (3), and (4) no string attached. Why does it return? Here's the (5). (Turn the page upside down.)

You threw it straight up in the air!

86

Write the missing words to this true story.

daylight   frightening   earthquake   weren't   into
happened   roofs   when   themselves

Soon after (1) on the morning of April 18, 1906,
people in the busy city of San Francisco heard a (2)
noise like thunder. An (3) had struck. The walls of buildings
crumbled (4) the streets, and (5) fell in on houses. People (6) sure
how to save (7) , and many were crushed. The shaking also cut off
the water supply. As a result, the most damage (8) after the quake (9)
fires spread throughout the city.

You're Invited

Write the missing words in the invitation below.

chorus   don't   occasion   orchestra   banjos   pianos

An Invitation to a Concert

You'll hear a symphony (1) with sixty
instruments including two grand (2) and a (3) of fifty
singers. The special guests are the Blackburn Family
who will strum on their (4) and lead the audience
in singing folk songs. Please (5) miss this enjoyable (6) !
January 15   7:30 P.M.   Music Society Hall

Horse Sense

quarter hoofs cliffs ridge horseback actually can't anything

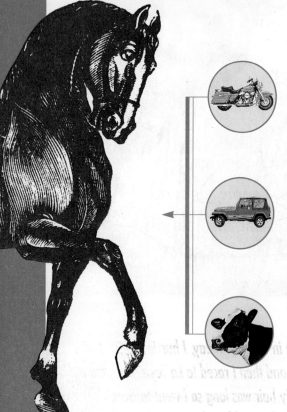

Kristen's class asked questions about animals and found their own answers. Complete Kristen's answer.

Question: What horse is both a worker and a racer?

Answer: The American Quarter Horse is both strong and fast. It can beat a motorcycle or __(1)__ else in a race that is a __(2)__ of a mile long. True, it __(3)__ beat a thoroughbred in a long race, but it will always win a short race. When you see cowboys on __(4)__ , they are probably riding a quarter horse. It is better than a jeep when it comes to herding cows. Its nimble __(5)__ can carry it along the edges of __(6)__ , over the __(7)__ of a hill, or through bramble bushes. They say that this horse rounds up cattle so well, it __(8)__ thinks like a cow!

Diagram of a Lunch

**sandwich halves length width
loaves Georgia sometimes**

The __(1)__ is four inches. The __(2)__ is five inches. Often this __(3)__ is cut in two __(4)__ . The bread may be from whole wheat or white __(5)__ . The peanut butter is from peanuts grown in __(6)__ or Alabama. People __(7)__ like jelly with the peanut butter.

4 inches

5 inches

Cut Here

How to Do Everything

Write the missing words below.

videos   library   potatoes raccoon   heroes
fireplace volleyball radios   tomatoes

The Soto family has a small __(1)__ of books and __(2)__ at home.

Here are their favorites.

Mr. Soto: How to grow __(3)__ and __(4)__ .

               How to clean a chimney and a __(5)__ .

Hector: How to draw warriors and __(6)__ .

               How to repair old __(7)__ .

Delores: How to track a __(8)__ in the snow.

               How to play __(9)__ .

Out of Breath

"Hi, everyone. I'm in a hurry. Today, I hurried to Dr. Jenks for my toothache, and then I raced to La Toya's to have my brakes checked. My hair was long so I went to Nora's shop. I zoomed to the market and bought a round orange squash. As I left, I ran right into my neighbor. I called out, 'Sorry, Your Honor,' and rushed home to make apples dipped in candy. I've got to go. Bye!"

Hurried Hal is telling us about his hectic day. Show that you know what he means by writing the list word that answers each question.

~~haircut~~ ~~judge~~ ~~pumpkin~~
~~mechanic~~ ~~caramel~~ ~~dentist~~

1. What job does Dr. Jenks have?
2. What job does La Toya have?
3. What did Nora give Hal?
4. What job does Hal's neighbor have?
5. What is the name of the squash?
6. What kind of candy goes on the apples?

Memory Tricks

DISCOVER THE STRATEGY Knowing which part of a word gives you problems may not be enough. This memory-tricks strategy will help you spell tricky words.

Mark the problem part of a word.

Think of other words with those letters.

dream?
beach?
eat?

Create a memory trick.

Don't eat the leaves!

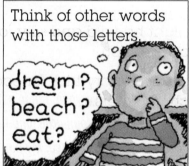

Your memory helper might be a phrase or a sentence. It might rhyme, or it might not. Just be sure you can spell your helper and that the problem letters match. Here are more memory tricks.

answer	We know the answer.
occasion	I can't come to that occasion.
meadow	dead flowers in the meadow
missiles	The missiles missed by two miles.

TRY IT OUT Now practice this memory-tricks strategy.

Complete the following memory tricks with words from the box. Write words with letters that match the underlined letters. Then circle the matching letters in your words.

| cat | Paul | rain | off |

1. ___ did the laundry.
2. fall ___ a cliff
3. a ___ on vacation
4. ___ on the brain

Your own memory tricks might be wild and silly, and that's just fine. Use what works best for you.

Work with a partner. Create a memory trick for each pair of words. Underline the matching letters.

5. Georgia   giant
6. friend   end

7. Create a memory trick for one of the words in the box. Mark the matching letters.

| frightening | aliens | potatoes |

LOOK AHEAD Look ahead at the next five lessons for list words that might give you problems. Create memory tricks for two of them. Share your tricks with the class.

Getting Letters in Correct Order

SPELLING FOCUS

Watch for letter combinations that are hard to keep in order and pay special attention to those parts: **beautiful**, **their**.

■ **STUDY**   Look at each word and take special notice of the underlined letters. Then read the sentence.

❋
WATCH OUT FOR FREQUENTLY MISSPELLED WORDS!

1.	lonely	I felt **lonely** after everyone left.
2.	hundred	One **hundred** cents is a dollar.
3.	friend ❋	My **friend** can depend on me.
4.	built	The beaver **built** the log dam.
5.	beautiful ❋	We stared at the **beautiful** sunset.
6.	heard ❋	I awoke when I **heard** the alarm.
7.	radio	We played loud music on the **radio.**
8.	their ❋	The couple bought **their** tickets.
9.	caught ❋	The fish was **caught** in the net.
10.	bored	His long story **bored** the audience.
11.	guard	The **guard** checks everyone's bag.
12.	pierce	A nail can **pierce** through a tire.
13.	shriek	We heard a **shriek** of surprise.
14.	receive	Did you **receive** my letter?
15.	horrible	The monster face was **horrible.**
16.	jewelry	I put my **jewelry** in the safe.
17.	tumble	We **tumble** on a mat for safety.
18.	northern	The **northern** lakes freeze first.
19.	acre	The farmer plowed an **acre** of land.
20.	museum	We toured the art **museum.**

CHALLENGE!

unbelievable
fluorescent
exclaimed
capitalize
emperor

■ **PRACTICE**   Look over the list and write the words that are hardest for you to spell. Take care as you write each of these words. Then write the remaining words.

■ **WRITE**   Choose two words to use in an advertisement.

ANTONYMS Write the list word that means the opposite of each word below.

1. give
2. ugly
3. wonderful
4. destroyed
5. enemy
6. released
7. southern
8. entertained

Take a Hint
Bored and **board** sound alike, but they aren't spelled alike. Remember, when you're b<u>ored</u>, you act t<u>ired</u>. You build something with a board.

MAKING CONNECTIONS Write the list word that fits each clue below.

9. If you startle someone, you may hear this.
10. People wear this as a decoration.
11. You do this with a fork, knife, or pin.
12. This is an area of land.
13. If you know about a noise, you did this.
14. If you do this on stairs, you could hurt yourself.
15. Turn on this to hear music, news, or weather reports.
16. This person usually wears a uniform and a weapon.
17. This may contain mummies, paintings, or inventions.

Using the Memory Tricks Strategy

Use memory tricks to help you spell. Write a list word to complete each trick. Underline the matching letters.

18. <u>Fr</u>ed counted a ___ <u>red</u> lights.
19. <u>The</u>y picked ___ own apples.
20. Number <u>one</u> is ___.

≡	Make a capital.
/	Make a small letter.
∧	Add something.
ℓ	Take out something.
⊙	Add a period.
¶	New paragraph

PROOFREAD A SIGN Mistakes look worse when they are on a huge sign. Find a spelling error in the sign below. Write it correctly.

Proofreading Tip
Here's a sign for <u>you</u> to read. *Before you hang up a sign, an announcement, or a poster, hang in there and* **P-R-O-O-F-R-E-A-D F-I-R-S-T!**

SE GIFT GALORE
SALES
EM • STEREOS • SPEAKERS • TOYS •
JEWLERY • PERFUME
COSMETIC • FLOWER
HAIR PRODUCTS • LAMPS

WRITE A SIGN Pick two items from the sign and advertise them on a new sign. To attract customers, add describing words. Use at least three list words.

Word List

beautiful	their	tumble	bored
heard	shriek	lonely	caught
guard	receive	northern	built
friend	horrible	hundred	radio
pierce	jewelry	acre	museum

Personal Words 1. ___ 2. ___

Review

CROSSWORD PUZZLE   Use the clues to help you fill in the puzzle with the words from the box.

Across
  3. very pretty
  6. a pal
  7. listened to
  8. grabbed
  9. uninterested

Down
  1. belonging to them
  2. ten times ten
  3. to have made
  4. feeling alone
  5. a device to hear sounds

lonely
hundred
friend
built
beautiful
heard
radio
their
caught
bored

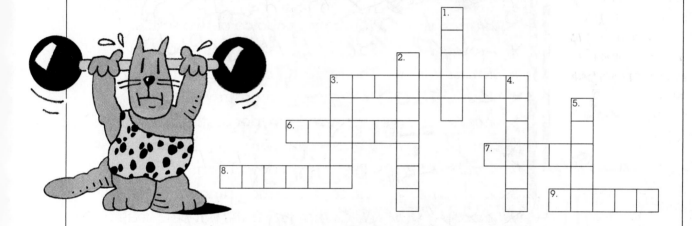

Using a *Dictionary*

FINDING WORDS   Is *shriek* spelled with **sh** or **ch?** When you have to look up a word that you don't know how to spell, check the Spellings of English Sounds chart in a dictionary or in the back of this book. It shows you all the ways that sounds in English are spelled. The most common spellings are listed first. Use the three steps at the right.

Use the three steps to find the correctly spelled word in each group below. Write the correct spelling.

1. cercos   cirkus   circus
2. beetle   beedle   beetel
3. museum   muesum   meusum

STEP 1 Sound out the word.

STEP 2 Look up sounds that you're unsure of in the Spellings of English Sounds chart.

STEP 3 Find the correct spelling in a dictionary.

95

Vowel Sounds in *boy* and *out*

SPELLING FOCUS

The vowel sound /oi/ can be spelled **oi** and **oy**: **ch<u>oi</u>ce, lo<u>ya</u>l**. The vowel sound /ou/ can be spelled **ow** and **ou**: **t<u>ow</u>el, <u>ou</u>r**.

■ **STUDY** Say the words and read the sentences. Look for the letters that spell the vowel sounds in **boy** and **out**.

1.	*choice* √	You have a **choice** of two soups.
2.	*noisy* √	Folding chairs is a **noisy** job.
3.	*loyal*	The fans are **loyal** to their team.
4.	*destroy*	A tornado can **destroy** homes.
5.	*powder*	I sprinkled **powder** on the baby.
6.	*towel*	We used a **towel** to dry the car.
7.	*downtown*	I like to shop **downtown**.
8.	*amount*	She saved a small **amount** of money.
9.	*our* ✳	We found **our** coats, but not theirs.
10.	*outside* ✳	They played **outside** in the park.

11.	*spoil*	Milk left out too long may **spoil**.
12.	*poison*	The bleach label warned of **poison**.
13.	*Illinois*	Soybeans and corn grow in **Illinois**.
14.	*annoy*	The loud jets overhead **annoy** us.
15.	*oyster*	This beach has many **oyster** shells.
16.	*voyage*	Our sea **voyage** will last one week.
17.	*drown*	One can **drown** in shallow water.
18.	*growl*	The dog's low **growl** frightened me.
19.	*couch*	This leather **couch** stains easily.
20.	*surround*	I built a fence to **surround** the pool.

■ **PRACTICE** Sort the words by writing
- ten words with a vowel sound /oi/
- ten words with a vowel sound /ou/

■ **WRITE** Choose two sentences to use in a paragraph.

CHALLENGE!

turmoil √
exploit
employer √
cauliflower √
foundation √

ANALOGIES   Write the list word that completes each analogy.

1. A hike is to land as a ___ is to sea.
2. Rind is to orange as shell is to ___.
3. Nourishing is to food as deadly is to ___.
4. Scrub is to brush as dry is to ___.
5. Bench is to park as ___ is to living room.
6. Floor is to inside as sidewalk is to ___.
7. Nation is to United States as state is to ___.
8. Picnicking is to park as shopping is to ___.

WORD MATH   Write the list word that completes each equation.

9. voice + animal + threat = ___
10. underwater + suffocate + sink = ___
11. harsh + sounds + loud = ___
12. my + your = ___
13. dusty + sprinkle + a puff = ___
14. count + add + sum = ___
15. decision + pick + one = ___
16. trouble + behavior + bother = ___
17. protect + fence in + enclose = ___

Take a Hint
To spell *poison*, remember this: Make sure the **poison is on** the top shelf.

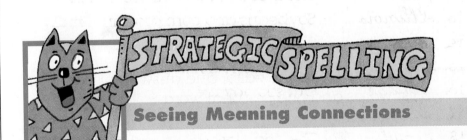

Seeing Meaning Connections

Write the list word that completes each sentence. The underlined word is a clue. Circle the letters in each word that are the same as those in the underlined word.

18. You can't ___ something that is <u>indestructible</u>.
19. Visitors who litter this <u>unspoiled</u> beach will ___ it.
20. The <u>disloyal</u> citizen wouldn't cheer for the ___ soldiers.

≡	Make a capital.
/	Make a small letter.
∧	Add something.
ℓ	Take out something.
⊙	Add a period.
¶	New paragraph

PROOFREAD A LETTER Al writes a column in a nature magazine. He received this letter. Fix the four spelling mistakes and three punctuation errors.

PROOFREADING TIP

The kids packed two complete ideas in the first sentence, but they forgot to add punctuation. Don't forget that this is a letter. What parts need checking?

April 6, 20_ _

Dear Al.

My brother and I think sharks are beutiful and we want to take a voage to see some. But are friends say sharks are ugly. They annoiy us! What can we do?

Sincerely.

Annette and Jeff Turk

WRITE A LETTER Be the editor and answer this letter. Use two list words and one personal word.

Word List

powder	amount	loyal	choice
drown	outside	spoil	voyage
towel	growl	oyster	noisy
couch	surround	poison	Illinois
our	downtown	annoy	destroy

Personal Words 1. ___ 2. ___

Review

choice
noisy
loyal
destroy
powder
towel
downtown
amount
our
outside

OPPOSITES   Write the words from the box that complete the phrases.

1. not inside, but ___
2. not quiet, but ___
3. not uptown, but ___
4. not their turn, but ___ turn
5. not to build, but to ___

CLASSIFYING   Write the list word that belongs in each group.

1. true, faithful, ___
2. selection, option, pick, ___
3. washcloth, bath mat, ___
4. ashes, dust, ___
5. sum, quantity, ___

Word *Study*

ONOMATOPOEIA   What sound does an angry dog make? You could say *growl.* You could actually sound like the dog when you say it. Try it. *Gr-r-r-o-owl!*

Words like *growl, screech,* and *oink* are examples of **onomatopoeia.** The word imitates the sound that you are trying to describe.

Write words that describe the sounds these objects make. Use a word that actually imitates the sound.

1. a little silver bell
2. noisy eating
3. opening a can of soda
4. a big cat
5. a huge church bell

Vowel Sounds with r

SPELLING FOCUS

The vowel sound /är/ can be spelled **ar**: g<u>ar</u>bage.
The vowel sound /ėr/ can be spelled **ur** and **our**:
ret<u>ur</u>n, j<u>our</u>nal.

■ **STUDY** Say each word. Listen for the vowel sound you hear in **scar** or **curl**. Then read the sentence.

1.	*army*	The **army** trained for battle.
2.	*starve*	You will **starve** without food.
3.	*scar*	The burn left a **scar** on his arm.
4.	*garbage*	Put the **garbage** in the trash can.
5.	*hamburger*	I like catsup on my **hamburger.**
6.	*return*	You must **return** the video today.
7.	*purpose*	What is the **purpose** of your call?
8.	*surface*	I sanded the rough table **surface.**
9.	*courage*	It takes **courage** to face danger.
10.	*journal*	Every day I make a **journal** entry.

11.	*argue*	Don't **argue** about who is first.
12.	*apartment*	They rented an **apartment.**
13.	*guitar*	He put new strings on the **guitar.**
14.	*Arkansas*	**Arkansas** is a south central state.
15.	*curl*	I wanted to **curl** my straight hair.
16.	*purse*	She put her keys in her **purse.**
17.	*furniture*	The empty room needed **furniture.**
18.	*courtesy*	It is a **courtesy** to say "please."
19.	*nourish*	Whole milk will **nourish** the baby.
20.	*journey*	Our Asian **journey** begins at dawn.

CHALLENGE!

departure
margarine
suburban
absurd
flourish

■ **PRACTICE** Sort the list words by writing
- eight words with **ar**
- five words with **our**
- seven words with **ur**

■ **WRITE** Choose a sentence to write a saying.

CLASSIFYING Write the list word that belongs in each group.

1. carpets, lamps, ___
2. navy, marines, ___
3 violin, banjo, ___
4. waste, trash, ___
5. bruise, cut, ___
6. ham, hot dog, ___

7. house, cottage, ___
8. wallet, pouch, ___
9. Illinois, Mississippi, ___
10. trip, voyage, ___
11. diary, notebook, ___
12. braid, ponytail, ___

SYNONYMS Write a list word that means the same as the underlined word or phrase.

13. What is the <u>object</u> of this lesson?
14. Be careful not to scratch the <u>top</u> of the wood.
15. Good food will <u>strengthen</u> you and help you grow.
16. The students will <u>go back</u> on the bus.
17. The cruel warlord let the prisoners <u>die of hunger.</u>

Seeing Meaning Connections

Write the list word that completes each sentence. The underlined word is a clue. Circle the letters in each word that are the same as those in the underlined word.

18. If I___ with a friend, I make up after the <u>argument</u>.
19. Lydia had the ___ to try racing after the <u>courageous</u> runner spoke to her.
20. The <u>courteous</u> children knew that ___ is kindness.

Did You Know?
A popular food in Hamburg, Germany, was finely chopped beef. People called it a "Hamburg steak." It became even more popular in the United States as a sandwich—the hamburger.

≡	Make a capital.
/	Make a small letter.
∧	Add something.
ℯ	Take out something.
⊙	Add a period.
¶	New paragraph

PROOFREAD AN EXPLANATION
Tom explained how he is different from others in his class. Find his five spelling mistakes. Two of them are plural nouns.

PROOFREADING TIP
You'll find one of the mistakes if you can answer this riddle. What word has an ending like *knife* when it is singular but a different ending when it's plural?

Most kids in my class have lived here in Arkansa all their lifes. I'm different because I've lived in three states and one foreign country. I've lived in an aparment and in houes. You see, my dad is in the arny. When they transfer him, we go too!

WRITE AN EXPLANATION
Think of a way in which you are different from Tom or from others in your class. Write an explanation about it. Try to use two list words.

Word List

curl	argue	journal	furniture
Arkansas	nourish	return	surface
army	purse	apartment	garbage
hamburger	courage	purpose	guitar
courtesy	starve	scar	journey

Personal Words   1. ___ 2. ___

Review

WORDS IN CONTEXT Write the word from the box that is missing from each person's statement.

1. Short-order cook: "One ___, well done, with onions."
2. Patient: "Doctor, do you think I will have a ___?"
3. President: "The ___ will protect the country."
4. Librarian: "Be sure to ___ the books on time."
5. Astronaut: "The moon's ___ is rough."
6. Artist: "I use ___ from the dump to make sculptures."
7. Soldier: "Thank you for this medal for ___."
8. Student: "I will write about the field trip in my ___."
9. Scientist: "The ___ of this experiment is clear."
10. Veterinarian: "If the bird does not eat, it will ___."

| army |
| starve |
| scar |
| garbage |
| hamburger |
| return |
| purpose |
| surface |
| courage |
| journal |

Word *Study*

FROM OTHER LANGUAGES Many English words that you use every day came from other languages.

In French, the word *jour* means "day." The French word *journée* was a trip that took one *day*. People who are journalists write the news of the *day*.

Use a word or phrase at the right to complete this telephone conversation.

"Bonjour, Ms. Kent. This is Luis. I arrived an hour ago. I'm happy that my job as a (1) has given me a chance to (2) all the way to France! Yes, I'll report on the bicycle races. I'll write about it in my (3) too. I'm going to a restaurant now. I wonder what the (4) will be. What did you say? Oh, that means 'good day.'"

English Words from French

soup du jour	soup of the day
journal	a record of the day
journey	traveling from one place to another
journalist	person who writes for a newspaper or magazine

More Vowels with r

The vowel sound /âr/ can be spelled **are** and **air**: sh**are**, st**air**way. The vowel sound /ir/ can be spelled **ear** and **eer**: d**ear**, car**eer**.

■ **STUDY** Say each word and listen for the vowel sound in **spare** or **dear.** Then read the sentence.

1. aware — I wasn't **aware** of a hidden camera.
2. prepare — He studied to **prepare** for the test.
3. share — I cut the cake so I could **share** it.
4. dairy — Yogurt is a **dairy** product.
5. stairway — Take the **stairway** to the top floor.
6. dear — My sons are **dear** to me.
7. beard — He shaved his **beard** for a new look.
8. appear — You **appear** shorter on television.
9. volunteer — We need a **volunteer** to go first.
10. career — I want to make teaching my **career.**

11. declare — The mayor will **declare** a holiday.
12. spare — I don't have a minute to **spare.**
13. beware — A sign warned us to **beware** of dogs.
14. prairie — The dry **prairie** grass caught fire.
15. repair — I stopped to **repair** the flat tire.
16. weary — The long trip made us **weary.**
17. smear — He had a **smear** of mud on his face.
18. cheery — Bright yellow is a **cheery** color.
19. pioneer — The **pioneer** explored the new land.
20. reindeer — Two **reindeer** pulled the sleigh.

CHALLENGE!

hardware
impair
millionaire
clearance
domineer

■ **PRACTICE** Sort the words by writing
- ten words with the vowel sound /âr/
- ten words with the vowel sound /ir/

■ **WRITE** Choose two sentences to use in a paragraph.

RHYMING WORDS Write the list word that rhymes
with the underlined word and makes sense in the sentence.

1. When you see a big furry <u>bear,</u> take care and ___!
2. Milk and cheese are <u>very</u> nourishing ___ products.
3. The golfer left the <u>fairway</u> and climbed up the ___.
4. The horse will <u>carry</u> the wagon over the ___.
5. Do you have a ___ <u>pair</u> of socks to lend me?
6. I <u>fear</u> Billy will be angry if you ___ paint on the wall.
7. A herd of ___ came <u>near</u> the barn.
8. This <u>year,</u> she started her ___ as a teacher.

RELATED WORDS Write the list word that is the base
word of each word below.

9. volunteering
10. appearance
11. dearly
12. sharing

13. declaration
14. pioneering
15. preparation
16. repairable

STRATEGIC SPELLING

Building New Words

Write the base words *beard, aware, weary,* and *cheery.*
Write the suffix to make a new word. **Remember:** When a
suffix is added to a word ending with a consonant and **y,**
the **y** is usually changed to **i.**

Base word	Suffix	New word
17. ___	-less	___
18. ___	-ness	___
19. ___	-ness	___
20. ___	-ness	___

Did You Know?
Smear comes from an Old English word that means
"grease." Things that smear are messy, gooey, or
sticky—just like grease!

☰	Make a capital.
/	Make a small letter.
∧	Add something.
ℓ	Take out something.
⊙	Add a period.
⌧	New paragraph

PROOFREAD RESEARCH Mandy discovered what children did in colonial days. Five words are misspelled in her research, and three verbs switch from past to present. Fix these errors.

PROOFREADING TIP

Since Mandy started with the **past tense,** she needs to stick with it. The first verb is right because she used *had* instead of *have.* Check the other verbs.

In pionere days, kids had to shar the work. Colonies even make laws about this. In 1640, a Massachusetts law says that both boys and girls have to be tought to spin cloth. Another law said that children who tended sheep had to spin or knit in there spair time.

WRITE ABOUT RESEARCH What do you think about children working in colonial times? Do you think children your age should work or do chores? Write your reaction. Use three list words and a personal word.

Word List

prairie	dairy	weary	beard
declare	stairway	career	pioneer
aware	prepare	dear	appear
repair	spare	cheery	volunteer
beware	share	smear	reindeer

Personal Words 1. ___ 2. ___

aware
prepare
share
dairy
stairway
dear
beard
appear
volunteer
career

Review

DEFINITIONS Write the word from the box that matches each clue.

1. to make ready
2. someone who offers to help
3. the hair growing on a man's face
4. products made from milk
5. having knowledge or realizing something
6. to seem or look as if
7. an occupation or profession
8. to use the same thing together
9. a way up and down by steps
10. much valued and highly respected

Word *Study*

SYNONYMS If you say a cat *dashed* across the floor, you are using a synonym for *ran*. A **synonym** is a word that means nearly the same as another word.

Write the synonym for *say* that fits best in each sentence. Choose from the synonyms below.

1. Do you *say* that you will obey the law?
2. Jason likes to *say* words to himself when he's drawing, but no one knows what he is saying.
3. Please do not say the rules. You've said them once.
4. Everyone heard the referee *say* that Gil won.

Say verb   **Say** means to make words with the voice. It is also used about written words. "Let's go to the store," said Dad. What time does the invitation say the party starts?
Declare means to say in public. Only Congress has the power to declare war.
Repeat means to say again. I promised not to repeat the secret.
Swear means to make a solemn statement or promise. I swear I will tell no one.
Murmur means to talk softly and unclearly. The murmur of the audience stopped when the curtain opened.

Homophones

SPELLING FOCUS

A homophone is a word that sounds exactly like another word but has a different spelling and meaning: **buy, by.**

■ **STUDY** Say each word and sentence. Notice which words in the list sound alike and how they are spelled.

1.	*write*	I **write** my name on each assignment.
2.	*right*	We learned the **right** way to e-mail.
3.	*buy* ✻	In August, I **buy** my school supplies.
4.	*by*	The locker room is **by** the pool.
5.	*to* ✻	She skated **to** the corner and back.
6.	*too* ✻	This boulder is **too** heavy to lift.
7.	*bored*	We were **bored** waiting for the bus.
8.	*board*	The carpenter sanded the **board.**
9.	*it's* ✻	I'll tell you when **it's** time to leave.
10.	*its*	The bird built **its** nest with twigs.

11.	*threw*	The pitcher **threw** a curve ball.
12.	*through* ✻	I pushed **through** the crowd.
13.	*knead*	Bakers **knead** bread dough by hand.
14.	*need*	The newborn kittens **need** milk.
15.	*main*	Every paragraph has a **main** idea.
16.	*mane*	I brushed the horse's long **mane.**
17.	*past*	Grandpa told stories from the **past.**
18.	*passed*	The parade **passed** by our school.
19.	*allowed*	Our dog is not **allowed** on the bed.
20.	*aloud*	An oral report is given **aloud.**

CHALLENGE!

symbol
cymbal
ascent
assent
slay
sleigh

■ **PRACTICE** Write the pairs that are most confusing for you. Then write the rest of the homophones.

■ **WRITE** Choose ten words to write in sentences.

SAME SOUNDS To complete each statement below, use list words that sound alike. Make sure that the sentences make sense.

A baker:"I (1) dough because people (2) bread."

A police officer: "I will (3) the directions on this card so you will know the (4) way to go."

A cook: "This dish is (5) hot (6) touch!"

A store clerk: "Some people stop and (7) things, but others just walk (8) my shop."

A builder: "I'm never (9) when I have nails and a (10)."

DIFFERENT MEANINGS Read the sentences. Then write the list word that matches each definition.

Maybe *it's* going to catch *its* own tail.
11. it is ___   12. belonging to it ___

She *threw* a frisbee *through* a hoop.
13. between the parts of ___   14. tossed ___

In the *past*, covered wagons *passed* this way.
15. went by ___   16. time gone by, yesterday ___

Using the Memory Tricks Strategy

main
allowed
aloud
mane

Use memory tricks to help you spell. Write a word from the box to complete each trick. Underline the matching letters.

17. Make the ___ idea interesting
18. A ___ is on a horse's neck.
19. They ___ all of us to go.
20. Speak ___ in a loud voice.

≡	Make a capital.
/	Make a small letter.
∧	Add something.
ℰ	Take out something.
⊙	Add a period.
⁋	New paragraph

PROOFREAD JOKES Read the jokes that students wrote for the class newspaper. Fix five spelling errors and three punctuation errors.

PROOFREADING TIP

Even jokes need proofreading. When you write items in a list, remember to use commas like this, this, and this. Get it?

Al: Did your frends become bakers?

Sal: No, but they aways need some dough!

Rick: What goes threw the woods without making a sound?

Nick: A path.

Have you ever seen: a board walk a fish bowl a scool trip or a poweder puff?

Ollie: What is more useful after it's broken?

Molly: An egg!

WRITE JOKES It's your turn to be funny. Write your favorite jokes or make up some. Try to use two list words too!

Word List

main	threw	buy	passed
mane	bored	by	to
it's	board	write	too
its	knead	right	allowed
through	need	past	aloud

Personal Words 1. ___ 2. ___

110

Review

RHYMES Write the word from the box that rhymes with the underlined word and ends with the same letter(s).

1. I am so excited for <u>my</u> birthday party.
2. The <u>guy</u> at the video store suggested it.
3. Maria could not find the <u>light</u> switch.
4. Jeremy bought another <u>kite</u> today.
5. Our team finally <u>scored</u>!

> write
> right
> buy
> by
> to
> too
> bored
> board
> it's
> its

POEM Write the words from the box that complete the haiku.

An erased black <u>(6)</u>
<u>(7)</u> message <u>(8)</u> the students
gone, <u>(9)</u> <u>(10)</u> late now

Multicultural *Connection*

GAMES People of all cultures enjoy games. Read about the board games below, and then write the answers.

Mankala   A game played in Africa and the Middle East

A board has two rows of six cups. Players transfer beans or pebbles from one cup to another. The object of the game is to win the most beans. Mankala means "transferring."

1. Think of games you play. Name one or more in which you move markers or count markers.

Stone Toss   An American Indian game

Players use a flat basket as a board and stones that are decorated on one side. A player shakes the basket to toss the stones. If the stone lands with the decorated side up, the player wins points.

2. What do you toss in many games to win points or to know how far to move your marker?
3. Name two board games that use this item.

111

Review

Lesson 19: Getting Letters in Correct Order
Lesson 20: Vowel Sounds in boy and out
Lesson 21: Vowel Sounds with r
Lesson 22: More Vowels with r
Lesson 23: Homophones

REVIEW WORD LIST

1. beautiful
2. caught
3. friend
4. guard
5. heard
6. jewelry
7. museum
8. northern
9. radio
10. their
11. tumble
12. drown
13. Illinois
14. loyal
15. noisy
16. outside
17. oyster
18. powder
19. apartment
20. Arkansas
21. army
22. furniture
23. garbage
24. guitar
25. hamburger
26. journey
27. return
28. surface
29. aware
30. career
31. pioneer
32. prepare
33. reindeer
34. repair
35. share
36. stairway
37. volunteer
38. weary
39. allowed
40. board
41. bored
42. buy
43. by
44. knead
45. main
46. passed
47. right
48. through
49. too
50. write

A Boy of Lapland

Write the missing words.

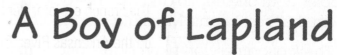

repair   northern   caught   outside   reindeer

My name is Nils-Ole. Here's what I did today. I hiked in the (1) region of Norway. I slept (2) in a tent on the tundra. I decided to tame a (3). I threw a lasso and (4) a white one. I helped Father (5) our snowmobile.

The Swimming Expert

Write the missing words in Safety Seal's message.

aware   **friend**   ~~main~~   **allowed**
guard   **drown**   **board**   **too**

"Learn to swim, pals! The (1) reason humans (2) is that they don't know how to swim. Be (3) of the rules. Make sure a (4) is on duty. Don't swim under a diving (5) . You are never (6) to swim alone so go with a (7) . Maybe you weren't born a swimmer like me, but it's never (8) late to learn!"

Arkansas

Land of the healing waters

Visit

Little Rock
The Ozark Mountains
Pine Forests

A Little Rock on a Big River

Use the list words to complete the brochure.

museum   **pioneer**   ~~by~~   ~~Arkansas~~   ~~furniture~~
journey   **weary**   ~~right~~

Come to Little Rock, the capital city of (1) !

History of Little Rock

The French explorer Bernard de la Harpe made a (2) up the Arkansas River. On the way, he noticed a place (3) a small rock. He thought it would be just the (4) spot for a trading post. Soon (5) travelers began to stop there. They called it Little Rock.

What to Do

Visit old homes of the (6) days. See the handmade chairs and other (7) the settlers would have used. Tour the old statehouse which is now a public (8) .

A Dazzling Hobby

People who do rock tumbling find stones and polish them in a machine. They often make jewelry and other pretty things with the stones. Aurora says that this hobby appeals to her senses. Read her reasons below and write the missing list words.

beautiful tumble through powder
surface jewelry their noisy

Hearing → You hear the rocks in the tumbler. Sometimes the rocks have to (1) night and day for weeks! It is very (2) !

Touch → You use grit, which can feel like sand or (3) . When you are (4) tumbling the rocks, you feel (5) smoothness.

Sight → You can see changing colors when light falls on the (6) of some stones. You can use them to make pretty (7) . Polished stones look very (8) !

Reporter's Notes

Sarah imagined that she was a reporter during the Civil War. Use the list words to complete her notes.

Illinois army share buy return loyal volunteer

I talked to Private Jeb Bullock Anderson who decided to join the Union (1) last year. He's a (2) from the state of (3) . He is nineteen. I saw his camp. He and nine other men (4) a tent. Jeb says he gets enough meat and bread, but he wishes he had money to (5) fruit from the trader. Jeb says he fights because he is (6) to the United States. He wants to (7) to his family and farm as soon as the war is over.

Daydreaming About the Future

Tamara gets ideas about what she wants to be from ordinary things she sees.
Write the missing words.

radio guitar heard garbage career bored write

TV and (1)

With my sense of humor, I could (2) jokes and advertisements.

banjo and (3)

I could choose a (4) in music. I'd never be (5) playing in a country and western band.

recycling bin

Maybe I should start a recycling business. I (6) that towns can't find places to dump their (7) .

What's for Dinner?

As he leaves his building, Ronnie figures out what people in other apartments will eat for dinner. Write the missing words.

apartment **hamburger** **stairway** **passed**
prepare **oyster** **knead**

The Nguyens in apartment 4B are having seafood. They let me taste an (1) . Mrs. Buksis is having French fries and a (2) . When I (3) her door, I could smell it. They're having fresh bread in (4) 2C. I saw Mrs. Goodman (5) the dough. I helped Mr. Harris carry groceries up the front (6) . He'll (7) green beans and fried chicken.

Meaning Helpers

DISCOVER THE STRATEGY Jody kept misspelling the sound /sh/ in *direction* so she thought of a way to remember it. She shared her strategy with the class.

> I think of the meaning helper
> direct because it has a similar
> meaning. When I hear the t in
> direct, I remember the t in
> direction.

TRY IT OUT Now try this meaning helper strategy.

The word pairs below are related in meaning. The top word is the helper. Write the words. Then explain why the top word helps you spell the bottom word. The first one is done for you.

1. photo
   photography

The **o's** in **photo** remind me that
photography has two **o's**.

2. acre
   acreage

3. tense
   tension

Caution: Don't forget to drop the final **e** from tense when you write **tension.**

Choose a meaning helper from the box to help you spell each word below. Write the word and mark the letter or letters that remind you how to spell the hard word. Circle the word in which the final **e** was dropped.

mean	compose	invent

4. invention   5. composition   6. meant

Write a meaning helper of your own for each word below. Mark the letter or letters that help you spell the words.

7. action   8. possession   9. factual

LOOK AHEAD Look over the words in Lesson 28. Write three hard words. Choose a meaning helper for each. Mark the letter or letters in each helper that remind you how to spell the hard word.

Related Words

SPELLING FOCUS

Related words often have parts that are spelled the same but pronounced differently: **cl<u>o</u>th, cl<u>o</u>thes.**

■ **STUDY**   Say each pair of related words. Notice how the pronunciation and spelling change. Read each sentence.

1.	*please*	A low price will **please** the buyer.
2.	*pleasant*	The weather was **pleasant** and mild.
3.	*cloth*	Use the **cloth** to wipe the table.
4.	*clothes*	I wore warm **clothes** for skiing.
5.	*sign*	The exit **sign** showed the way out.
6.	*signature*	I wrote my **signature** on the check.
7.	*dream*	During the night, I had a **dream.**
8.	*dreamt*	I **dreamt** I was a bird flying.
9.	*part*	We found the lost **part** of the toy.
10.	*partial*	A deposit is a **partial** payment.

11.	*moist*	The jungle air was **moist** and hot.
12.	*moisten*	I **moisten** my dry skin with lotion.
13.	*breathe*	A swimmer must **breathe** evenly.
14.	*breath*	The diver took a deep **breath.**
15.	*create*	We used clay to **create** sculptures.
16.	*creature*	The hairy **creature** was terrifying.
17.	*elect*	We voted to **elect** a new president.
18.	*election*	The mayoral **election** is today.
19.	*practice*	Baseball **practice** is every Tuesday.
20.	*practical*	Gardening is a **practical** skill.

✳
**WATCH OUT FOR
FREQUENTLY
MISSPELLED
WORDS!**

■ **PRACTICE**   Which pairs of related words do you already know how to spell? Write these words first. Then write the word pairs you don't know as well.

■ **WRITE**   Choose two sentences to use in a paragraph.

C**HALLENGE!**

politics
politician
authority
authorize
compete
competition

■ **RELATED PAIRS**   Write the list word that matches each clue. Then write the list word that is related to it.

1–2. a share of something
3–4. to choose by voting
5–6. slightly wet
7–8. to make something that has not been made before

■ **EXACT MEANINGS**   Write the list word that makes sense in each sentence below. The answer will be a form of the word in parentheses.

9. Make a big (signed) to announce the winner.
10. Sturdy shoes with thick soles are (practiced) for hiking.
11. How long can you hold your (breathing)?
12. The band will (practiced) today for two hours.
13. The doctor told me to (breathing) deeply.
14. I can read every letter in John Hancock's (signed).

STRATEGIC SPELLING

Using the Meaning Helper Strategy

15–20. Use meaning helpers to help spell hard words. Write *cloth, please, elect, dream, moist,* and *practice.* Write the list word that goes with each of these meaning helpers. Mark the letters that match the underlined sound clues.

Take a Hint
Spelling creature is easy if you remember that it has to **eat.**

≡	Make a capital.
/	Make a small letter.
∧	Add something.
ℓ	Take out something.
⊙	Add a period.
⁋	New paragraph

PROOFREAD AN INTERVIEW

Andre wrote about a volleyball player.
Fix five spelling mistakes and two
sentence errors in her interview.

PROOFREADING TIP

Two sentences are out of
bounds because two complete
thoughts run into each other.
Write a complete thought as a
separate sentence.

> Andre: How often do you pratice volleyball?
>
> Laura: I usualy play every day.
>
> Andre: What was your most exciteing game?
>
> Laura: It was the game with Stone School I
> made the winning point.
>
> Andre: I saw that game I was holding my
> breth at the end. Do you ever dreem about
> playing in the Olympics?

WRITE AN INTERVIEW Pretend you are Laura.

Answer Andre's last question. Then write another question
and answer for the interview. Use a list word and a
personal word.

Word List

moist	signature	breathe	election
moisten	dream	breath	part
cloth	dreamt	create	partial
clothes	please	creature	practice
sign	pleasant	elect	practical

Personal Words 1. ___ 2. ___

Review

ASSOCIATIONS   Write the word from the box that is associated with each set of items.

1. material, fabric
2. piece, section
3. fantasy, nightmare
4. you're welcome, thank you
5. enjoyable, delightful

MAKING CONNECTIONS   Write the word from the box that completes each sentence.

6. Susan packed a sweater, jeans, and other ___.
7. It was raining so hard, we could barely read the ___.
8. Last night, I ___ I was eating a giant apple.
9. A parent's ___ is a requirement for joining the league.
10. Lin made a ___ payment on a drum set.

please
pleasant
cloth
clothes
sign
signature
dream
dreamt
part
partial

Using a *Dictionary*

INFLECTED FORMS and RUN-ONS

Here's how to be sure of spelling **inflected forms,** or words with the ending **-s, -es, -ed, -ing,** or **-est.** Look up the base word in a dictionary. If the spelling changes when an ending is added, you'll see a new spelling. Notice **breathed** and **breathing** in the entry for **breathe.** If you don't see inflected forms, just add the ending to the base word.

breathe (brēŦH), **1** draw air into the lungs and force it out. **2** stop for breath; rest. *v.*, **breathed, breath•ing.**

pleas•ant (plez′nt), **1** that pleases; agreeable. **2** easy to get along with. *adj.*—**pleas′•ant•ly,** *adv.* —**pleas′•ant•ness,** *n.*

Look for **run-on entries,** or words with suffixes such as **-ly** or **-ness,** as in the entry for **pleasant.** To figure out the meaning of a run-on entry, just put the meaning of the entry word and the meaning of the suffix together.

Read the two definitions at the right. Write the inflected form or run-on entry that completes each sentence below.

1. The volleyball players were ___ hard.
2. After riding in a bus for two days, we enjoyed the ___ of our home.
3. Joel ___ in deeply after he returned the serve.
4. The neighbors greeted us ___.

Prefixes dis-, un-, mid-, pre-

SPELLING FOCUS

A prefix is a group of letters added to the beginning of a word to change the meaning or to make a new word. When adding **dis-**, **un-**, **mid-**, or **pre-**, make no changes to the base word: **mid + way = midway**.

■ **STUDY** Read the word in each column. Notice what happens to the base word when a prefix is added.

dis + covered =	1.	*discovered*
dis + order =	2.	*disorder*
un + sure =	3.	*unsure*
un + clear =	4.	*unclear*
un + able =	5.	*unable*
mid + week =	6.	*midweek*
mid + year =	7.	*midyear*
mid + way =	8.	*midway*
pre + test =	9.	*pretest*
pre + school =	10.	*preschool*

dis + appoint =	11.	*disappoint*
dis + obey =	12.	*disobey*
dis + approve =	13.	*disapprove*
un + buckle =	14.	*unbuckle*
un + limited =	15.	*unlimited*
mid + night =	16.	*midnight*
mid + stream =	17.	*midstream*
pre + cook =	18.	*precook*
pre + paid =	19.	*prepaid*
pre + recorded =	20.	*prerecorded*

CHALLENGE!

disadvantages
uncertainty
unnecessary
Midwestern
premature

■ **PRACTICE** Sort the list by
- alphabetizing ten words with **dis-** or **un-**
- alphabetizing ten words with **mid-** or **pre-**

■ **WRITE** Choose ten words to write in sentences.

■ **ADDING WORD PARTS** Write the list words that contain the words below.

1. approve
2. way
3. recorded
4. cook
5. stream

6. appoint
7. night
8. limited
9. test
10. paid

■ **CONTEXT SENTENCES** Write the missing list words. Here's a hint: The underlined word in each sentence is the base word of the answer.

11. Robin and Roger go to __, not to grade <u>school</u>.
12. They enrolled for a <u>year</u>; they had a break at __.
13. They were __ of where to sit; now they are <u>sure</u>.
14. They were __ to tie shoes; now they are <u>able</u> to.
15. They could __ a belt; now they can <u>buckle</u> one also.
16. They left toys in __; now they put them in <u>order</u>.
17. Sometimes they would __ the rules; now they <u>obey</u>.
18. The words to songs seemed __; now they are <u>clear</u>.
19. Robin does a chore for a <u>week</u>; Roger switches at __.
20. They __ an old bookcase; they <u>covered</u> it with paint.

Building New Words

21–24. Write *historic* and *afraid*. Add either the prefix **un-** or **pre-** to each word. Remember the rule you just learned. Check the words in your Spelling Dictionary.

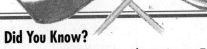

Did You Know?
When it's **midnight** on Sunday in Austin, Texas, it's 8 A.M. on Monday in Jerusalem, Israel.

≡	Make a capital.
/	Make a small letter.
∧	Add something.
℮	Take out something.
⊙	Add a period.
⨍	New paragraph

PROOFREAD A LIST Gina was in a hurry when she wrote this reminder list for her sister. Fix five misspellings and two adjective errors.

PROOFREADING TIP

When Gina wrote *won't* and *no*, she used two "no" words in one sentence. Use only <u>one</u> word such as *not, never, nothing,* or *no one* in a sentence.

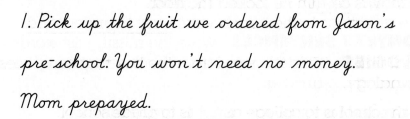

1. Pick up the fruit we ordered from Jason's pre-school. You won't need no money. Mom prepayed.

2. Wind the clock in the hallway. It stoped at mid-night.

3. Put the basketballs and skates in the closet. We do't want no one to trip on them.

WRITE A LIST Would you like to do the kind of chores that Gina's sister does? Write a list of chores that you would enjoy doing at home. Try to use a list word and a personal word.

Word List

disappoint	unsure	pretest	midnight
disobey	unbuckle	precook	midweek
disorder	unclear	prepaid	midyear
discovered	unable	preschool	midway
disapprove	unlimited	prerecorded	midstream

Personal Words 1. ___ 2. ___

Review

ANTONYMS Write the word from the box that most nearly means the opposite of the underlined word or words in each sentence.

discovered
disorder
unsure
unclear
unable
midweek
midyear
midway
pretest
preschool

1. We took <u>a test after</u> reading about reptiles.
2. The pirates <u>buried</u> the treasure.
3. Ashley is <u>qualified</u> to coach the team.
4. Jake was <u>certain</u> he locked the door.
5. The directions to the beach were <u>easy to understand</u>.

ANALOGIES Write the word from the box that completes each analogy.

6. High school is to college as ___ is to grade school.
7. June is to December as ___ is to the year end.
8. Litter is to mess as clutter is to ___.
9. Saturday is to weekend as Wednesday is to ___.
10. Finish is to end as halfway is to ___.

Word *Study*

WORD WEBS Cory wanted to show how midnight indoors is different from midnight outdoors. Making a word web helped her. Read Cory's web, and then make your own web to describe midnight *outdoors*.

night light   creaking

snores   (**midnight inside**)   shadowy shapes

soft pajamas   clock chiming

(**midnight outdoors**)

125

Suffixes -able, -ible, -ant, -ent

SPELLING FOCUS

When suffixes **-able, -ible, -ant,** and **-ent** are added, often the base word stays the same: **comfortable.** In most words that end in **e,** the **e** is dropped: **sensible.** In most words that end in **y, y** is changed to **i: defiant.**

■ **STUDY** Notice what happens to each base word.

comfort + able	=	1. *comfortable*
reason + able	=	2. *reasonable*
wash + able	=	3. *washable*
response + ible	=	4. *responsible*
sense + ible	=	5. *sensible*
contest + ant	=	6. *contestant*
defy + ant	=	7. *defiant*
serve + ant	=	8. *servant*
study + ent	=	9. *student*
reside + ent	=	10. *resident*

agree + able	=	11. *agreeable*
value + able	=	12. *valuable*
convert + ible	=	13. *convertible*
flex + ible	=	14. *flexible*
reverse + ible	=	15. *reversible*
observe + ant	=	16. *observant*
occupy + ant	=	17. *occupant*
urge + ent	=	18. *urgent*
confide + ent	=	19. *confident*
oppose + ent	=	20. *opponent*

CHALLENGE!

knowledgeable
biodegradable
collapsible
participant
correspondent

■ **PRACTICE** Sort the list by writing
- seven words, each having no spelling change when a suffix is added
- thirteen words, each with a spelling change

■ **WRITE** Choose ten words to write in sentences.

■ **DEFINITIONS** Write the list word that matches each clue.

1. someone who learns from books or a teacher
2. someone who waits on a master
3. someone who lives in a town or country
4. someone who is on the other side in a fight
5. someone who participates in a race or contest
6. someone who occupies a place for a time
7. quick to notice things
8. feels very sure or certain
9. standing up against authority
10. must be done immediately

■ **SUFFIX SEARCH** Add a suffix to each word in parentheses to form a list word and complete the sentence.

11. (wash) This cotton dress is <u>(11)</u>.
12. (sense) Eating soup with a fork isn't <u>(12)</u>.
13. (flex) A gymnast has a <u>(13)</u> body.
14. (response) A <u>(14)</u> citizen does not litter.
15. (value) Is this jewelry <u>(15)</u>?
16. (comfort) When I'm tired, I like a warm, <u>(16)</u> bed.
17. (reason) The rule that says students must be on time for school is <u>(17)</u>.
18. (reverse) This <u>(18)</u> jacket is red on the outside and blue on the inside.
19. (convert) Have you ever ridden in a <u>(19)</u>?
20. (agree) Aunt Sue is a friendly and <u>(20)</u> person.

STRATEGIC SPELLING

Building New Words

21–23. Write *honor, understand,* and *defend.* Add the suffix **-ant** or **-able** to each base word. Use your Spelling Dictionary.

☰	Make a capital.
/	Make a small letter.
∧	Add something.
ℰ	Take out something.
⊙	Add a period.
¶	New paragraph

PROOFREAD A SIGN This sign has only eleven words, but one of them is misspelled. Find the spelling mistake and write it correctly.

PROOFREADING TIP

If you want to score big points with a sign, plan it out on a piece of paper. Check the spelling of the words. Then have fun creating the sign.

CAR BAZAAR

555-4950

SALES - PORTERING

LOT PAVING SPECIALS $
NO RESONABLE OFFER REFUSED

WRITE A SIGN Create a sign that uses one or more list words. Begin by thinking of what the words might describe or relate to. Plan the sign on a piece of paper first.

Word List

comfortable	convertible	contestant	student
valuable	responsible	occupant	resident
reasonable	sensible	defiant	opponent
washable	flexible	observant	confident
agreeable	reversible	servant	urgent

Personal Words 1. ___ 2. ___

128

Review

WORDS IN CONTEXT Write the word from the box that is missing from each person's statement.

comfortable
reasonable
washable
responsible
sensible
contestant
defiant
servant
student
resident

1. King: "I will have my ___ bring dessert now."
2. Mail carrier: "Is Ms. Jenkins a ___ of this house?"
3. Bus driver: "The seats in the front are more ___."
4. Mother: "Come back at a ___ hour."
5. Tailor: "You don't dry-clean this dress; it is ___."
6. Game Show host: "Let's find out who our next ___ is."
7. Lifeguard: "The ___ boaters wear life jackets."
8. Principal: "The ___ council elections are on Tuesday."
9. Police officer: "The suspect was ___ and rude."
10. Baby-sitter: "It's not ___ to cancel at the last minute."

Word Study

DIAMOND POEM This diamond poem shows how one student felt about a school year. The poem has seven lines and sixteen words. The top part of the poem describes the beginning of the year, and the bottom describes the end of it. Write your own diamond poem about your school year.

One Student's Year

September
nervous, excited
hoping, preparing, starting,
friendships, teams, projects, bells,
working, practicing, trying,
confident, free
June!

Suffixes -ous, -ion, -ation

SPELLING FOCUS

When adding the suffixes **-ous**, **-ion**, and **-ation**, often the base word stays the same: **inform, information**. For most words ending in **e**, drop the **e**: **fame, famous**. For most words ending in **y**, change **y** to **i**: **mystery, mysterious**.

■ **STUDY**   Notice what happens to each base word.

fame + ous	=	1. famous
nerve + ous	=	2. nervous
mystery + ous	=	3. mysterious
danger + ous	=	4. dangerous
select + ion	=	5. selection
educate + ion	=	6. education
inform + ation	=	7. information
organize + ation	=	8. organization
converse + ation	=	9. conversation
imagine + ation	=	10. imagination

joy + ous	=	11. joyous
marvel + ous	=	12. marvelous
humor + ous	=	13. humorous
instruct + ion	=	14. instruction
attract + ion	=	15. attraction
reject + ion	=	16. rejection
inflate + ion	=	17. inflation
decorate + ion	=	18. decoration
admire + ation	=	19. admiration
prepare + ation	=	20. preparation

CHALLENGE!

contagious
ambitious
interception
appreciation
civilization

■ **PRACTICE**   Sort the list by writing
- eleven words with a spelling change when a suffix is added
- nine words with no spelling change

■ **WRITE**   Choose ten words to write in sentences.

■ **ANTONYMS** Write the list word that means the opposite of each underlined word. Use the Spelling Dictionary if you need to.

1. Everyone wanted an autograph of the <u>unknown</u> baseball player.
2. The audience laughed at the <u>serious</u> clown.
3. The guard warned us that it was <u>safe</u> to swim alone.
4. A visit to the moon would be a <u>dull</u> experience.
5. When we celebrate a holiday, it is a <u>sad</u> occasion.
6. During the storm, the dog was very shaky and <u>calm</u>.
7. The disappearance of our cow was <u>understandable</u>.
8. Writers feel discouraged when they send stories to magazines and receive letters of <u>acceptance</u>.

■ **WORD FORMS** Add **-ion** or **-ation** to each verb below to create a list word.

9. inform
10. organize
11. select
12. converse

13. prepare
14. decorate
15. attract
16. imagine

STRATEGIC SPELLING

Using the Meaning Helper Strategy

Use meaning helpers to help spell hard words. Write the list word that goes with each meaning helper. Mark the letter that matches the underlined sound clue.

17. admi<u>r</u>e
18. infla<u>t</u>e

19. educa<u>t</u>e
20. instru<u>ct</u>

Did You Know?
The highest military **decoration** is the Congressional Medal of Honor. It is awarded to persons in the military for acting "above and beyond the call of duty."

☰	Make a capital.
/	Make a small letter.
∧	Add something.
ℯ	Take out something.
⊙	Add a period.
¶	New paragraph

PROOFREAD A BUSINESS LETTER

Find the five misspellings in this imaginary letter. Fix three careless errors.

PROOFREADING TIP

The Mayor is writing to tell the wolf that he's in deep water, but he may just laugh at her careless mistakes. Where should she have divided *houses*? Read carefully to catch her other mistakes.

```
                                   101 Main Street
                                   Pig Town, UT 84002
                                   April 1, 20--
B. B. Wolf
R. R. 1
Spring Grove, UT 84001

Dear Mr. B. B. Wolf:

   We, the homeowners of Pig Town, have
imformation that you plan to blow down are hou-
ses. Every residint is nervos. You must stop
this this dangerus activity Immediately.

                                   Yours truly,
                                   Mayor Ima Pig
```

WRITE A BUSINESS LETTER
Write Mr. Wolf's reply to the Mayor. Include all the parts of a business letter as in the example. Use three list words and a personal word.

Word List

famous	dangerous	selection	organization
nervous	humorous	rejection	conversation
joyous	education	inflation	admiration
marvelous	instruction	decoration	imagination
mysterious	attraction	information	preparation

Personal Words 1. ___ 2. ___

MAKING CONNECTIONS Write the word from the box that completes each unfinished sentence in the letter.

famous
nervous
mysterious
dangerous
selection
education
information
organization
conversation
imagination

Dear Skip,

How's college? As Dad would say, "I hope you're getting a good (1)." I joined the service (2) at school. My new school has a good (3) of activities.

I really enjoyed the (4) we had on the telephone last week. The (5) that you provided, made me feel less (6) about flying to Grandma's. Although you said riding in a car is more (7) than flying in an airplane, I feel more safe in a car. Remember, I have a wild (8) and sometimes awful pictures form in my mind.

I probably watch too much TV. Last night I watched an old detective show with a lot of (9) characters in it. Mom said the show made many of the actors (10).

I should finish packing. I miss you.

Love,
Melissa

Multicultural Connection

ENVIRONMENT Nature can be marvelous to see, feel, and hear. The country of Brazil has many amazing marvels of nature. Picture the scenes at the right. Imagine that you're a film director making a nature film called *Marvelous Brazil.* Pick a scene and send a camera crew to film it. Write directions for three close-up camera shots.

Scenes in Brazil

the largest river, the Amazon

the largest tropical rain forest

the greatest waterfalls, the Iguaçu Falls

many gold mines

some of the largest frogs and snakes

Film this scene _____

Close-up #1 _____

Close-up #2 _____

Close-up #3 _____

Possessives

■ **STUDY**   Read the sentence. Notice the two kinds of endings: **'s** or **s'**.

✳
WATCH OUT FOR FREQUENTLY MISSPELLED WORDS!

1.	*friend's*	My **friend's** brother is in college.
2.	*today's*	Chili is **today's** lunch special.
3.	*Dad's* ✳	I used **Dad's** new computer.
4.	*Mom's* ✳	She borrowed **Mom's** earrings.
5.	*sister's*	I played my **sister's** video game.
6.	*sisters'*	We borrowed the two **sisters'** skis.
7.	*child's*	A **child's** dinner includes a toy.
8.	*children's*	Tag is a **children's** game.
9.	*person's*	That is only one **person's** opinion.
10.	*people's*	It is the **people's** right to vote.

11.	*grandmother's*	I made my **grandmother's** bed.
12.	*grandfather's*	His **grandfather's** hobby is golf.
13.	*uncle's*	My mother is my **uncle's** sister.
14.	*uncles'*	Both **uncles'** cars were identical.
15.	*doctor's*	I value my **doctor's** opinion.
16.	*doctors'*	Those **doctors'** offices are closed.
17.	*cousin's*	I cut my **cousin's** hair.
18.	*cousins'*	Our **cousins'** hamsters are cute.
19.	*woman's*	This **woman's** suitcase was lost.
20.	*women's*	The **women's** team won.

CHALLENGE!

pedestrian's
pedestrians'
principal's
principals'
bicyclist's
bicyclists'

■ **PRACTICE**   Sort the list words by writing
- seven plural possessive nouns
- thirteen singular possessive nouns

■ **WRITE**   Choose ten words to write in sentences.

■ **RIDDLES** Complete each sentence by writing the possessive form of each word in the riddle.

1. *How to Operate:* a book in a (doctor) office.
2. A biography: the story of a (person) life.
3. *Bedtime Stories*: a book in my (grandmother) house.
4. Nursery songs: (children) music.
5. The second Sunday in May: (Mom) special day.
6. A banjo: my (grandfather) favorite instrument.
7. My uncle: (Dad) brother.
8. A photo of my parents' daughter: my (sister) picture.
9. My uncle's son's jacket: my (cousin) coat.
10. The date of the day after yesterday: (today) date.
11. A Chinese restaurant: my (uncle) business.

■ **WORD FORMS** Write the list words by writing the possessive form of each word below.

12. friend
13. sisters
14. woman
15. child
16. doctors

17. cousins
18. uncles
19. women
20. people

FREQUENTLY MISSPELLED WORDS

Capitalize **Dad's** and **Mom's** only when they are names. *Get Dad's coat and Peg's hat.* Notice the difference: *Here are your mom's books.*

STRATEGIC SPELLING

Building New Words

Write the words that complete the chart. Remember what you learned.

Singular	Plural Possessive
21. man	——
22. student	——

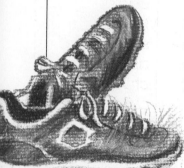

═══	Make a capital.
/	Make a small letter.
∧	Add something.
ℓ	Take out something.
⊙	Add a period.
¶	New paragraph

PROOFREAD A FORM Vanessa decided to fill out a form at a store. Find the four misspelled words and three handwriting errors. Write them correctly.

PROOFREADING TIP

Vanessa wrote an important message, but will the workers at the store be able to read her handwriting? They will if she closes certain letters.

GIANT DEPARTMENT STORE

Comment Card

Name ___Vanessa Hightower___   Phone ___555-1769___

Is your comment about a

☐ suggestion   ☑ problem   ☐ compliment

Tell us about it!

Your ud in todays newspaper was wrong. It sead that childrens' shoes are on sale for $14.99. I can only find shoes that cost more. Do you usely check your uds?

WRITE A FORM Think about your shopping experiences in large stores. Then write your comments. Use at least two list words and a personal word.

Word List

Dad's	children's	person's	sisters'
Mom's	woman's	people's	cousin's
today's	women's	uncle's	cousins'
friend's	grandmother's	uncles'	doctor's
child's	grandfather's	sister's	doctors'

Personal Words 1. ___ 2. ___

Review

MEANING MATCH Write the word from the box that means the same as the underlined word or words.

1. On Friday, I am going to a <u>buddy's</u> birthday party.
2. He's too old to pay the <u>young boys' and girls'</u> admission.
3. Cindy put a <u>kid's</u> jacket in the lost and found bin.
4. That <u>individual's</u> car has its lights on.
5. <u>Men's, women's, and children's</u> luggage did arrive.

friend's
today's
Dad's
Mom's
sister's
sisters'
child's
children's
person's
people's

PARAGRAPH COMPLETION Complete the journal entry with the words from the box.

I am so excited! Tomorrow, my three aunts are coming to visit from Puerto Rico. They are (6) _____ sisters. She has not seen them since last year. Her (7) _____ flight will arrive while I am at school. Her oldest (8) _____ daughter is my same age. I see (9) _____ relatives all the time. He grew up here. Hopefully, the weather tomorrow will be as nice as (10) _____ weather.

Word *Study*

ALLITERATION This small town has a strange newspaper! The reporters always write about their relatives and they always use **alliteration** in the headlines like the one at the right. Alliteration is the use of the same consonant sound at the beginning of most of the words in a sentence or phrase.

Write other headlines with alliteration using the possessive nouns below. To use alliteration, start all the important words with the same consonant.

Mom's	cousin's	team's

Review

Lesson 25: Related Words
Lesson 26: Prefixes dis-, un-, mid-, pre-
Lesson 27: Suffixes -able, -ible, -ant, -ent
Lesson 28: Suffixes -ous, -ion, -ation
Lesson 29: Possessives

REVIEW WORD LIST

1. breath
2. breathe
3. clothes
4. create
5. creature
6. dream
7. dreamt
8. elect
9. election
10. part
11. pleasant
12. practical
13. practice
14. sign
15. disappoint
16. discovered
17. midweek
18. midyear
19. preschool
20. unable
21. unclear
22. unsure
23. confident
24. flexible
25. observant
26. opponent
27. student
28. admiration
29. attraction
30. conversation
31. dangerous
32. education
33. famous
34. humorous
35. imagination
36. information
37. instruction
38. joyous
39. nervous
40. organization
41. preparation
42. selection
43. children's
44. Dad's
45. doctor's
46. friend's
47. Mom's
48. people's
49. person's
50. today's

Exercise to Feel Great!

Write list words that complete the instructions.

~~breathe~~   ~~instruction~~   ~~breath~~
~~practice~~   ~~pleasant~~

Here is an easy exercise. You need no special (1), and you can do it while you are on a (2) walk. Take a deep (3) and hold it for four steps. Then (4) out on the next four steps. If you (5), you should be able to inhale for eight steps and exhale for eight.

138

Birthday Greetings

The parents of Jimmy and Drew share a birthday.
Write list words that complete their card.

joyous   Mom's   admiration
Dad's   sign   dream

A Greeting for (1) and (2) Birthday

We hope you have a (3) day.

We hope a (4) comes true.

We (5) this card (and we mean it too)

With love and (6), Jimmy and Drew.

Playground Plans

Use the list words to complete these notes from a meeting.

part   organization   children's   create   today's
midyear   practical   preparation   unclear

The parents at Two Oaks School formed an (1) to help their (2) school. At (3) meeting, they talked about playground equipment. Here's what they said:

Mr. Leggat: Let's (4) a design and ask the students to help us build the equipment.

Mrs. Oakson: That isn't (5) because we wouldn't finish until (6) or later. Let's buy equipment.

Mrs. Casco: It's (7) to me where the money will come from.

Mr. Chung: We can raise (8) of the money by having a car wash and a fun fair.

Ms. Falk: It will take a lot of (9). Let's start now!

Campaigning

These campaign ads are missing some words. Write them.

clothes
election
disappoint
unsure
selection
people's
opponent
elect

Ray is the (1) candidate.
If you (2) Ray,
he won't (3) you.

Make a smart (4) .
Pick Jenny in this (5) !
Don't be confused, don't be (6) .
Decide to cast your vote for her!

Meg disagrees with the rule about what
(7) you can wear to school. Libby, the other
candidate, agrees with the rule. Vote for Meg,
not her (8) .

Pet Volunteer

Use the list words to complete this letter.

conversation
confident
doctor's
education
student
midweek
nervous
dreamt

March 30, 20_ _

Dear John,
    I have some news! Last Saturday, I had a (1) with
my neighbor Bret. He works at an Animal Hospital as a
(2) assistant. I asked him if a (3) could be a volunteer
at the hospital. By (4) , he had asked the doctor if I
could help. Wham! I'm starting tomorrow. I feel (5) that
I can do the job, but I feel a little (6) too. I've (7) about
becoming a veterinarian, but I never thought my (8)
would start this soon!

                    Your friend,
                    Marissa

140

Big Bird

Write the missing words in these fascinating facts.
Use the list words.

attraction observant information unable
creature discovered dangerous flexible

Does an ostrich bury its head in the earth?

For a long time, the habits of this large __(1)__ were not known.
Ostriches are very __(2)__ and can see movement over long
distances because of their long, __(3)__ necks. To get close enough
to gather __(4)__ about these birds, two zoologists hid in a mound
where the ostriches were __(5)__ to see them. The team __(6)__ that
when this bird is on its nest and sees something __(7)__ , it lowers its
head until the neck is almost on the ground. In this position,
the ostrich is not an __(8)__ to a predator. An ostrich doesn't really
bury its head!

Pick a Card

To move ahead in a game, players
have to follow instructions on these
cards. Write the missing words.

friend's imagination famous
person's preschool humorous

Spell your best __(1)__
name backwards, and
then sing a song
that you learned when
you were a toddler
or in __(2)__ .

Make your opponent
laugh. Tell a __(3)__
story while imitating
another __(4)__ voice.

Name a __(5)__ athlete.
Use your __(6)__ and
tell about one day in
his or her life.

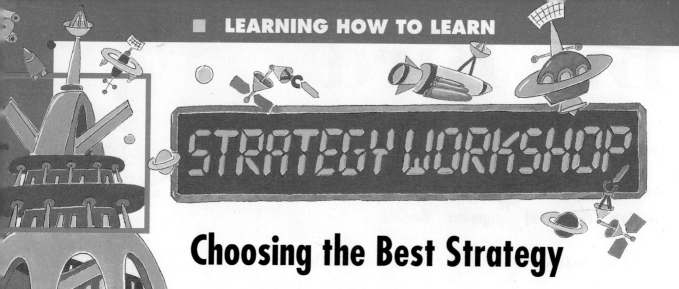

Choosing the Best Strategy

DISCOVER THE STRATEGY Remember that you can always use the Steps for Spelling strategy when you study most spelling words. Don't forget that if a word gives you problems, you can try another strategy. Read about the strategies in the chart below.

Steps for Spelling Use the step-by-step strategy for studying most spelling words. 1. Look. 2. Spell. 3. Think. 4. Picture. 5. Look. 6. Cover and write.	**Divide and Conquer** Divide long words into shorter pieces. Sep/tem/ber night/time	**Memory Tricks** Link the tricky word with a helper that you can spell. a <u>cat</u> on va<u>cat</u>ion Don't <u>eat</u> the l<u>ea</u>ves!
Problem Parts Mark the problem part and study it extra hard. bri<u>d</u>ge glass<u>es</u>	**Pronouncing for Spelling** Pronounce the word correctly or change a sound. Say "**k**-not." Say "clo-**the**-s."	**Meaning Helpers** Find a related word that gives you a sound clue. h<u>ea</u>l—h<u>ea</u>lth sof<u>t</u>—sof<u>t</u>en

TRY IT OUT Now practice choosing strategies. Do the exercises below and on the next page.

Read the description of the strategy each person below has used. Then write the name of the strategy. Use the chart.

1. Heather: The **t** in *select* reminds me that *selection* is spelled with a **t** too._____

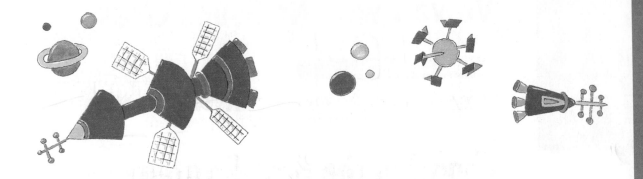

2. Michael: I kept misspelling the first part of *guitar* until I studied that part extra hard: gu̲itar. ____

3. Frank: I always remember the silent **b** in *comb* because I pronounce it "com-**b**."____

Read the reasons why some words are hard to spell. Then write the strategy that you think would work best for each.

4. *Convertible* is hard because it's so long.

5. *Know* is hard because you might forget about the **k.**

6. *Occasion* is hard because one letter is doubled.

Compare your results with a partner or in a group. You may have chosen different strategies for the same word. That's fine, as long as you can explain your choice.

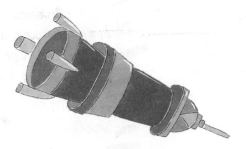

LOOK AHEAD Look ahead at the lessons in the next unit. Find three words that look hard to spell. Which strategy would you choose to help you spell each word? Write the words and strategies you chose.

Vowels with No Sound Clues

SPELLING FOCUS

In some words the vowel sound you hear is schwa /ə/. It gives no clue to its spelling: **president**.

■ **STUDY** Say the words. Pay attention to the underlined letters. Then read the sentence.

WATCH OUT FOR
FREQUENTLY
MISSPELLED
WORDS!

1.	manager	I complained to the store **manager**.
2.	president	We elected a new club **president**.
3.	different ✳	He tried on three **different** suits.
4.	terrible	The garbage had a **terrible** odor.
5.	finally ✳	My refund **finally** came in the mail.
6.	really	Did you **really** meet an astronaut?
7.	supposed	I was **supposed** to leave by noon.
8.	probably ✳	Dark clouds **probably** mean rain.
9.	California	San Francisco is in **California**.
10.	especially ✳	This test is **especially** difficult.

11.	balance	A high diver needs great **balance**.
12.	constant	The **constant** rain kept us indoors.
13.	innocent	The **innocent** man was set free.
14.	realize	We didn't **realize** it was so late.
15.	opportunity	I have an **opportunity** to audition.
16.	pollute	Car exhaust fumes **pollute** the air.
17.	prisoner	One **prisoner** was in the jail cell.
18.	celebrate	Let's **celebrate** your birthday.
19.	grocery	I wrote milk on my **grocery** list.
20.	elevator	The **elevator** stops at each floor.

CHALLENGE!

diamond
government
miniature
refrigerator
veterinarian

■ **PRACTICE** First write the words that you know best. Then write words that are more difficult for you.

■ **WRITE** Choose two sentences to use in a paragraph.

ASSOCIATIONS Write the list word that is associated with the items below.

1. locks, bars, jail
2. toxic waste, litter, smog
3. election, candidate, White House
4. gold rush, sunshine, ranches
5. up, down, floors
6. party, festival, happiness
7. organizer, business, leader

Take a Hint
Students often make the mistake of writing **supposed to** as one word. Remember that it takes **two** words to write **supposed to**.

POEMS Write the list words that complete the poem.

A Flood of Trouble

I was (8) to do dishes—Mom had said, "Get right to it!"
I hate doing dishes, but I decided to do it.
I had turned on the water (it was a (9) flow),
When I heard the doorbell—it was my good pal Joe.

He was offering me an (10) to play.
While we played, I didn't (11) that time was slipping away.
When I (12) went home, I got a shocking surprise:
Water covered the floor and was (13) on the rise!

Just then Mom splashed in, carrying her (14) bags.
"This is (15)!" she yelled. "Get a mop and some rags!"
Suddenly she lost her (16) and plopped right on the floor.
"From now on," she gasped, "you may do a (17) chore."

STRATEGIC SPELLING

Choosing the Best Strategy

18–20. Write *probably, especially,* and *innocent.* Choose a strategy from page 142 that would help you spell each word. Write the name of the strategy next to each word.

Challenge
mean
Range
mode
median

≡	Make a capital.
/	Make a small letter.
∧	Add something.
ℓ	Take out something.
⊙	Add a period.
¶	New paragraph

PROOFREAD OPINIONS Read Kelly's opinions of two books she read. Correct the five spelling errors and one mistake concerning paragraph form.

PROOFREADING TIP
You actually read two paragraphs, but they look more like one. Where would you tell Kelly to start a new paragraph?

I belive we'll probly colonize another planet soon. That's why I expecially liked Day of the Earthlings by Eve Bunting. Now I relize how differnt life on Mars might be. I also liked Wanted: UFO. It showed what aliens might want from Earth.

WRITE OPINIONS Write your opinions of one or two books you have read. Explain your reactions. Try to use some list words and a personal word.

Word List

different	really	especially	celebrate
manager	realize	prisoner	grocery
balance	innocent	terrible	elevator
constant	opportunity	California	supposed
president	pollute	probably	finally

Personal Words 1. ___ 2. ___

146

Review

CROSSWORD PUZZLE   Use the clues to fill in the puzzle with the words from the box.

Across
2. actually
5. Sacramento is this state's capital.
8. more than others
9. more likely than not
10. the chief officer

Down
1. person who manages
3. not alike
4. awful
6. at last
7. considered true

Word box:
- manager ✓
- president ✓
- different
- terrible
- finally
- really
- supposed
- probably ✓
- California ✓
- especially

Multicultural Connection

CELEBRATIONS   People everywhere celebrate when a new year arrives. The Chinese people celebrate the new year on the first day of the lunar, or moon, calendar, which falls between January 21 and February 19. The holiday is also called the Spring Festival. To prepare, people clean the house and pay their debts. On Chinese New Year, people wish each other good luck, good health, success, and other good things.

If you were invited to a Chinese home for a typical New Year's celebration, you would notice a sign on the front door like the one at the right. The sign says "Welcome to the new spring! May good fortune be yours."

Create your own Chinese New Year door sign. Write the message that you would use on your sign. Include any of the wishes mentioned above and one of your own.

Vowels in Final Syllables

SPELLING FOCUS

Vowels in final syllables often sound alike even when they are spelled differently: anot**her**, calend**ar**; ev**il**, canc**el**; capt**ain**, froz**en**.

■ **STUDY** Say each list word. Pay special attention to how the last syllable is spelled. Read the sentence.

❋

WATCH OUT FOR FREQUENTLY MISSPELLED WORDS!

1.	*either*	Choose **either** toast or a bagel.
2.	*another* ❋	I need to meet you **another** day.
3.	*calendar*	Circle the date on your **calendar.**
4.	*evil*	The villain had an **evil** plan.
5.	*cancel*	Please **cancel** my book order.
6.	*label*	The shirt size was on the **label.**
7.	*eaten*	I have **eaten** at this restaurant.
8.	*frozen*	We skated on the **frozen** pond.
9.	*curtain*	The **curtain** covered the window.
10.	*captain*	The team **captain** called a meeting.

11.	*computer*	This **computer** has more memory.
12.	*solar*	The sun provides **solar** energy.
13.	*particular*	That **particular** book is sold out.
14.	*fossil*	The archaeologist found a **fossil.**
15.	*civil*	Voting is a **civil** duty.
16.	*channel*	Large ships use the deep **channel.**
17.	*quarrel*	We shook hands after our **quarrel.**
18.	*siren*	The loud **siren** signaled a tornado.
19.	*fountain*	Water gushed from the **fountain.**
20.	*bargain*	I made a **bargain** with the trader.

CHALLENGE!

cylinder
scholar
sentinel
hydrogen
villain

■ **PRACTICE** Sort the words by writing
- six words ending with the letters **ar** or **er**
- seven words ending with the letters **il** or **el**
- seven words ending with the letters **en** or **ain**

■ **WRITE** Choose ten words to write in sentences.

ANALOGIES Write a list word that completes each analogy.

1. Drip is to faucet as gush is to ___.
2. Lunar is to moon as ___ is to sun.
3. Clock is to hour as ___ is to date.
4. Bedspread is to bed as ___ is to window.
5. Lieutenant is to navy as ___ is to army.
6. Melted is to soft as ___ is to hard.
7. Dinner bell is to calling as ___ is to warning.
8. Hero is to good as villain is to ___.
9. Train is to railroad track as boat is to river ___.
10. Neither is to nor as ___ is to or.
11. Agreement is to peace as ___ is to fight.

*FREQUENTLY MISSPELLED WORDS * FREQUENTLY MISSPELLED WORDS*

Here's a way to remember the spelling of *another*, a word that stumps a lot of students. It's made up of three words: **a not her.**

MAKING CONNECTIONS Write the list word that answers each question.

12. What word means "exact" or "special"?
13. What is often attached to clothing?
14. What is a rock that has an image of an insect?
15. What do you do to an order if you don't want it?
16. What has a keyboard, a monitor, and a memory?
17. What is a costly item that you bought for a low price?
18. What has a person done when he or she is full?
19. What do you ask for when one is not enough?

STRATEGIC SPELLING

Seeing Meaning Connections

20. Write the list word that is related in spelling and meaning to the words in the box. Then complete the sentences with the words from the box.

| civilized |
| civilian |
| civilization |

Col. Rankin spoke to our class. He wore (21) clothes, not a uniform. He said that education has helped him to become more (22). His hobby is learning about the ancient (23) of Egypt.

☰	Make a capital.
/	Make a small letter.
∧	Add something.
ℓ	Take out something.
⊙	Add a period.
¶	New paragraph

PROOFREAD A SIGN Here's another big mistake that a store owner did not notice. Which word needs fixing? Write it correctly.

PROOFREADING TIP
One sign maker has this checklist. You can use it too.
√ Plan the sign first.
√ Check the words in a dictionary.
√ Proofread your work.

"BARGIN" DAY

CREATE A SIGN Write a sign that begins with the words in the sign above. Use two more list words and a personal word in your sign. Check all words for correct spelling.

Word List

bargain	another	label	quarrel
eaten	either	solar	captain
evil	calendar	fountain	siren
curtain	cancel	particular	computer
fossil	channel	frozen	civil

Personal Words 1. ___ 2. ___

Review

CONTEXT CLUES Use the context in each sentence to help you write the correct word from the box.

either
another
calendar
evil
cancel
label
eaten
frozen
curtain
captain

1. It will take hours to thaw the ___ chicken.
2. The horror movie was about a boy and his ___ twin.
3. The rain caused the officials to ___ our soccer game.
4. My science project had a ___ to explain what it was.
5. The ___ of the ship gave orders to the sailors.
6. The ___ on the left window is longer than the others.
7. If Paulo had ___ lunch, he wouldn't be hungry now.
8. While cleaning the attic, we found a ___ from 1938.
9. Dad could take ___ the train or the bus to work.
10. Jo caught ___ fish before she rowed back to shore.

Using a *Dictionary*

USING EXACT WORDS When Charles said, "I'm thinking of something red," each of his friends pictured a different shade of red. Read what they pictured below. Then write the items in order. Begin with the item that is the lightest red and end with the one that is darkest. Compare answers with a partner.

raspberries   **a stop sign**   **a person's red hair**

Words may be about one topic, but the meanings may be weaker or stronger, just as shades of a color are lighter or darker. The words below are about the same topic. Write the words in order. Begin with the weakest and end with the strongest. Use the Spelling Dictionary.

quarrel   **war**   **contest**

Capitalization

■ **STUDY** Read the names of the cities and states. Then add the city, or town, and state where you live.

1. Houston
2. Alaska
3. Kentucky
4. Little Rock
5. Duluth
6. Arizona
7. Miami
8. Indiana
9. Alabama
10. South Carolina
11. Baltimore
12. Detroit
13. Los Angeles
14. Hawaii
15. Memphis
16. Virginia
17. Oregon
18. Pittsburgh
19. _____
20. _____

■ **PRACTICE** Sort the words by writing
- ten words that name cities or a town
- ten words that name states

■ **WRITE** Choose three places and write a paragraph about visiting them.

CHALLENGE!

Louisiana
Juneau
Philadelphia
San Francisco
Cincinnati

RIDDLES   Write the list word that answers each riddle.

1. Which city is smaller than a boulder?
2. Which state has the first and last letters of the alphabet?
3. Which state could have the nickname "Ginny"?
4. Which city sounds like a sandwich when you add **-er?**
5. Which city has a ball but not a bat?
6. *I am* in the middle of this city. Which city am I in?
7. In which city can you find an angel?
8. Which state means "land of the Indians"?
9. Which city ends this rhyme: Ruth lost a tooth in ___?
10. Which state's name has two words?
11. The name of this state makes you think that there is no more iron ore and other minerals left. Which is it?

MATCHING PARTS   Write the list word that has the same beginning letter and the same number of syllables as each word below.

12. appreciate
13. history
14. karate
15. horseback
16. magnet
17. astronaut
18. dinner

19–20. Now write the name of your city and state. Think of words whose first letters and number of syllables match them.

STRATEGIC SPELLING

Divide and Conquer Strategy

21–24. Sometimes it helps to study long words piece by piece. Write four list words that are hard for you. Draw lines between the syllables and study them. Check a dictionary.

Did You Know?
Arizona probably comes from the Papago Indian word *arizonak*, which means "small spring." *Alaska* comes from the Eskimo word *alakshak*, which means "mainland."

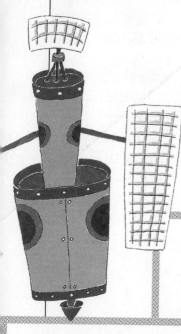

≡	Make a capital.
/	Make a small letter.
∧	Add something.
ℯ	Take out something.
⊙	Add a period.
¶	New paragraph

PROOFREAD AN ITINERARY

Itineraries are plans for traveling. This is part of Rose's itinerary for her family's vacation. Correct five spelling errors. Fix three careless errors.

June 28–30 We'll leave Mephis and and drive to Lexington, Kentucy. We'll stay at at our grandmothers house.

July 1–3 We'll drive Indianapolis for the Baker family reunion.

July 4 We'll eather go too the parade or visit the planetarium.

PROOFREADING TIP

One of Rose's careless errors is her repeated words. Another is dropping words. We all need to fix careless errors after writing a first draft.

WRITE AN ITINERARY Plan a trip that would take a week and write an itinerary like the one above. Use one list word and two personal words.

Word List

Baltimore	Indiana	South Carolina	Hawaii
Miami	Houston	Virginia	Alabama
Kentucky	Little Rock	Oregon	Pittsburgh
Alaska	Arizona	Duluth	
Detroit	Memphis	Los Angeles	

Personal Words 1. ___ 2. ___

Review

Houston
Alaska
Kentucky
Little Rock
Duluth
Arizona
Miami
Indiana
Alabama
South Carolina

TONGUE TWISTERS Write the word from the box that would best complete each tongue twister. Here's a clue: The answer will start with the same letter as the first word in each sentence.

1. Mornings in ___ are magnificent.
2. Houses in ___ are huge.
3. Kind kids keep kittens in ___.
4. Dinosaurs don't dig in ___.
5. Let's look at the landmark in ___.
6. Some say the ___ sun is soothing.
7. Insects in ___ are interesting.

MAKING INFERENCES Write the word from the box that fits each clue.

8. In this northwestern state, sleds carry people and supplies in the snow.
9. In this southwestern state, most people live in the desert.
10. This southeastern state is known as the *Heart of Dixie.*

Using a *Dictionary*

WORD HISTORIES The history of a word is its **etymology.** When you look up a word's etymology, you might find that it comes from another language. Many words come from people's names. For example, Houston, Texas, was named after Sam Houston, who was the president of Texas before it became a state.

Read at the right how the Ferris wheel got its name. In a dictionary entry, the etymology is in brackets [ ].

These riddles show how some common words came into English. Write the answers. Use the Spelling Dictionary.

1. **Adolphe Sax:** I am the inventor of a musical instrument. What is it?
2. **Amelia J. Bloomer:** Back in the 1800s, I wrote about a new style of women's pants. What were they called?
3. **King Louis XIV:** The explorer La Salle named land in America after me. What did he call it?

Ferris wheel (fer′is), a large, revolving wheel with hanging seats, used in carnivals, amusement parks, fairs, etc. [The *Ferris wheel* was named for George W. *Ferris,* 1859-1896, an American engineer who invented it.]

Easily Confused Words

SPELLING FOCUS

Some words are easily confused because they have similar pronunciations and spellings: **except, accept.**

■ **STUDY** Say each pair of words. Notice how each one looks and sounds. Then read the sentences.

* **WATCH OUT FOR FREQUENTLY MISSPELLED WORDS!**

1.	*of*	I am a member **of** my family.
2.	*off* ✳	The books fell **off** the desk.
3.	*except* ✳	I like all colors **except** yellow.
4.	*accept*	We **accept** your invitation.
5.	*which* ✳	Please decide **which** one to buy.
6.	*witch*	She wore a **witch** costume.
7.	*where* ✳	Hide the gift **where** it will be safe.
8.	*were* ✳	The twins **were** identical.
9.	*weather*	The **weather** report predicted rain.
10.	*whether*	I must decide **whether** to stay or go.

11.	*plant*	The drooping **plant** needed water.
12.	*planet*	Mars is the **planet** nearest to Earth.
13.	*bounds*	The foul ball was out of **bounds.**
14.	*bounce*	I love to **bounce** on a trampoline.
15.	*desert*	Cacti grow in the hot, dry **desert.**
16.	*dessert*	We ordered ice cream for **dessert.**
17.	*rise*	I saw the balloon **rise** in the sky.
18.	*raise*	He will **raise** the flag at dawn.
19.	*dinner*	Let's have spaghetti for **dinner.**
20.	*diner*	The **diner** was eating alone.

■ **PRACTICE** Some word pairs are more confusing than others. Write the word pairs that you use correctly. Then write the pairs that you aren't sure of.

■ **WRITE** Choose ten words to write in sentences.

CHALLENGE!

respectively
respectfully
adapt
adopt
conscious
conscience

WORD EQUATIONS   Write the list word that completes the equation.

1. temperature + moisture + air =
2. Mars + space + sphere =
3. hot + sand + dry =
4. woman + fairy tale + magic powers =
5. sweet + food + after dinner =
6. leaves + stalk + root =
7. line + limit + edge =
8. food + meal + filling =

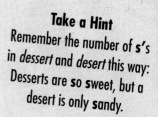

Take a Hint.
Remember the number of **s**'s in *dessert* and *desert* this way: Desserts are **so** sweet, but a desert is only **s**andy.

WORDS IN CONTEXT   Some words are missing in the paragraphs below. Write the list words that complete them.

The snow falling outside was beginning to (9) above the the front-porch steps. Soon Grandpa would say, "Do you want to shovel the snow (10) the path?" He always asked her politely, but Lee Ann knew that she had to (11) the job.

She wished that robots (12) able to do her chores. On TV she had seen robots that could (13) and lower heavy objects and pick up containers. "They can do almost anything (14) read your mind," Lee Ann thought. "If I had a robot (15) my own," she said to herself, "I'd give it these commands: Pick up the shovel (16) is on the porch. Lift the snow off the path. Stop (17) the path meets the road and return to the house."

STRATEGIC SPELLING

Choosing the Best Strategy

18–20. Write *whether, diner,* and *bounce.* Which strategy could help you spell each word? Write the name of the strategy next to each word. Then compare choices with a partner. For a list of strategies, see page 142.

═	Make a capital.
/	Make a small letter.
∧	Add something.
ℓ	Take out something.
⊙	Add a period.
¶	New paragraph

PROOFREAD AN INVITATION Holly thought of a theme for her party and made invitations. Fix five spelling mistakes and three handwriting errors.

PROOFREADING TIP

Holly spent a lot of time on this clever invitation, but her handwriting isn't always clear. Will her guests be able to read her address and other words?

Come to an intergalactic party!

Place: 560 Third St.   Date: March 3

Time: 6 p. m.   Given by: Holly Broz

We'll be blasting of to have diner on Pizzatron Two, a friendly plant. For desert, we'll have Saturn Slush. Radio a message if you except my invitation.

WRITE AN INVITATION Imagine a party you would like to have. Then write an invitation to a friend. Use three list words and one personal word.

Word List

of	whether	except	dessert
off	which	accept	rise
where	witch	bounds	raise
were	plant	bounce	dinner
weather	planet	desert	diner

Personal Words   1. ___ 2. ___

Review

RHYMES   Write the word from the box that rhymes with the underlined word and ends with the same letters.

1. That football player is a <u>rich</u> man.
2. Dad gave Mom <u>leather</u> gloves for her birthday.
3. The prisoner dug a <u>ditch</u>.
4. The goat had broken its <u>tether</u> and was in the shed.

SYNONYMS   Write the word from the box that means nearly the same as the underlined word or phrase in each sentence.

5. The house was made <u>from</u> bricks.
6. I was <u>away</u> at camp for the whole summer.
7. <u>In what place</u> should we meet?
8. My aunt will <u>take</u> the award for my uncle.
9. <u>Other than</u> Jerome, everyone is here.
10. Mickey and Sue <u>had been</u> at the playground.

of
off
except
accept
which
witch
where
were
weather
whether

Using a *Dictionary*

IDIOMS   Olivia used the idiom *bounce back* in a sports article. She wrote:

> If our runners lose a meet, they always bounce back.

An **idiom** is a phrase that means something different from the usual meaning of the words. This idiom means "begin again with enthusiasm." An idiom is found in the dictionary under its most important word—in this case, *bounce.*

Idioms
let the cat out of the bag
shell out
pass out

Rewrite the sentences below by substituting an idiom at the right for some words. Use the Spelling Dictionary.

1. Would you faint if you met a creature from outer space?
2. We had to pay five dollars to see *Lost Satellites.*
3. Edward told everyone about the surprise.

Compound Words 2

SPELLING FOCUS

Some compound words are written as one word: **everybody.** Others are written as two words: **all right.**

■ **STUDY** Say each compound word and look at the two words that form it. Then read the sentence.

1. *bookshelf*   I put the books on the **bookshelf.**
2. *someone*   This job requires **someone** strong.
3. *everybody*   I need **everybody** to line up now.
4. *nowhere*   My hat is **nowhere** to be found.
5. *cupcake*   The baker frosted the **cupcake.**
6. *home run*   Her **home run** won the game.
7. *each other*   We helped **each other** do chores.
8. *hot dog*   I like mustard on my **hot dog.**
9. *all right*   She was **all right** after falling.
10. *high school*   I am a senior in **high school.**

11. *grandparent*   I am named for a **grandparent.**
12. *wristwatch*   I prefer a digital **wristwatch.**
13. *everyone* ✳   He invited **everyone** in the class.
14. *blindfold*   The **blindfold** covered her eyes.
15. *typewriter*   He wrote a letter on a **typewriter.**
16. *pen pal*   I wrote to my **pen pal** in Sweden.
17. *living room*   We relaxed in the **living room.**
18. *peanut butter*   I love **peanut butter** sandwiches.
19. *no one*   He saw **no one** that he knew.
20. *first aid*   I learned **first aid** in the Scouts.

■ **PRACTICE** Alphabetize the compounds in which two words are joined. Then alphabetize the compounds with a space between the two words.

■ **WRITE** Choose two sentences to use in a paragraph.

CHALLENGE!

splashdown
drawbridge
remote control
bulletin board
scuba diving

PUZZLE Read the clues. Then complete the puzzle by writing the words across.

1. no person; nobody
2. in no place, at no place
3. some person
4. each one; everybody
5. every person
6. one another

1. _ _ ■ _ _ _
2. _ _ _ _ _ _ _
3. _ _ _ _ _ _ _
4. _ _ _ _ _ _ _ _
5. _ _ _ _ _ _ _ _ _
6. _ _ _ _ ■ _ _ _ _ _

DRAWING CONCLUSIONS Write the list word that matches each clue.

7. The father or mother of your mom or dad is this.
8. Children often spread this on bread.
9. This machine has every key from A to Z.
10. In some games you use this to cover someone's eyes.
11. This food was named after an animal.
12. This might have hands, an alarm, and numbers.
13. This makes the numbers on a scoreboard change.
14. Peel off the paper before you eat this sweet treat.
15. This person expects to receive letters.
16. When you finish this, you'll receive a diploma.
17. This can be an answer to the question "How are you?"
18. This is where you often find chairs, a sofa, and lamps.
19. Look for stories, poems, and photo albums in this place.

STRATEGIC SPELLING

Seeing Meaning Connections

Use the related words from the box to complete the paragraph.

first aid
firsthand
first lady

Mrs. Racky, our principal, says that the governor and the (20) will visit our school. She got (21) information from the governor himself. They will visit a social studies class and a health class where students are learning (22).

Take a Hint
You may say **all right** as if it is one word, but you must write it as <u>two words</u>.

■ PROOFREADING AND WRITING

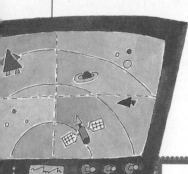

≡	Make a capital.
/	Make a small letter.
∧	Add something.
ℯ	Take out something.
⊙	Add a period.
¶	New paragraph

PROOFREAD A JOURNAL ENTRY

Maybe you will write a journal entry like this one in the near future. Fix five spelling errors and three verb errors.

PROOFREADING TIP

This driver needs to watch out for endings on action words. Notice the phrase *It look*. It should be *It looks*. Can you find similar mistakes?

> June 29, 2015   I'm writing as my car take me to Red Lake, Utah. It look as if noone is driving, but I'am safe as can be. Computer maps guides cars like these so drivers cann't get lost or into accidents. My car is so simple that some one could drive it with a blind fold on.

WRITE A JOURNAL ENTRY
Choose a date in the future or before you were born. Write about an experience on that day. Use at least two list words.

Word List

everybody	everyone	home run	living room
bookshelf	nowhere	no one	peanut butter
grandparent	blindfold	each other	all right
someone	typewriter	pen pal	high school
wristwatch	cupcake	hot dog	first aid

Personal Words   1. ___ 2. ___

Review

CLASSIFYING Write the word from the box that belongs in each group.

1. grade school, college, ___
2. cookie, brownie, ___
3. desk, chair, ___
4. peanuts, popcorn, ___
5. strike, safe, out, ___

bookshelf
someone
everybody
nowhere
cupcake
home run
each other
hot dog
all right
high school

MAKING INFERENCES Write the word from the box that fits each clue.

6. Other than Rudy, ___ likes the new coach.
7. The two teachers saw ___ at the mall.
8. Will ___ open a window, please?
9. I didn't plan for company, but it was ___.
10. We stopped at a gas station in the middle of ___.

Word *Study*

ANTONYMS You can create "tangle talk" with **antonyms,** or words that have opposite meanings. In tangle talk, you say one thing and then the opposite. Read this tangle-talk poem.

> No one was inside of
> that merry, crowded house.
> Everyone was very noisy
> And just as quiet as a mouse.

Find two pairs of antonyms in the poem. Write the words.

Now read another tangle-talk poem. Write the missing words. Here's a hint: Each missing word is an antonym of another word in the same line.

> On a summer day in (3),
> We met a young man who looked (4),
> From a planet somewhere near to (5),
> Where the sea was hot and the sun was (6).

Review

Lesson 31: Vowels with No Sound Clues
Lesson 32: Vowels in Final Syllables
Lesson 33: Capitalization
Lesson 34: Easily Confused Words
Lesson 35: Compound Words 2

REVIEW WORD LIST

1. celebrate
2. different
3. finally
4. grocery
5. manager
6. opportunity
7. president
8. probably
9. realize
10. really
11. supposed
12. terrible
13. another
14. calendar
15. captain
16. computer
17. eaten
18. fossil
19. frozen
20. label
21. particular
22. quarrel
23. siren
24. Alaska
25. Arizona
26. Detroit
27. Indiana
28. Oregon
29. accept
30. bounce
31. bounds
32. dessert
33. dinner
34. except
35. off
36. plant
37. rise
38. weather
39. were
40. where
41. which
42. all right
43. bookshelf
44. cupcake
45. each other
46. hot dog
47. peanut butter
48. pen pal
49. someone
50. wristwatch

Robo-pet

Use the list words to complete this explanation.

grocery   dinner   quarrel   computer   particular

Hello. I am Robo-pet. I look like a toy, but I have a (1) brain. I am useful and fun. I will remember the (2) list and create (3) menus. I also play games. You can program me to do a (4) job just for you, and I will never (5) with you. I am ready. What do you want me to do?

Scavenger Hunt

Walt went on a scavenger hunt. Read what he had to look for and what he found. Write the missing words.

wristwatch	**president**	**calendar**	**bookshelf**
Arizona	**another**	**which**	**someone**

Find something __(1)__ is older than 1970.
I found a dictionary dated 1965 on the __(2)__ .

Find something new that __(3)__ gave you.
I'm wearing my new __(4)__ that Uncle Peter gave me.

Find a __(5)__ for this year.
I've got one that has a picture of
every __(6)__ of the United States.

Find a souvenir from __(7)__ state.
My dad lent me a turquoise ring that he bought in __(8)__ .

A newspaper had these sport reports. Write the missing words.

Sports News

Good Bye, Rudy!

Rudy Rios, the __(1)__ of the Miracles, has retired. At his farewell party, he said, "I plan to return to my home in Portland, __(2)__ , and watch baseball on TV."

Winners
The Scramblers have won the softball league championship! Team captain Julie Glover will __(3)__ the trophy tonight. "We __(4)__ are a great team," she said. "My teammates and I will __(5)__ at the banquet!"

Nervous Player
Sheila Olsen's serves kept going out of __(6)__ at her tennis match yesterday in __(7)__ , Michigan. "From now on, I'll __(8)__ the ball a couple of times before I serve," said Sheila. "If I could be calmer, I'd __(9)__ play better."

bounds
Oregon
manager
really
accept
bounce
celebrate
Detroit
probably

Postcard from the Hoosier State

Write the missing words in this postcard.

except   weather   Indiana   where   all right   rise   supposed

Dear Indra,

So far, our trip to _(1)_ has been fine _(2)_ for the flat tires and the hailstorm. Now the car is _(3)_ and the _(4)_ is sunny. We went near Madison _(5)_ Mounds State Park is located. I walked around the temple mounds that _(6)_ above the ground. The Woodland Indians were _(7)_ to have built them as burial places about 1,000 years ago. See you soon!

Eric

The Word That Came from a Myth

This myth tells the story of an everyday word. Write the missing words.

terrible   realize   were   off   finally   siren   captain

A _(1)_ has a loud, piercing sound, but long ago the word meant a lovely sound.

In a Greek myth, sirens _(2)_ bird-women who lived on a rocky island. Their sweet songs were as deadly as a _(3)_ storm. Sailors heard the songs and sailed their ships closer until they crashed on the rocks.

The hero Ulysses was the _(4)_ of a ship that had to pass the island. His crew didn't _(5)_ what the danger was, but clever Ulysses did. He put wax in the sailors' ears and had the crew tie him to the mast. When Ulysses heard the sirens' song, he struggled to take _(6)_ the ropes, but he couldn't. The ship _(7)_ sailed past the island to safety.

From Across the Ocean

Read the letter Sanna received from a friend from the United States. Write the missing words.

peanut butter	label	pen pal	hot dog
cupcake	dessert	each other	different

July 28, 20_ _

Dear Sanna,

I received your letter. Yes, I'd like to be your (1). Let's write to (2) often.

I'm sending you a package of our food. You'll get a jar that contains something we spread on bread. Look for the (3) that says "(4)." You will also get a type of sausage which we often eat at picnics. It is a (5). I like to eat cookies or a (6) for (7). If you visit me, I'll bake some for you.

Write to tell me if the food you eat in Finland is (8) from ours.

Your friend,
Yolanda

Buried in Ice

Write the missing words.

Alaska	frozen
fossil	opportunity
eaten	plant

A (1) can be the remains of a tiny (2) or a huge creature.

Giant fossils of woolly mammoths have been found (3) in the

ice in Siberia and in (4). The meat of these huge animals was

often (5) by dogs belonging to Eskimos. A giant fossil may be

in a museum near you. Don't miss an (6) to see one close up!

Vocabulary, Writing, and Reference Resources

Cross-Curricular Lessons

Writer's Handbook

Spelling Dictionary

Writer's Thesaurus

English/Spanish Word List

Cross-Curricular Lessons

Geography

When you use these words about geography, you show that you know about your world. Use your Spelling Dictionary if you need to check the meanings of these words. Add your own words about geography.

■ GETTING AT MEANING

Many Kinds of Maps   Complete each statement with the correct list word.

Name: Gwen Palkowski   **Profession:** Mapmaker

Experience: In school my favorite subject was (1) . Now I create the maps that students and adults use.

On this physical map you can see the Midwest where I grew up. The land there is flat. I dreamed of seeing mountains and other different (2) .

When I was ten, my family and I hiked in the mountains. I felt short of breath and dizzy. Later I checked the (3) key on a map to find how high we had climbed above sea level.

When I was older and we'd go on car trips, I was in charge of reading (4) . I'd figure out the route and estimate the (5) we had to cover as we traveled from town to town.

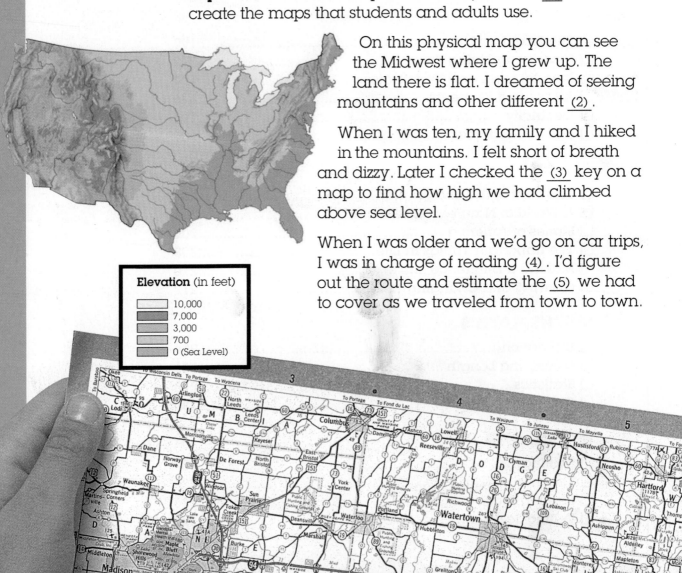

Elevation (in feet)

☐ 10,000
☐ 7,000
☐ 3,000
☐ 700
☐ 0 (Sea Level)

On freezing cold days, I used to think about people who were in a sunny place complaining that the (6) was 95 degrees.

Together with other (7), I now use facts about temperature to create (8) maps. These maps also show rainfall, or (9), in different regions.

We also study (10) maps to find out how people are spread out over the land.

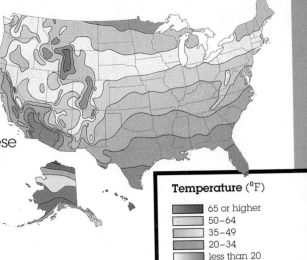

Temperature (°F)

	65 or higher
	50–64
	35–49
	20–34
	less than 20

■ SPELL WELL

Suffixes The spelling of the base word may change when the suffix **-ion** is added. Add **-ion** to each word below to form a list word. What letter was dropped in each word?

11. precipitate

12. populate

13. elevate

Population
(people per square mile)

	90 or more
	45–89
	18–44
	6–17
	less than 6

A Puzzling State

Draw an outline of your state on a large sheet of paper. Label the state capital, major cities, and important landforms. Then turn your finished map over. Draw lines on the back to create a jigsaw puzzle of about twenty pieces. Cut the puzzle pieces apart. Trade puzzles with a classmate and put each other's state back together!

Iroquois
longhouse
corn
Sioux
nomads
pueblo
Anasazi
tepee
agriculture
buffalo

North American Indians

The words in the list describe a few American Indian cultures. Use your Spelling Dictionary to check the meanings of words. Think of other words that belong on the list.

■ GETTING AT MEANING

Working American Indians were as different as their names. Most of the year, the Sioux were nomads, moving around to hunt herds of buffalo. The Anasazi depended on agriculture so they stayed in one place to tend their crops. The Iroquois hunted, fished, and farmed.

This man is a Sioux. Members of his tribe were

1. _____

The Anasazi grew corn and other crops. This tribe knew much about

2. _____

Dwellings Tribes had many varieties of homes. The Iroquois Indians lived in longhouses and the Anasazi lived in pueblos that resembled apartment houses. Some Sioux lived in tepees.

Write the list words that name the dwellings in the pictures.

3. _____

4. _____

5. _____

176

Food An important crop to most American Indian farmers was corn. Buffalo provided food, clothing, and shelter for Plains Indians like the Sioux.

Write the list words that name the items below.

6. _____

7. _____

Tribes The words below name things that were important to tribes on the list. Write the correct tribe's name below each group of words.

longhouse, hunting, fishing, and farming

8. _____

pueblos, agriculture

9. _____

tepees, buffalo

10. _____

■ SPELL WELL

Including All the Letters
Sometimes words contain letters that are not pronounced. Say each word below and write it.

Underline the letters you don't hear.

11. Sioux

12. Iroquois

Did You Know?

The game of lacrosse grew out of an old North American Indian ball game called baggataway. *Each player on a team held a stick with a net at the end of it and tried to scoop up the ball and toss it. The French traders took up the game, giving it the name* lacrosse.

navigation
captain
course
exploration
crew
sailor
expedition
voyage
treasure
discover

Exploration

The sixteenth century was a time of intense European exploration. The list words describe that exciting time. Use the Spelling Dictionary if you need to. Add your own words to the list.

■ GETTING AT MEANING

A Ship's Log Write the list words that complete each item in the log of the *Seabird* by Captain William Goodwin.

| course   treasure   crew   captain   expedition |

21 June 1609 — I am in charge of a daring (1) into unexplored seas. As (2) of this ship, I am hopeful that we will return with (3) and riches.

An astrolabe used in the 1600s

9 July 1609 — Fierce storms have blasted us for two days. The (4) worked around the clock. Now gentle winds are blowing. We are heading straight on (5) again.

navigation	voyage

14 July 1609 — Each day I use my astrolabe, the new (6) instrument that I bought in Portugal. Each day I chart where the ship has been. When I return to Europe, I know that geographers will be eager to learn where this long (7) has taken us.

exploration	discover	sailor

1 September 1609 — Every (8) aboard the ship is grumbling because we have not seen land. Their fears do not bother me. My goal is the (9) of unknown places. I will not turn back!

10 September 1609 — It is a wonderful day! Land has been sighted. We will go ashore tomorrow. What will we (10) when we explore this land?

SPELL WELL

Suffixes The spelling of a base word may change when the suffix **-ion** or **-ation** is added. Add **-ion** or **-ation** to each word below to form a list word. What letter was dropped in each word?

11. expedite

12. navigate

13. explore

A modern compass

Operation Preparation!
You and a partner are in charge of an expedition. Choose a destination such as Antarctica, a mountain, or another place. You can take only eight items from the list of supplies below. Write them and then number them in order of importance.

compass
insect repellent
matches
warm clothing
rope
canned foods
fishing line
tent
wristwatch
water

shipbuilding
whaling
grains
rice
tobacco
glassware
furniture
cloth
silverware
indigo

Colonial Life

People in the English Colonies were busy making goods and growing crops. The list words name some of their important products. Use the Spelling Dictionary to check the meanings. Can you add words to the list?

■ GETTING AT MEANING

Workers Read what the workers say about the products they make or grow.

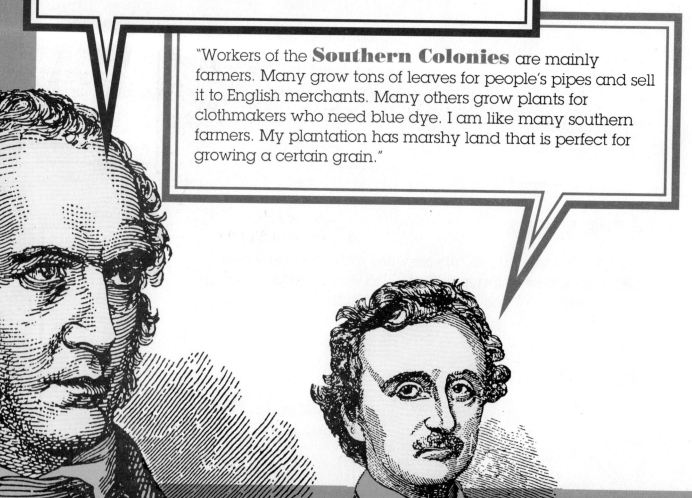

"Workers of the **New England Colonies** produce most of the whale oil used to light lamps. Thousands work building all kinds of boats. Our smiths make the best knives, forks, and platters in all the colonies."

"Workers of the **Southern Colonies** are mainly farmers. Many grow tons of leaves for people's pipes and sell it to English merchants. Many others grow plants for clothmakers who need blue dye. I am like many southern farmers. My plantation has marshy land that is perfect for growing a certain grain."

"Workers of the **Middle Colonies** like me weave linen and wool at home. It is sold both here and in England. Many others build fine chairs and tables for a living. The windows, lamps, and bottles that our workers make are the finest in the colonies, and our farmers are successful growing oats, wheat, and barley."

Chart Complete the chart below. Each list word is one of the products or industries. Find clues in the statements.

Products and Industries of the Colonies

New England	Middle	Southern
_____	_____	_____
_____	_____	_____
_____	_____	_____
	_____	

■ SPELL WELL

Double Consonants Write the two list words that have double consonants. Underline the double letters in each.

Did You Know? A big city in colonial times would be just a small town today. In 1760, Philadelphia had 23,000 people and was the biggest city in the English Colonies. Today towns of that size are common. Is your community bigger than Philadelphia was in colonial times?

By the way, Philadelphia's population today is
1,586,000

177

legislative
   branch
Congress
Senate
House of
   Representatives
executive
   branch
President
Cabinet
judicial branch
justices
Supreme Court

Government

What if one branch of a government becomes too powerful? Americans found a solution to this problem. Add more words about American government. Use the Spelling Dictionary if you need to.

■ GETTING AT MEANING

Reading a Diagram Study the following diagram. Then complete the sentences.

Executive Branch:

The President + members of the Cabinet who give advice

• **makes sure laws are carried out**
• **can veto, or disapprove, bills**

Legislative Branch:

Congress, made up of the Senate and the House of Representatives

• **makes laws**
• **can override President's veto**

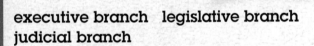

executive branch   legislative branch
judicial branch

One group of people says a law about fishing rights is fair. Another group says it is unfair. The (1) of government will decide who's right.

Congress passes a new law making the national speed limit 45 miles per hour. The (2) of government will make sure that new highway signs go up.

Some students want a law that will let them vote when they are 16 years old. They should go to the (3) of government.

Judicial Branch:

Nine justices of the Supreme Court

- **decide whether laws have been broken**
- **decide what laws mean**
- **can strike down a law that does not agree with the Constitution**

Imagine that yesterday Congress passed a new law. Now everyone in the nation can have a free college education. Taxes will go up to pay for the costs.

Complete the statements below. Remember that each branch has certain powers over the others.

Congress   House of Representatives   Senate   President   Cabinet   justices   Supreme Court

Citizen #1: "I heard members of Congress give speeches about this bill in the (4) and in the (5) . Most of them voted for it."

Citizen #2: "I can't afford more taxes. I wrote to the (6) and asked him to veto it. I also wrote to his adviser in the (7) and asked her to speak against the bill."

Citizen #3: "I think that the (8) of the (9) should decide that this law is prohibited by the Constitution."

Citizen #4: "I'm a college student. I was worried when the President vetoed this bill, but the lawmakers in (10) voted to override his veto."

■ SPELL WELL

Related Words Can you spot words in the list that are related to the ones below? Find them and write them.

11. execute   12. Senator   13. legislate

Who's in Power? Get together with others and draw a diagram that shows how your school is governed. Show who has the power to make rules. Also show the powers of groups such as the student council, class representatives, and ordinary students.

The Civil War

sectionalism
slavery
Union
representatives
compromise
secede
Confederacy
abolish
Emancipation
  Proclamation
surrender

The people of the United States fought against one another in the Civil War. The words in the list tell about this bitter war. Use the Spelling Dictionary if you need to check any meanings. Can you add your own words about the war?

■ GETTING AT MEANING

Letters of Peace These letters could have been written during the Civil War by cousins—one from the North and one from the South. Complete them with words from each list.

compromise   Union   representatives   abolish   slavery

Boston, Massachusetts

September 20, 1862

Dear Cousin Sarah,

My heart is heavy as I write to you. My son Joshua has quarreled with his father and run off to join the ___ Army.

You know that my husband Henry was one of the ___ to Congress. He wanted a peaceful solution to the issue of ___ . Henry wanted to ___ with the South. Joshua disagreed. He said that the President should ___ slavery immediately. I could see that he was determined to fight for his beliefs.

Pray with me that he will return alive.

Your loving cousin,

Rebecca

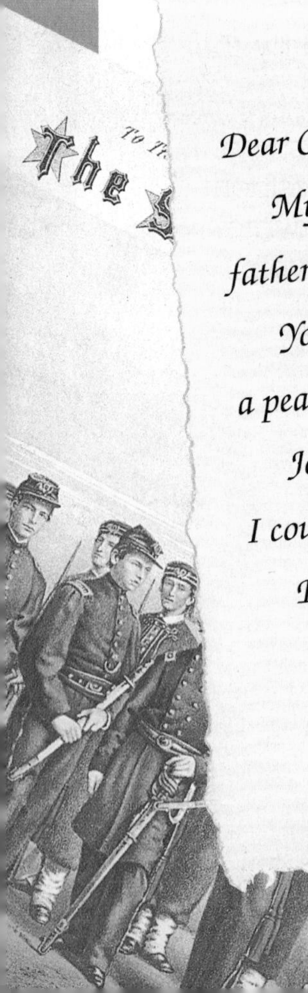

sectionalism   Confederacy   secede   surrender   Emancipation Proclamation

Atlanta, Georgia
January 20, 1863

My dear Cousin Rebecca,

Our worries are the same. Your son is a Union soldier and mine is an officer of the ___. Our sons are enemies.

I once believed that the South needed to ___ from the United States and be separate. I did not foresee that hate would grow in each section of the country. I now fear that ___ will destroy us all.

News has come that your President Lincoln signed an ___ proclaiming that our slaves are free. My neighbors say that our troops must fight harder now, but I see our troops growing weaker. The Confederacy may have to ___ .

Yes, I too am praying for our sons.

Your cousin,
Sarah

▇ SPELL WELL

A Capital Idea Write the three list words that begin with capital letters.

_____   _____   _____

After the War When the Civil War was over, the people of the North and the South had to unite as one nation. It took many years for the North and the South to forget that they had been enemies. Design a button that celebrates peace or the end of the war. Show designs or words that both sides would agree with.

Peace

invention
mass
 production
machine
natural
 resources
industries
factories
labor unions
strike
wages
railroads

The Industrial Revolution

The Industrial Revolution was a time of great change in society. Some list words tell about progress and some tell about problems. Check the Spelling Dictionary if you need to. Add your own words.

■ GETTING AT MEANING

Progress Complete each statement with the correct list word below.

**natural resources   mass production   industries   machine
invention   railroads**

1. During the Industrial Revolution, workers produced goods such as furniture by machine in mass quantities. This process was called ____.

2. Manufacturing and mining were two ____ that expanded rapidly.

3. Factories used great amounts of ____ like iron and coal.

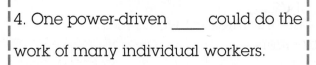

4. One power-driven ____ could do the work of many individual workers.

5. Factory products were sent overland on ____ to distant places.

6. The steamboat was an ____ that allowed factories to transport goods faster over the waterways.

182

Hardships Complete each statement with the correct word below. The pictures may give you a clue to the answers.

factories   strike   labor unions   wages

7. Many people found jobs in

_____, but they were often unsafe and unhealthy.

8. People earned low _____ at factory jobs.

9. Workers joined together to form _____ to fight for safer workplaces and more pay.

10. To get shorter hours and better pay, the union workers would refuse to work, or _____.

Inventions in Your Desk There are inventions around your classroom and in your desk that you couldn't live without. Have you ever wondered when and how paper clips, erasers, sticky notes, markers, and crayons were invented? Choose an item from your classroom and find out when and how it was developed.

cerebrum
cerebellum
atrium
diaphragm
inhale
exhale
ventricle
oxygen
trachea
esophagus

How Your Body Works

The list words are about that amazing machine, the body. Use the Spelling Dictionary if you need to. Try to add words to the list.

■ GETTING AT MEANING

Busy Body Study the diagram and the paragraph below. Use the list words to complete the captions.

Your brain is your body's boss. It tells the parts of your body to do different jobs. It makes sure that **oxygen** coming in the nose goes down the **trachea** to the lungs. It makes sure that food goes down the **esophagus** to the stomach. It tells each **atrium** in the upper part of the heart to pump blood to each lower part called a **ventricle.**

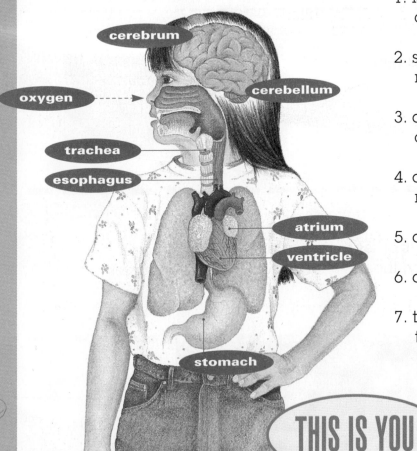

cerebrum

oxygen

cerebellum

trachea

esophagus

atrium

ventricle

stomach

THIS IS YOU

1. largest part of brain; controls thought

2. smaller part of brain; keeps muscles working together

3. air that enters the mouth or nose

4. a tube that leads from the nose and throat to lungs

5. an upper part of the heart

6. a lower part of the heart

7. tube that connects mouth to stomach

184

Take a Breath Use list words to complete the statements below. Read the chart to find clues to the answers.

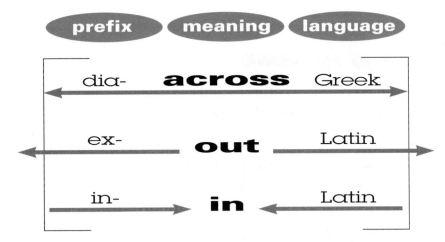

prefix	meaning	language
dia-	**across**	Greek
ex-	**out**	Latin
in-	**in**	Latin

When you breathe in, you __(8)__ .

Your __(9)__ tightens across your ribs. Air is pulled into your lungs.

When you breathe out, you __(10)__ .

■ SPELL WELL

Including All the Letters Sometimes words contain letters that you don't expect to see. Write each word below. Underline the letters you think you might forget.

11. trachea

12. diaphragm

Did You Know?
The body of an eighty-pound child contains about two and one-half quarts of blood.

2.5

The heart pumps this blood through the body continuously.

In a single day, this incredible machine pumps over 7,000 quarts of blood!

7,000

pedestrian
accidents
crosswalk
escape plan
prevent
emergency
smoke detectors
crawl
choking
windpipe

Keeping Safe

Use the words in the list when you talk or write about safety. The Spelling Dictionary will tell you more about their meanings. Add others to the list.

■ GETTING AT MEANING

Posters Read the award-winning safety posters below. Use the list words to complete the statements.

Do You Know What to Do

?

Do call an adult if someone is __(1)__ on food or another object.

Do learn how to help someone who has an object stuck in the throat or __(2)__.

Do have a list of __(3)__ phone numbers ready.

1

Prepare to Stay Cool if a Fire Starts

Draw a diagram of your home. Show two places where people can get out safely. Explain this __(4)__ to your family.

Check the fire alarms in your home. If there are none, think of two places to put __(5)__ . Tell your family.

2

Leave quickly if a fire starts. If the air is smoky, stay low and __(6)__ on the floor to the exit.

Rules of the Road for Everyone

Do you usually ride a bicycle?

Rule | Practice making quick stops to avoid _(7)_ .

Do you usually walk? Are you a _(8)_ ?

Rule | Cross streets only at a _(9)_ or corner.

Do you usually drive a car?

Rule | Obey traffic signs to _(10)_ accidents.

■ SPELL WELL

Divide and Conquer Break long words into smaller pieces to help you remember their spellings. Say each word slowly so you can hear the syllables. Then write the words.

11. e ▪ mer ▪ gen ▪ cy   12. pe ▪ des ▪ tri ▪ an

Poster Parade

We all need to be reminded to act safely. Draw a poster that reminds people to follow safety rules about wearing seat belts, swimming and boating, bicycling, or other safety topics. Catch your reader's attention by writing a slogan, a warning, or a poem. Illustrate the poster.

carpools
solar energy
sewage
scrubbers
landfills
incinerators
recycling
treatment plant
solid waste
air pollution

Community Concerns

The words in the list are about protecting the environment. Can you add other words? Use the Spelling Dictionary if you need to.

■ GETTING AT MEANING

Problems and Solutions Read the paragraphs below. Then write the missing list words in each problem and solution.

Cars give off harmful gases that cause **air pollution.** Someday cars may use clean **solar energy** from the sun instead of gasoline.

Some factories use devices called **scrubbers** to remove ashes from smoke. The waste water, or **sewage,** from homes and buildings is cleaned at a sewage **treatment plant.**

Garbage and trash is **solid waste** that is often buried in **landfills.** Some communities use large **incinerators** to burn solid waste. Some towns encourage **recycling** so that newspapers, cans, and bottles can be made into useful items again.

See a Problem?

Students noticed that a factory wasn't using ❶ to remove ashes.

Also, it didn't have bins for ❷ cans.

Often people leave water running or waste it in other ways. They should know that it is expensive to clean ❹ , or waste water.

Food and other things we buy have a lot of packaging. This turns into garbage and other ❻ that fills up ❼ .

The roads are crowded with cars that cause ❾ .

Most cars on the road have only one person in them.

■ SPELL WELL

Double Letters Four list words have double letters. The double letters stand for only one sound, but to spell them correctly, you must use two letters. Write the words and underline the double letters.

Did You Know?

This familiar symbol was designed in 1973 by a Dutch paper company. It means "This can be recycled." If you see a circle around the arrows, it usually means "This was made from recycled materials."

Find a Solution!

They invited the factory manager to school to see their recycling project and a display showing how sunlight is turned into ③.

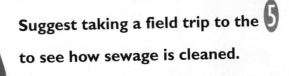

Suggest taking a field trip to the ⑤ to see how sewage is cleaned.

Write to a town official. Ask if your community has enough landfills to bury garbage or ⑧ for burning it.

Plan with your friends to ride together in ⑩.

scientific
  method
observations
data
hypothesis
experiment
problem
control
senses
conclusion
theory

The Scientific Method

The list words are about experimenting and the scientific method. The Spelling Dictionary will tell you more about their meanings. Add other words to the list.

■ GETTING AT MEANING

Using the Scientific Method Read the paragraphs that follow. Use words from the list to complete the statements.

98° **?** 66° 35°

The scientific method is a step-by-step way to find answers to questions. First, ask the question, or state the problem.

1

Erin wanted to practice the steps of the (1). She stated this (2): "Will water evaporate faster or slower in different temperatures?"

Predict the answer, then test your prediction, or hypothesis. A good test is to do an experiment and set up a control to compare the results.

2

She predicted that water would evaporate faster in warm air. She needed to test her (3) by doing this (4).

Three identical jars are filled with equal amounts of water. One jar is placed in a warm spot, another in a cold spot, and a third in regular room temperature for comparison. It is the (5).

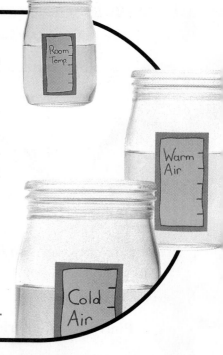

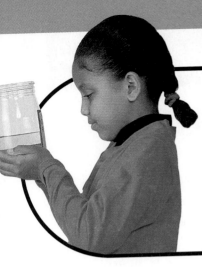

Her sight was the most important of her (6) for this experiment. Erin made (7) by looking at the water level of each jar once a day. She recorded the data on a chart.

3 Use **senses** such as sight, sound, or touch to make **observations** during the experiment. Keep a record of the **data**, or information.

After three days, she read the (8) . She found that the water level was lowest in the jar in the warm spot and highest in the jar in the cold spot. She drew the (9) that her hypothesis was correct. She wondered if her conclusion could be a (10) .

4 Finally, study all the data and draw a **conclusion**. Scientists who test a hypothesis many times may say their conclusion is a **theory**, or an accepted explanation of the problem.

■ SPELL WELL

Divide and Conquer Break long words into smaller pieces to help you remember their spellings. Say each word slowly so you can hear the syllables. Then write the words.

11. hy ▪ poth ▪ e ▪ sis   12. sci ▪ en ▪ tif ▪ ic   meth ▪ od

Did You Know?
High school students designed eleven of the experiments done by astronauts in Skylab, the first laboratory in space. Two of these experiments tested if spiders could spin webs and if fish could swim normally without the force of gravity. They could!

animals
classify
traits
kingdom
genus
species
scientific name
common name
life span
endangered
  species

Classifying Living Things

Scientists use the words in the list when they talk about grouping living things. Check their meanings in the Spelling Dictionary. Think of other words to add.

■ GETTING AT MEANING

Diagrams Read about the groups. Complete the sentences with words from the list.

Scientists (1) living things into two main groups called kingdoms. Each kingdom is further divided into smaller and smaller groups. Animalia is the name of this (2) . All (3) belong to this kingdom.

Group: kingdom
Name of living thing:
Animalia

A smaller group in a kingdom is called a (4) . All the animals in this genus resemble cats.

Group: genus
Name of living thing:
Panthera

The smallest group in a kingdom is called a (5) . The only animal in this species is the tiger.

Group: species
Name of living thing:
Panthera tigris

All About a Tiger Write list words to complete the paragraph below. Use the information at the right.

"Tiger" is this cat's _(6)_, but *Panthera tigris* is its _(7)_. Scientists have observed its color, what it eats, and its other _(8)_. They learned that no other animal is exactly like it. If you see this animal in a zoo, a sign will tell you that it's an _(9)_ because few are left in the wild. The living ones have a _(10)_ of only twenty years.

common name: tiger

scientific name: *Panthera Tigris*

endangered species: not many are left

traits: colorful, striped coat, good swimmer, keen senses, preys on other animals

life span: may live up to 20 years

■ SPELL WELL

Secret Pronunciations Making up a secret pronunciation can help you spell the words below. Pronounce or exaggerate the sounds of the underlined letters. Then write each word as you say its secret pronunciation.

11. kingd<u>o</u>m

12. spe<u>c</u>ies

Here *Felis*, Here *Felis*

"Cat" is the common name of a favorite family pet. The scientific name is *Felis domesticus*. Look up the name of another pet or animal in an encyclopedia to find out its scientific name.

invertebrates
vertebrates
sponge
jellyfish
tentacles
backbone
mollusks
fish
alligator
gills

Invertebrates and Vertebrates

The words in the list are about two groups of animals and their differences. Use the Spelling Dictionary if you need to. Add other words to the list.

■ GETTING AT MEANING

Captions Read the paragraph below. Then write the list words to complete the captions about each picture.

Scientists divide all animals into **invertebrates** and **vertebrates.** Animals without **backbones** are invertebrates; animals with backbones are vertebrates. **Jellyfish** and **mollusks,** such as clams and oysters, are invertebrates. Some vertebrates, like the **alligator,** live on the land and breathe air. Others, like **fish,** live underwater and take oxygen from water through **gills.**

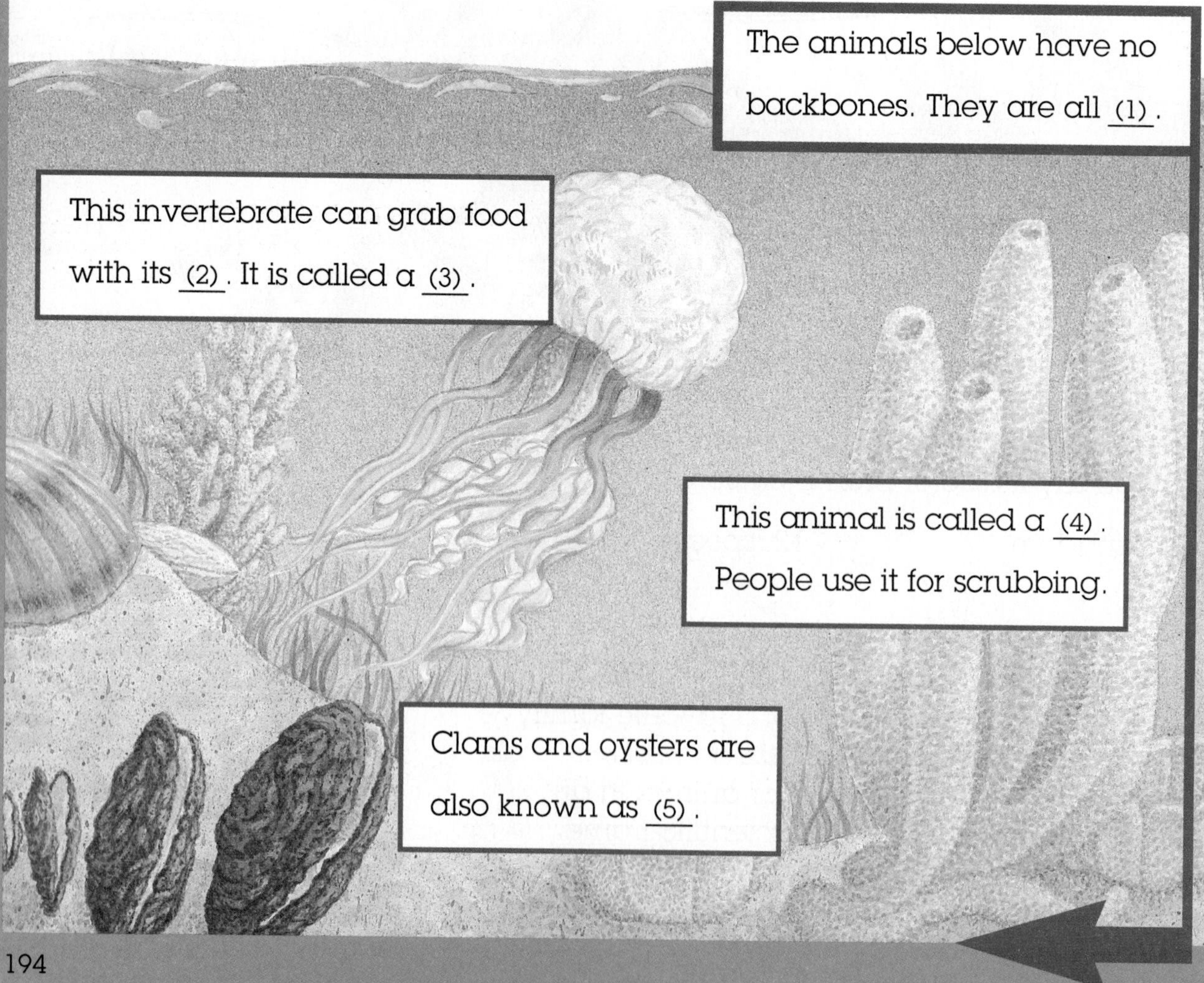

The animals below have no backbones. They are all (1) .

This invertebrate can grab food with its (2) . It is called a (3) .

This animal is called a (4) . People use it for scrubbing.

Clams and oysters are also known as (5) .

194

■ SPELL WELL

Including All the Letters Sometimes we spell words wrong because we say them wrong. Say each word below and write it. Be sure to pronounce the sounds of the underlined letters.

tent<u>a</u>cles   mollu<u>sk</u>s

Did You Know? All **tomato clown fish** are male when they are hatched! Later the ones that grow larger and more dominant turn into females. The males are red-orange except for a wide white stripe around the middle. The females are black.

These animals have backbones. They are all (6) .

This (7) is a vertebrate. If you took an X ray of it, you could see its (8) .

Water passes through the (9) of a (10) so that it can get oxygen.

atom
electron
proton
neutron
nucleus
elements
molecule
metals
nonmetals
symbol

Atoms and Elements

The list words are about parts of matter. Can you add words to the list? Check the Spelling Dictionary.

■ GETTING AT MEANING

Read the chart to find the names and symbols of a few elements. Then read the information below the chart.

Kinds of Elements	Names of Elements		Symbols	
Metals	gold	silver	**Au**	**Ag**
Nonmetals	oxygen	hydrogen	**O**	**H**

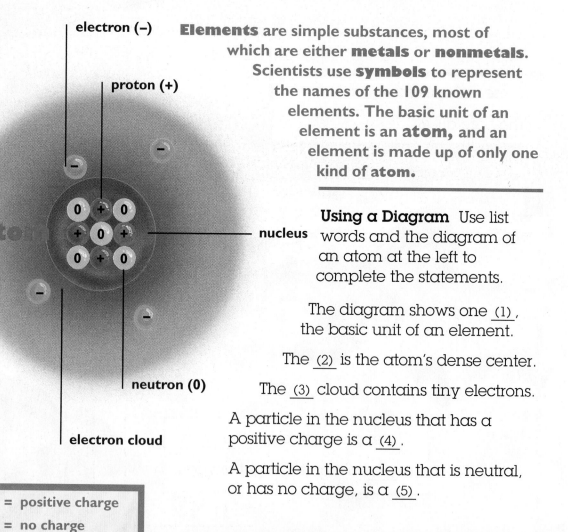

electron (−)

proton (+)

An Atom

nucleus

neutron (0)

electron cloud

Elements are simple substances, most of which are either **metals** or **nonmetals**. Scientists use **symbols** to represent the names of the 109 known elements. The basic unit of an element is an **atom,** and an element is made up of only one kind of **atom.**

Using a Diagram Use list words and the diagram of an atom at the left to complete the statements.

The diagram shows one (1) , the basic unit of an element.

The (2) is the atom's dense center.

The (3) cloud contains tiny electrons.

A particle in the nucleus that has a positive charge is a (4) .

A particle in the nucleus that is neutral, or has no charge, is a (5) .

➕ = positive charge

0 = no charge

➖ = negative charge

196

A Water Molecule (H₂O)

Water is made up of two elements, hydrogen and oxygen. The smallest unit of water is a **molecule.** The diagram above shows that hydrogen and oxygen atoms bond to form water.

Elements Use list words to complete the statements. The chart of elements and the diagram above will help you.

Oxygen and gold are names of (6) .
H is the (7) for the element we call hydrogen.
Hydrogen and oxygen are elements that are (8) .
Silver and gold are elements that are (9) .
Oxygen and hydrogen are the elements in a water (10) .

■ SPELL WELL

Divide and Conquer Sometimes it helps to study words syllable by syllable. Say each word below slowly so that you can hear the syllables. Then write the words.

11. nu ▪ cle ▪ us

12. mol ▪ e ▪ cule

more than 1,000 feet

Did You Know?

Atoms are extremely small, but the nucleus of an atom is even smaller. To get an idea of the difference in size, picture this: If a nucleus were the size of a dime, then the atom it was in would be as big as a skyscraper!

less than an inch

SCIENCE

Electricity

The list words help us discuss electricity. Can you add others?
Use your Spelling Dictionary if you need to.

■ GETTING AT MEANING

Energy is the ability to do work. **Electricity** is one form
of energy. A **conductor** is a material through which
electricity flows. **Insulators** are materials through which
electricity cannot flow. The continuous flow of electricity
creates a **current.** Electric current moves through a
closed **circuit.**

Fuses are safety devices that open circuits if too much
current is flowing through them. **Batteries** change
chemical energy into electric energy. At a power plant, a
huge **generator** produces electricity for a town. Electrical
power is measured in **watts.**

Inside a Flashlight Use list words and the paragraphs above
to complete the explanation of how a flashlight works.

Two (1) provide the power for this flashlight. The metal strip
is a (2) of the electric (3). When you switch the flashlight on,
the circuit is closed, allowing the current to flow and the light
bulb to glow. When you switch the flashlight off, the (4) is
open and the light goes out.

How a Flashlight Works

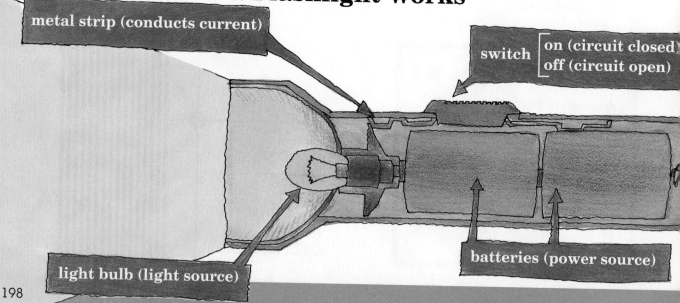

metal strip (conducts current)

switch [on (circuit closed)
off (circuit open)

light bulb (light source)

batteries (power source)

Power House Use the following list words to complete the statements about electricity in the home.

> fuses   watts   electricity   energy   insulators   generator

Many items in the home use the form of energy called (5) .

A large (6) at the power plant produces electricity for many homes.

Electricity is measured in (7) .

Safety devices like (8) prevent too much electric current from flowing through circuits.

Electric cords, like those on household appliances, are coated with rubber (9) to prevent electric current from flowing outside the wires.

Some toys and appliances use batteries to supply electric (10) .

■ SPELL WELL

Double Consonants Double consonants can sometimes cause problems. Write the three list words that have double consonants. Underline the double consonants to help you remember them.

11. ____

12. ____

13. ____

Meter Readers

With the help of an adult, find the electric meter in the building or house where you live. Read the numbers on the dials from left to right. Write the numbers down. Look at the meter at the same time every day for a week. How do the numbers change from day to day?

199

Energy Resources

nonrenewable
resources
fossil fuels
turbines
dam
nuclear energy
renewable
resources
hydroelectric
power
solar energy
windmills
conservation

The list words are about the earth's resources. Add more words if you can, and use the Spelling Dictionary if you need to.

◼ GETTING AT MEANING

*Not long ago, people used energy resources as if they would last forever. Now people practice **conservation**, or the careful use of resources, so they will last longer. **Nonrenewable resources** can't be easily replaced. **Fossil fuels** are nonrenewable. Coal, oil, and natural gas are fossil fuels we use. **Renewable resources** can be easily replaced. Some renewable resources we can use for energy are sun, wind, and water.*

*The sun's heat is **solar energy,** which can be stored in solar collectors. The wind can turn **windmills,** which turn the blades of **turbines** to produce electricity. Falling water from a **dam** turns turbines to produce electricity, or **hydroelectric power**.*

*Atoms can be split in a nuclear reactor to release **nuclear energy** and create heat.*

Energy Users Read what people in the community say about using energy. Use list words to complete their statements.

> ### *Ursula Walker, Mayor*
>
> *A nuclear power plant is on the outskirts of Greenville, so we use the __(1)__ it releases. Our town is growing. Since we'll need more energy, workers are building a __(2)__ with a power plant on the Catfish River. When it's finished, we can use the __(3)__ it produces. We think that it's a good idea to get power from __(4)__ like water.*

Mayor Ursula Walker

Wendy & Rob Anderson, homeowners

Our whole family recycles newspapers because we believe that _(5)_ of natural resources is important. We also have built solar collectors on the roof so we can use _(6)_ to heat our water.

Ms. Alicia Garcia, factory manager

This factory gets some electricity from wind energy. There are two _(7)_ nearby. A caretaker will show you the _(8)_ turning around on them. We do use some _(9)_ , or resources that are running out, but we are trying to use fewer _(10)_ like coal and gas.

■ SPELL WELL

Divide and Conquer Sometimes it helps to study long words syllable by syllable. Say each word slowly so that you can hear the syllables. Then write the words.

11. non■re■new■able re■sources

12. hy■dro■e■lec■tric pow■er

Ms. Alicia Garcia

Did You Know?

Here are three ways to save energy. Can you think of more?

- Turn the thermostat down in winter and up in summer.
- Turn off the lights, radio, and TV when you aren't using them.
- Turn used paper, cans, and glass into useful objects by recycling them.

201

imagine
brainstorm
illustrations
illustrator
instruments
rhythm
characters
conflict
fantasy
setting

Journeys of the Imagination

We can express what our imagination creates by using words like those on the list. Can you add your own words? Use the Spelling Dictionary if you need to.

■ GETTING AT MEANING

Flights of Fancy Elly wanted to use the ideas that were running through her imagination to plan a story. She decided to write notes about her ideas. Use the list words to complete Elly's plans and ideas.

The story is a **(1)**. I'm imagining some animals who are musicians. They'll be the main **(2)**. I need to **(3)** more ideas. Here goes:

The animals form a rock 'n' roll band called The Furry Five. The raccoon, the baboon, the rabbit, and the walrus play different **(4)**, and the lion is the lead singer.

Every story has to have a problem, or **(5)**. I **(6)** this happening:

The band practices hard. They have good **(7)** and they've even written their own songs. One day the raccoon hears that a music festival is coming to town. The Furry Five want to perform, but Mr. Budny, the festival director, won't even let them audition!

What does the band do next? I'm stuck! Maybe I should think about where the animals will play their music. I'm thinking of an outdoor **(8)** . Since I'm going to be the **(9)** of this book, I'll draw some pictures. Maybe I'll get ideas from my own **(10)**.

■ SPELL WELL

Related Words Knowing the meaning and spelling of one word may help you spell another word. Write the two list words that are related in spelling and meaning to *illustrate*.

11. _____   12. _____

The Final Chapter

Can you imagine how Elly's story will end? Write your ideas of what happens next and how the story ends.

resource
majestic
destructive
traditions
nurture
appreciation
share
harmony
droughts
habitat

A World of Nature

The list words express ideas about nature. Can you add other words to the list? Use your Spelling Dictionary if you need to.

■ GETTING AT MEANING

Nature in Literature Read about each illustration. Then complete the statements. Use the list words.

Poseidon, ruler of the sea, had a bad temper. When he struck the ground with his trident, the earth shook. When he struck the sea, waves rose high and winds howled.

In ancient Greek myths, gods and goddesses were like (1) kings and queens who ruled nature. People feared nature because it could be (2) and send earthquakes, floods, or (3). The myths show how powerless people felt against nature.

An old American folk tale tells of Johnny Appleseed, a poor man who understood nature and lived in (4) with it. He knew how to (5) seeds and saplings so they would grow into trees. This tale shows how people can help nature provide fruit to eat and a (6), or place to live, for animals and birds.

Johnny Appleseed was nature's friend. He planted trees along the American frontier as the settlers moved west. He gave apple seeds and small apple trees to everyone he met.

American Indian (7) teach that people and animals should (8) the land and take only what is needed from it. The Indians of the Plains knew that the buffalo was an important (9). They showed respect and (10) for nature by honoring the buffalo's spirit and making use of every part of the buffalo.

After killing a buffalo, the Indians of the Plains thanked its spirit for helping them survive. They knew that the buffalo was a gift from nature. They used every part of the buffalo they killed for food, clothing, and shelter.

■ SPELL WELL

Pronouncing Words Carefully We sometimes spell words wrong because we say them wrong. Say each word below carefully. Be sure to pronounce the sounds of the underlined letters. Then write the words.

11. environment

12. habitat

Your View of Nature

Do you think nature is a friend, an enemy, or both? Draw an illustration and write a caption to show your view of nature.

adventurous
wranglers
settled
homespun
Cherokee
longhorn
roundups
saddle
frontier
lariat

Stories of America

The words in the list are about cowboys and the western frontier. Add other words to the list. Remember to use the Spelling Dictionary.

■ GETTING AT MEANING

This brief biography is missing some words. Write them.

The Joking Cowboy

Will Rogers, a famous cowboy showman, was part (1) Indian. From the age of nine he worked as a cowboy on his father's ranch, herding (2) steers and going on cattle (3) . You might say his home was in the (4) . Will discovered his talent for roping when an African American cowboy named Dan Walker taught him to use a (5) . He became a rope artist himself by practicing daily and copying tricks that he saw other (6) do.

When Will was a young man, he joined a Wild West show. The shows were popular in the (7) areas of the East because people believed that the life of a

206

cowboy on the western __(8)__ had been exciting and __(9)__ . Will's roping and riding made him a star, but audiences also loved his jokes. In his friendly drawl, he'd make wisecracks and give funny advice. His __(10)__ style of humor won Will Rogers worldwide fame.

■ SPELL WELL

Compound Words Three list words are compounds made up of two words written as one. Write them.

Word Detectives

Much of the western United States was Spanish or Mexican territory at one time. That's why many words about cowboys' work are Spanish words. Read the following English words. Then write the Spanish word that each English word came from. The Spelling Dictionary will help.

buckaroo calaboose mustang lariat

freedom
sacrifice
health
heritage
proud
possession
courage
disability
opportunities
adventure

The Important Things in Life

Many of these words are about important ideas. Add some words to the list. The Spelling Dictionary will help you.

■ GETTING AT MEANING

Dreaming and Hoping Read what three people say about what is important to them. Write the missing words.

My parents love Korea, but there they did not have many (1) to work and get an education. Their dream was to live where people had more liberty because they believe that (2) is precious. Finally, they decided to move to Canada. It took a lot of (3) to leave the land of their (4) and to learn new ways, but it was worth it.

*I'm hoping to win a medal
in the intercity wheelchair marathon this year. Since I have a
physical (5), I can't walk, but I can race. I train hard and I'm in
very good (6). If I win, that medal will be my most prized (7).*

*The greatest (8) of my life was not climbing a mountain or
going deep-sea diving. It was receiving my master's degree in
engineering. Since I was going to school at night, I had to (9)
my free time and fun for a while. My family kept
encouraging me, and now they're (10) of me.*

■ SPELL WELL

Double Letters Double letters can cause
spelling problems. Write the three list
words with double letters. Underline the
double letters. Notice that one word has
two doubles.

*The Best Things in Life
You can figure out what is
valuable to others by observing
their actions. Think of three
people who became famous and
figure out what they might
have thought was important.
List several things each did that
showed this.*

courageous
comfortable
faithful
careful
exceptional
confidently
carefully
reassuring
obediently
skillful

Making a Difference

Can the words in the list be used to describe you or the way you do things? Think of other describing words and add them. Use the Spelling Dictionary.

■ GETTING AT MEANING

People You Should Know Write the words that are missing in the descriptions of Jack and Angela. Use the word lists next to each description.

courageous
confidently
reassuring
skillful
comfortable

Girls and boys! Get ready to see Jack, the star lion-trainer of the **TIP TOP CIRCUS!** Jack's (1) performance will **astound** you as he commands the lions to do amazing tricks. Yet Jack is not just courageous. He is a well-trained, (2) expert. **Observe him!** He will seem *relaxed* and (3), but he's aware of every move the lions make. He shows **NO** fear, and he always handles the lions (4). Don't be afraid when Jack enters the cage. Just look as his (5) smile, sit back, and **enjoy** the show!

Meet Angela, the girl with an (6) **ability** to care for pets! Mr. Kelly's dog Fireball is like a blast of <u>WHITE-HOT ENERGY</u>, yet Angela loves caring for him. At first, the owner warned her to be (7) because Fireball is so **strong**. This **experienced** girl listened (8) to all his instructions, and began to work. From the start, Fireball has (9) followed Angela's commands, and Angela has <u>never missed</u> her day to walk the dog. Now Mr. Kelly tells everyone that Angela is a (10) worker and a **talented** dog-walker!

faithful
exceptional
careful
carefully
obediently

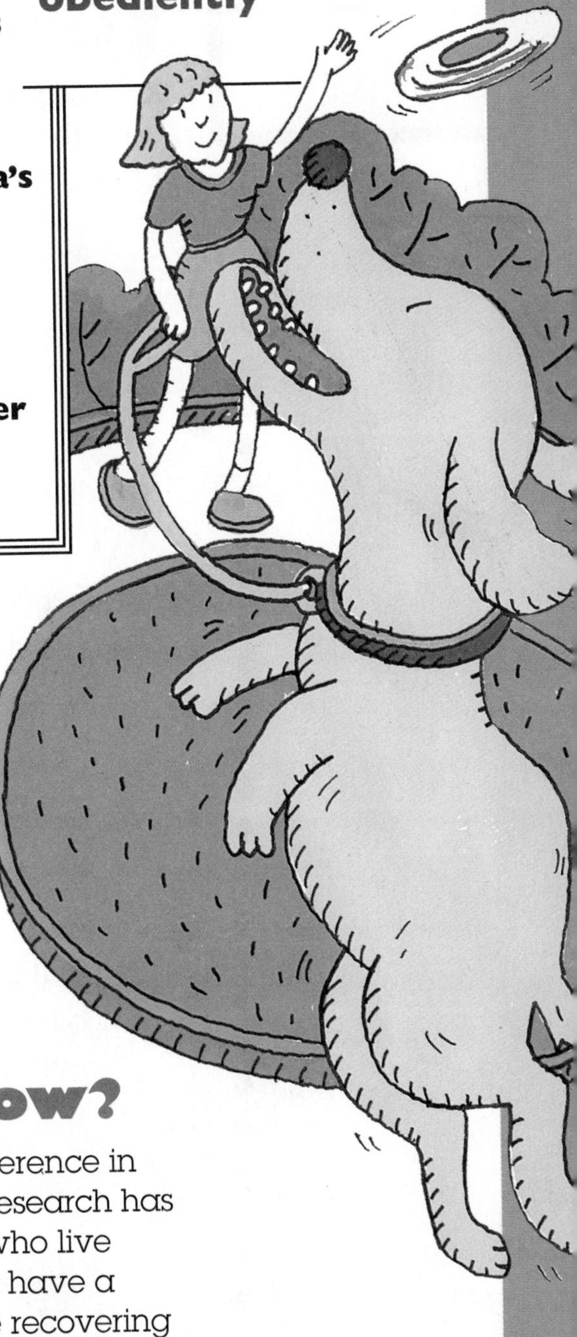

■ SPELL WELL

Suffixes Add **-ly** to the the base words below to form list words. Does the base word change? Write the new words.

11. confident

12. obedient

13. careful

Did You Know?

Pets can make a positive difference in the quality of people's lives. Research has shown that many people who live alone are happier if they have a pet, and many who are recovering from an illness get well faster.

admit
vow
talent
memories
commotion
cafeteria
miserable
emotional
dismay
childish

Growing and Changing

Good and difficult experiences are part of growing up.
Use the list words when you talk about your experiences
and add some of your own. The Spelling Dictionary will
help you.

■ GETTING AT MEANING

Keeping a Journal Betsy wrote in her journal about two
days that were important to her. Write the missing words.

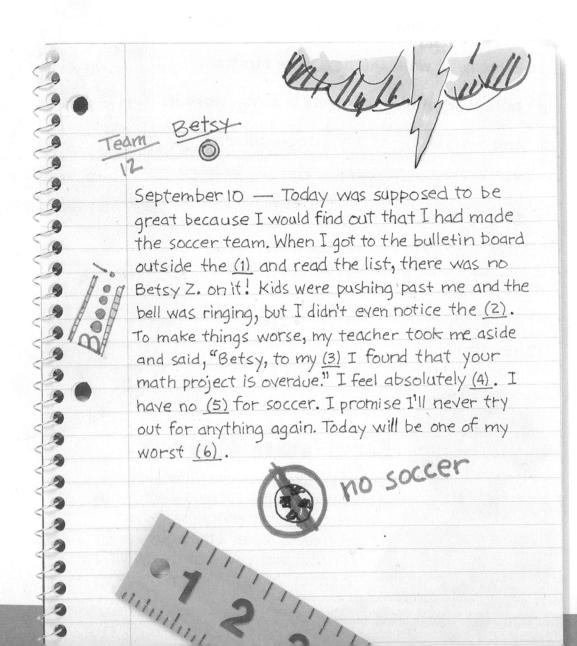

Team Betsy
12

September 10 — Today was supposed to be
great because I would find out that I had made
the soccer team. When I got to the bulletin board
outside the (1) and read the list, there was no
Betsy Z. on it! Kids were pushing past me and the
bell was ringing, but I didn't even notice the (2).
To make things worse, my teacher took me aside
and said, "Betsy, to my (3) I found that your
math project is overdue." I feel absolutely (4). I
have no (5) for soccer. I promise I'll never try
out for anything again. Today will be one of my
worst (6).

no soccer

212

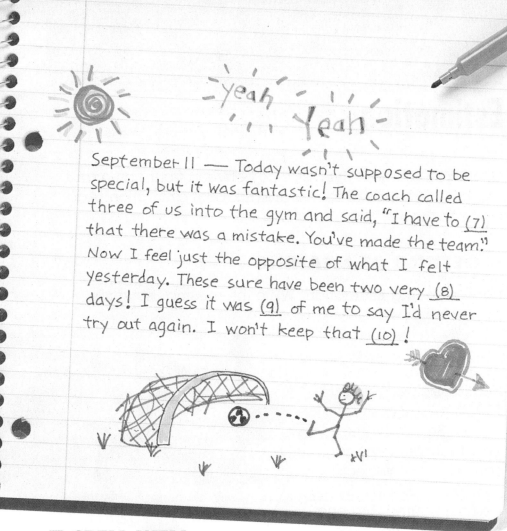

yeah *Yeah*

September 11 — Today wasn't supposed to be special, but it was fantastic! The coach called three of us into the gym and said, "I have to (7) that there was a mistake. You've made the team." Now I feel just the opposite of what I felt yesterday. These sure have been two very (8) days! I guess it was (9) of me to say I'd never try out again. I won't keep that (10) !

■ SPELL WELL

Syllables It is easier to spell longer words if you break them up into syllables. Say each word below so you can hear the syllables. Then write the words.

11. mis ▪ er ▪ a ▪ ble   12. caf ▪ e ▪ ter ▪ i ▪ a

Did You Know?
People played soccer in ancient times in European towns, but they didn't have to worry about trying out. The game was played right through the streets because the goals were at either end of town. Anyone who wished to play joined in, and there were no rules!

estimating
exact
nearest
reasonable
front-end digits
rounding
approximate
strategy
comparing
reference point

Estimation

Could you estimate the distance between your home and school? The words in the list are all about estimation. Add others to the list.

■ GETTING AT MEANING

Understanding Estimation Write the missing list words.

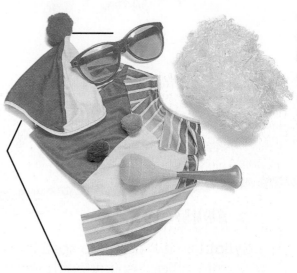

Sometimes you have to be **exact** when you work with numbers. At other times, **estimating** will give you a number that's close enough.

Heather's class needed $99.76 to buy costumes for a play. She knew the _(1)_ amounts they had earned in two projects: $33.90 and $31.04. By _(2)_, Heather figured that one more project would be enough.

To find an **approximate** amount, try **rounding** numbers to the **nearest** hundred.

A classmate asked Tony to guess the number of kids' shoes in the school. He knew that 581 students were enrolled and that the _(3)_ hundred was 600. Tony figured that the _(4)_ amount was 1,200 shoes. His strategy is called _(5)_.

Use this **strategy** to come up with a **reasonable** answer. Add the **front-end digits** of large numbers.

Patti saw three enormous watermelons that weighed 110, 105, and 240 pounds each. She used this (6) to estimate the total weight. She added 1, 1, and 2, which were the (7). Her answer of 400 pounds is very (8).

Try **comparing** numbers to a number you can work with easily. That number is called the **reference point.**

Stephanie began saving to buy three animal puppets that cost $4.75 each. By (9) the price to the (10) of $5.00, she estimated that she needed about $15.00.

SPELL WELL

Related Words Knowing the spelling of one word may help you spell longer words that are related to it. Write the list word that is related to each word below.

11. refer

12. reason

Stocking the Shelves

Before school begins each fall, store managers must guess how many school supplies people will buy. Work in a group to estimate the number of pencils, pens, and markers that students and adults have in your school on a regular day. Do you see why stores sometimes run out?

Measuring Length

customary units
inches
feet
yards
miles
metric units
meter
millimeter
centimeter
kilometers

The words in the list are all about systems of measuring.
Add others to the list if you can and check the spellings in
the Spelling Dictionary.

■ GETTING AT MEANING

Measuring Length In Spain, Anna used metric units such as
millimeters and kilometers. Now that she is in the United
States, she uses customary units, such as inches and feet.
Use the words and the pictures to complete the statements.

When Anna figured the distance between Chicago
and Cleveland, she used (1) . When she figured the
distance between Los Angeles and New York, she
used (2) .

When she first saw a baseball bat, she said it was
about one (3) long.

She prefers metric units like a (4) and a (5) to
measure tiny things like the thickness of a dime
and the size of a mosquito.

To measure the size of her room and her dog, she
used customary units like (6) and (7) .

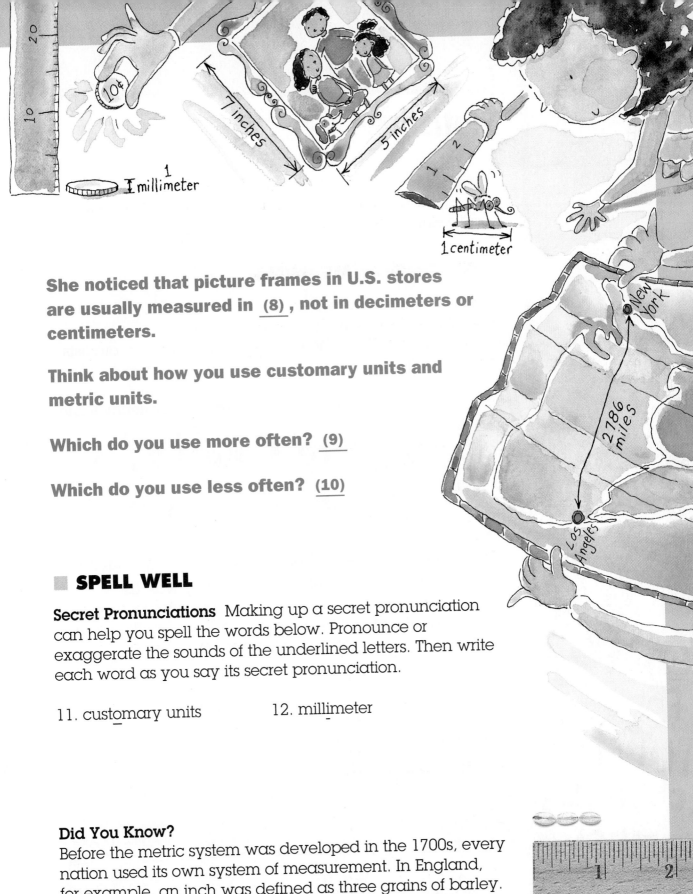

1 millimeter

1 centimeter

She noticed that picture frames in U.S. stores are usually measured in (8) , not in decimeters or centimeters.

Think about how you use customary units and metric units.

Which do you use more often? (9)

Which do you use less often? (10)

SPELL WELL

Secret Pronunciations Making up a secret pronunciation can help you spell the words below. Pronounce or exaggerate the sounds of the underlined letters. Then write each word as you say its secret pronunciation.

11. cust<u>o</u>mary units

12. milli<u>m</u>eter

Did You Know?
Before the metric system was developed in the 1700s, every nation used its own system of measurement. In England, for example, an inch was defined as three grains of barley. Since the size of any two grains was slightly different, measurements tended to be quite imprecise!

collect
sample
survey
data
organize
compare
percentage
frequency table
bar graph
circle graph

Statistics

Statistics are numerical facts that can help us make decisions. Add words about statistics to the list. You can check your words in the Spelling Dictionary.

■ GETTING AT MEANING

Working with Statistics Before a school election for student council president, Kay did some research and reported what she found. Write the missing words. Use the word lists on each page.

collect data organize survey sample frequency table

Your Vote Counts!

"Who is your choice for president?"

That was the question I asked in my pre-election (1). The school has 229 students, but my survey was just a (2) of 24 kids who ride my bus. It took four rides to (3) all 24 opinions. I wrote all the information, or (4), in the table below because a (5) is a good way to (6) data.

Frequency Table

Candidate	Tally	Number of Students
M. Bhatia	卌 IIII	9
A. Porto	卌 卌 II	12
J. Smith	III	3

percentage   compare   bar graph   circle graph

Here's how I analyzed the results of my survey. First, I made a __(7)__ so people could easily __(8)__ one candidate to another. Then I made a __(9)__ to show what __(10)__ of the 24 kids would vote for a certain candidate. I passed out copies on the bus.

Even with this data, I can't say who will win, but I can make some good predictions!

Did You Know ?

Some groups of people vote more often than others. For example, more women vote than men, and people between the ages of 55 and 75 are more likely to vote than other age groups.

▓ SPELL WELL

Related Words Can you spot words in the list that are related to the ones below? Find them and write them.

11. organization

12. collection

quadrilateral
pentagon
hexagon
octagon
right triangle
acute triangle
obtuse triangle
vertex
vertices
segment

Geometry

The words in this list are all about the surfaces of objects. Can you think of other words to add? Check the Spelling Dictionary if you need to.

■ GETTING AT MEANING

The Shape of a City What shapes, angles, and lines do you see in this view of a city? Write the list word that names each numbered item.

If you need help, look at the clues below. The word parts will help you remember the meanings of the list words.

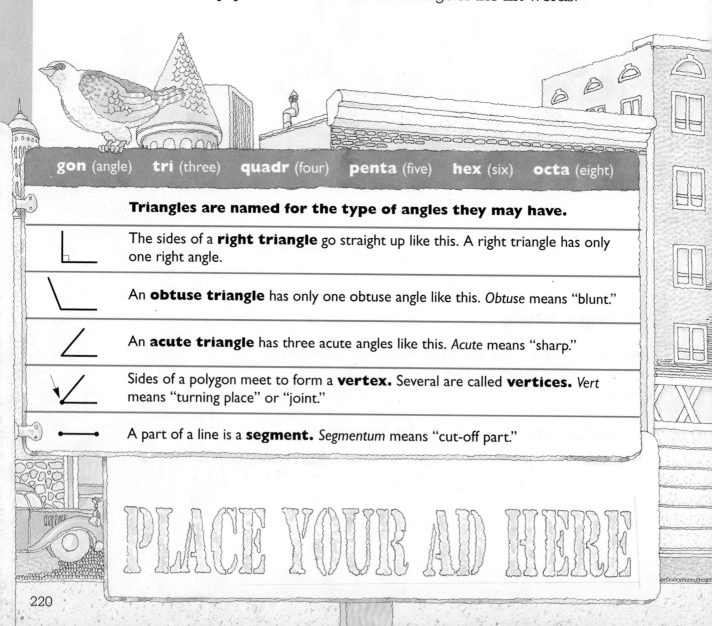

| **gon** (angle) | **tri** (three) | **quadr** (four) | **penta** (five) | **hex** (six) | **octa** (eight) |

Triangles are named for the type of angles they may have.

The sides of a **right triangle** go straight up like this. A right triangle has only one right angle.

An **obtuse triangle** has only one obtuse angle like this. *Obtuse* means "blunt."

An **acute triangle** has three acute angles like this. *Acute* means "sharp."

Sides of a polygon meet to form a **vertex.** Several are called **vertices.** *Vert* means "turning place" or "joint."

A part of a line is a **segment.** *Segmentum* means "cut-off part."

Did You Know?

■ SPELL WELL

Divide and Conquer It is easier to spell longer words if you break them up into syllables. Say each word below so you can hear the syllables. Then write the words.

ver ▪ ti ▪ ces   quad ▪ ri ▪ lat ▪ er ▪ al

Does it seem strange that **October**, the tenth month of the year, has a name that means "eight"? In the Roman calendar, March was the first month of the year, so **October** was the eighth. In the modern calendar, January and February begin the year, so **October** is the tenth month.

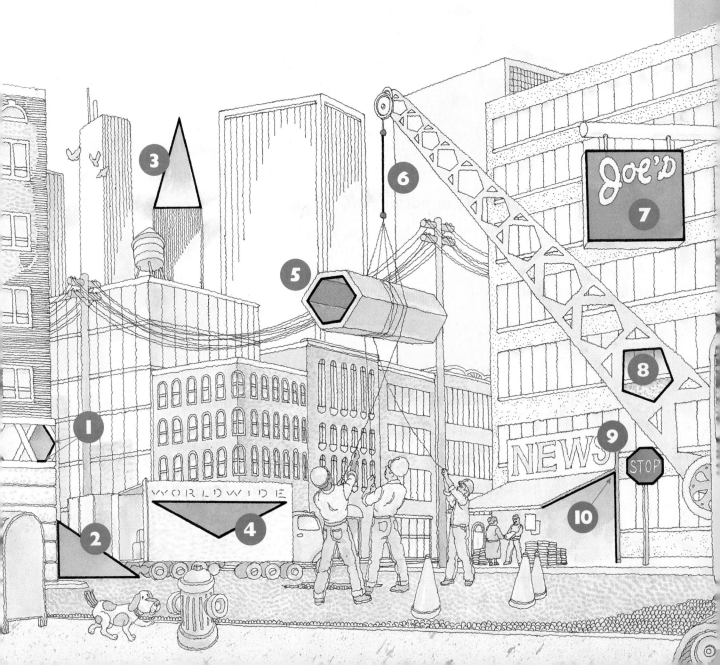

skateboard
roller skates
in-line skates
brakes
pumping
gliding
pavement
helmet
pads
protection

Skating

About ten million people in the United States like to skate.
Are you one of them? Add words about skating to the list.
Use your Spelling Dictionary if you need to.

■ GETTING AT MEANING

Using Diagrams Complete the descriptions near each
picture.

*People have enjoyed roller-skating since
1760, but today's (1) look different and
work much better than the first ones did. No
matter what kind of skates they use, skaters
start with the same simple movements. They move
by (2) , or pushing off, one skate and (3) on the other. They
stop by using toe stops, which are like (4) .*

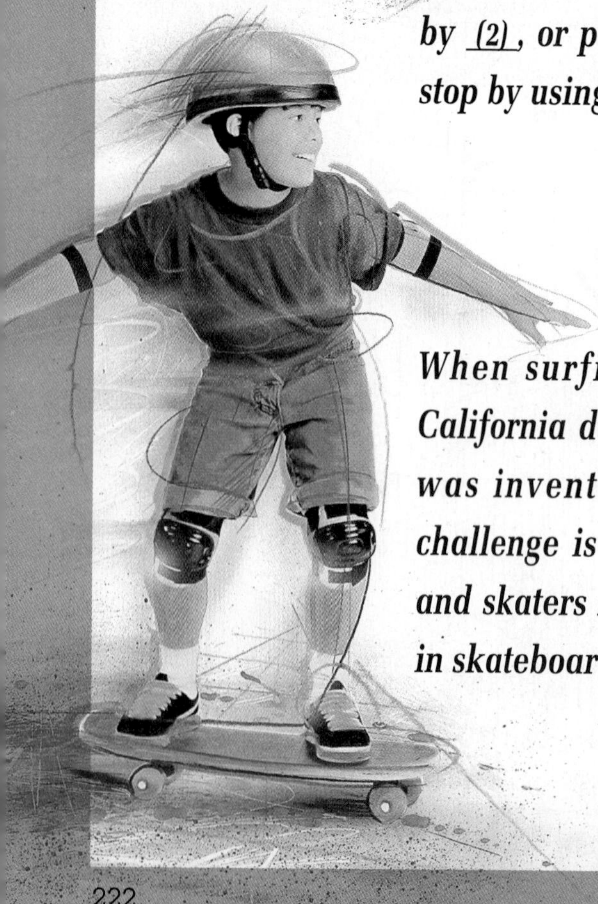

*When surfing became such a popular water sport in
California during the late 1950s, it wasn't long before the (5)
was invented. In both surfing and skateboarding, the
challenge is keeping your balance. Surfers ride the waves,
and skaters roll along the (6) or on specially designed rinks
in skateboard parks.*

In the 1980s, skates were designed with wheels in a single line like the blade on an ice skate. Both adults and kids like these _(7)_ because they are fast, smooth, and thrilling. They also give a skater a good workout. People who use all types of skates have many injuries if they don't use proper _(8)_. A smart skater always wears a _(9)_ for the head and _(10)_ for the elbows, knees, and wrists.

■ SPELL WELL

Compound Words Some of the words in the list are compound words. Write two compounds. First write the word parts and then write the whole word.

11. _____ + _____ = _____

12. _____ + _____ = _____

Did You Know?

The original roller skates were very difficult to control, so inventors came up with improved designs like the one at the right. The first roller skate that really worked was developed in 1863 when James L. Plimpton made a skate similar to modern roller skates. Could you improve on the design of your skate or skateboard? Make a sketch of your ideas.

Teacher

students
attendance
research
textbook
assignment
project
grading
portfolios
record
conferences

Teachers do a lot of preparation and planning. Can you add other words about teaching to the list? Use your Spelling Dictionary if you need to.

■ GETTING AT MEANING

Planning Calendar Ms. Romero likes to plot out her teaching plans on a calendar that she keeps on her desk. Read her plans and write the missing list words.

M	T	W	T	F
Begin the unit on birds. Ask the students what they'd like to find out, and (1) their answers on a chart.	Explain that each student will complete a science (2) about birds in flight.		Prewriting: Take the (3) outdoors to observe birds and to write questions.	Science: Students read "Different Habitats," pp. 98-99 in the (4).
Group Activity: Groups of students discuss their questions in (5).	Writing: Students write a report about birds. This (6) is due on Thursday.	Students go to the library to do (7) for their projects.	Students revise their reports and file them in their writing (8).	Check the (9) records and prepare the absentee report.
	Science projects are due.		Display students' projects.	It is the end of the (10) period. Distribute report cards.

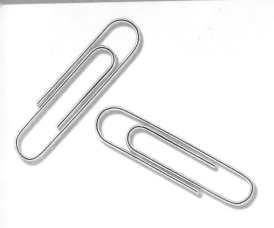

as ice-free fresh water permits.

female

BELTED
KINGFISHER.

■ SPELL WELL

Ending It Right One list word is spelled with **-ance.**
Another list word is spelled with **-ence.** Write each word.
Underline the **-ance** or **-ence** in each word. Since these
word parts sound the same, think of your own way to
remember each spelling.

Student Teacher

**Ms. Romero's calendar has no plans for
certain days. Choose two of those days and
write what you would do if you were the
teacher. Make sure your plans fit with the
theme of "birds."**

baby-sit
lawn mowing
pet-sitter
housework
car washing
tutoring
available
hire
provide
experience

Earning Money

How can a young person earn money? The words in the list
are about work. Add your own words. Use the Spelling
Dictionary if you need to.

■ GETTING AT MEANING

Workers for Hire Some ambitious fifth graders wrote job
ads so they could earn extra money. Read the ads
they passed out to their neighbors, and write the
missing list words.

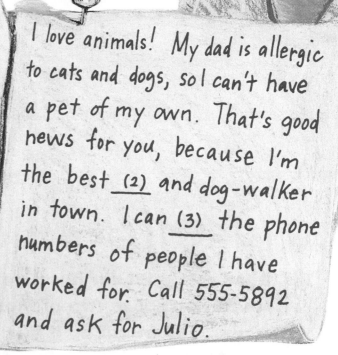

Straight-A student with a talent for helping others learn seeks a _(1)_ job after school. I'll help your child make the grade in math or language arts. Phone Rosa at 555-9163.

I love animals! My dad is allergic to cats and dogs, so I can't have a pet of my own. That's good news for you, because I'm the best _(2)_ and dog-walker in town. I can _(3)_ the phone numbers of people I have worked for. Call 555-5892 and ask for Julio.

Do you need a strong and sturdy go-getter who can do outdoor chores? I'm your worker! I'll do snow shoveling in winter. I'll do (4) and (5) in summer. If you (6) me, you'll have more free time! Call kim today at 555-8792.

I'm David, a ten-year-old who is (7) on weekends to be a parent's helper. I have lots of (8) taking care of my little brother and helping at home. I can (9) for your child while you do a project. I'll also help you sweep, dust, or do other (10). You can reach me at 555-6784.

■ SPELL WELL

Getting Letters in the Correct Order It's easy to get the underlined letters in the wrong order so concentrate on them. Write each word.

11. experience

12. available

It Pay$ to Adverti$e

If you wanted to earn some extra money, what kind of job would you like to do? Write your own advertisement for a job. Be specific about the kind of work you want to do and when you are available.

Your Ad Here !

comedy
comedians
humorous
punch line
audience
hilariously
laughter
knock-knock
   joke
riddle
pun

Telling Jokes

What kinds of jokes make you laugh? Do you like to make others laugh? If you know other words about telling jokes, add them to the list. Use your Spelling Dictionary.

■ GETTING AT MEANING

Teaming Up Read the dialogue and jokes, and write the missing list words.

Mary: Hey, Harry, you're a funny guy and I'm a funny gal. Maybe we should perform in the school talent show as stand-up (1).

Harry: That's a terrific idea, Mary! If we're going to be a (2) team, we need to practice some jokes. What kinds of jokes do people like?

Mary: I've noticed that people love to hear a (3) because they have to guess the answer. Here's one!

What always tastes hot and always has ice in it? → Spice!

Harry: That's pretty (4), all right. Now listen to this (5). A good play on words always gets a laugh.

Two tomatoes were racing to the hamburger bun. One fell behind but said he'd ketchup later.

228

Mary: You said, "He'd ketchup later"? I hope that pun doesn't make the (6) groan. Let's think of a joke that has a good (7) at the end.

Harry: I've got it! What about a (8)? The audience can participate by shouting out "Who's there?"

Knock! Knock! ⟶ Who's there?
Joe King. ⟶ Joe King who?
I'm Joe King around. Why aren't you laughing?

Mary: That's a good one! The audience will roar with (9)! Harry, old friend, I have a feeling that we'll be (10) funny together!

■ SPELL WELL

Suffixes Two words in the list end in the suffixes **-ous** and **-ly.** Write the words. Underline the suffix in each word.

Did You Know?

The comedienne and actress Lucille Ball starred in over 500 individual performances as the comical, red-headed "Lucy" in the "I Love Lucy" show and other television shows. Since 1951, the shows have been so popular throughout the world that more people have probably seen Lucille Ball's face more often than the face of any other human.

Writer's Handbook

INTRODUCTION

Spelling well is a basic part of writing well, but good spelling is not all you need to become a good writer. This handbook covers some of the other skills good writers use.

CONTENTS

Writing Traits

FOCUS/IDEAS

Good writers focus on a **main idea** and develop this idea with strong supporting details. In addition, they know their purpose for writing. This purpose may be to persuade, to inform, to describe, or to entertain. Deciding on your purpose can help you focus on your main idea and develop it effectively.

When you prepare to write, first consider possible topics. Choose the one that interests you the most. Then decide whether you want to inform, persuade, or entertain your audience. Write possible main ideas, and let your ideas flow as you plan. Don't be afraid to change your mind. Select the idea that makes the most sense as you consider who your audience is.

List **details** that focus your topic and support your main idea. Add interesting information that will appeal to your audience. Now decide which details are the strongest.

Look at the following example. This writer has listed details and then eliminated those that do not focus on the main idea.

Main Idea Persuade Mom to adopt a dog

Details

Will teach me responsibility

Will play with me

Promise to walk it every day

~~I saw cute dog in park~~

Will keep me company

~~Some dogs fluffy~~

Will take care of it

~~Could wear sweater in cold weather~~

STRATEGIES FOR FOCUS AND IDEAS

- Choose a topic you will enjoy writing about. If you care about your topic, you will be able to write with enthusiasm.
- If you cannot think of many supporting details, or find them through research, change your main idea.

ORGANIZATION

> When you write, put your ideas in an order that will help readers understand them. **Organization**—a composition's structure, or the way its ideas are put together—allows writers to show the connections among those ideas.

Here are examples of ways you can organize your writing to help readers understand the points you want to communicate:

- As a story, from beginning to middle to end
- As a comparison/contrast essay, describing likenesses and differences
- As a persuasive argument, expressing one convincing reason after another
- As a description, providing vivid details as you move from top to bottom of the subject
- As a how-to report, clearly presenting a series of steps

When you begin writing, pay attention to how you organize each paragraph. The sentences in a paragraph should fit together and appear in an order that makes sense. Use words and patterns that help a reader see how ideas are related. For example, one sentence can pose a question, and the next sentence can begin to answer it.

STRATEGIES FOR ORGANIZING YOUR WRITING

- Create a graphic organizer such as a web, outline, Venn diagram, or sketch to help you organize your ideas.
- Describe events in the order in which they happened, from first to last.
- Begin a paragraph with a topic sentence that expresses the main idea, and then write details that support the main idea.
- Use order words (*first, then, after, finally*) so your writing flows smoothly.
- Use transitions (*in addition, for example, however*) to connect ideas, sentences, and paragraphs.
- End with a concluding sentence that ties ideas together.

VOICE

> Good writers usually have a strong **voice**—a personality that comes through in the tone and style of their writing. A strong voice speaks directly to readers and keeps their attention.

Notice the difference in voice in the sentences below.
- Today began nicely. I felt happy. (weak voice)
- Today I leaped out of bed with a big smile on my face. (strong voice)

When you write, just as when you speak, you can choose the tone of voice you use. Voice helps you communicate with a certain audience for a particular purpose. The style of your writing and your choice of words can make the writing interesting to each reader, whether the tone is serious or humorous, formal or informal. If you care about your subject, your writing will reflect your voice.

STRATEGIES FOR DEVELOPING A WRITER'S VOICE

- Choose a voice that matches your audience and purpose. For example, a light, carefree voice probably would not work for writing an essay about your state's government. Instead, you would need to use a more formal tone.
- Use words and phrases that match the type of writing. For example, in a letter to the editor of your local newspaper, you should avoid using slang or casual language. In a letter to a friend, however, you would use informal and friendly words or even slang. Depending on your message, you might use a voice that is thoughtful, humorous, angry, excited, or sarcastic.
- Use vivid adjectives (*nervous, excited, calm*) to elaborate your ideas and give your writing a personal voice.
- Find your voice by reading aloud things you have written, or by having others read your own writing to you. In other words, learn to listen to yourself.
- Different types of sentences add to a voice. Engage readers by asking a question or giving a command.
- Be consistent. Establish your writer's voice in the opening paragraph of your work. Then stay with it until the end.

WORD CHOICE

> Good writers choose their **words** carefully. They use specific words to make their meanings clear. They also use vivid words to elaborate on their ideas and add excitement to their writing.

Sentences with strong, well-chosen words help the reader imagine people, places, and things in vivid detail. The sentences below show how word choice can make a sentence lively.

- Nat threw the ball to the batter. (dull)
- Nat grunted as he hurled a curve ball to the batter. (lively)

STRATEGIES FOR CHOOSING THE RIGHT WORDS

- Replace ordinary words with vivid words. A thesaurus, which lists synonyms, can help you. Choose words with caution, however: not all synonyms are interchangeable.
- Choose exact nouns. (*hotel* instead of *place*, *oil painting* instead of *picture*)
- Use strong verbs. (*flinch* instead of *move*, *barked* instead of *said*)
- Use vivid adjectives to elaborate on your descriptions. (*tattered* instead of *old*, *drenched* instead of *wet*)
- Avoid vague words such as *great, nice, thing,* and *stuff.* (*I smell roses* instead of *I smell things*)
- Use strong images or figurative language to appeal to your readers' senses. (*Gillian's face blushed tomato-red* instead of *Gillian was embarrassed*)
- Decide if some sentences that have linking verbs would be stronger with action verbs. (*My heart thumped* instead of *I was excited*)
- Avoid wordiness. (*I think we will win the game because we have better players* instead of *In my opinion, I think we will win the game due to the fact that we have better players*)
- Elaborate with specific details. (*Dan slurped up soup and ate crackers* instead of *Dan was a noisy eater*)

SENTENCES

Good writers express their thoughts in lively, varied **sentences.** They make reading a pleasure by using sentences that create a special rhythm and style.

Look at the short paragraph below. Note how the writer varies sentence type and length to make the writing interesting.

What should you keep in mind when adopting a dog? One important thing to remember is that some dogs are better than others for certain people. For example, hunting dogs need plenty of exercise. Do not get a hunting dog if you can't take her for long walks. Instead, think about adopting a small dog that needs less exercise. Enjoy your new pet!

STRATEGIES FOR IMPROVING YOUR SENTENCES

Use these guidelines to help you revise a piece of your writing.
- Write sentences that flow logically from one to the next.
- Vary sentence length by mixing short and long sentences.
- Avoid sentences that are too long or wordy. You might rewrite a very long sentence as two or more shorter sentences.
- Avoid writing a series of short, choppy sentences. Use connectors such as *and, but, or, because, although,* and *until* to join two simple, related sentences.
- Include different kinds of sentences to add variety and life to your writing. Although most sentences will be statements, include some questions, commands, and exclamations, too.
- Vary the beginnings of sentences. Avoid starting every sentence with words such as *I, she, he, then,* or *the.*
- Read what you write aloud to yourself. Listen for a rhythm as if you are listening to a song. Rewrite sentences that interrupt the flow.

CONVENTIONS

> **Conventions** are rules that people agree to follow. Written language follows special conventions. For example, sentences begin with capital letters and end with some kind of punctuation. Conventions also set rules for spelling and grammar.

How many conventions can you identify in the sentences below?

- Greg Harding was born in Nashville, Tennessee, on March 3, 1996.
- He is a student at Griffin Elementary School, and his favorite classes are English and math.

Proofreading Marks
Use these marks to edit your work.

⌿⌿	New paragraph
≡	Capital letter
/	Lowercase letter
◯	Correct the spelling.
∧	Add something.
℘	Remove something.

STRATEGIES FOR FOLLOWING WRITING CONVENTIONS

- Learn the rules for spelling. For example, add -s or -es to form the plural of most nouns.
- Use a dictionary or spell checker to help you with the spelling of difficult or new words.
- Capitalize the first word in a sentence and each important word in proper nouns.
- Use punctuation correctly.
- Make sure each verb you use agrees with its subject.
- Check that verb tenses are correct.
- Check that pronouns in subjects and predicates are correct.
- Do not run sentences together without proper punctuation.

Taking Writing Tests

Does the thought of taking a writing test make you uneasy? The tips that follow should help you take such tests with confidence.

GENERAL GUIDELINES FOR WRITING TESTS

- **Listen carefully to test instructions.** How much time do you have? Do you need a pen or pencil?
- **Read the assignment and identify the key words.** Make sure you write about exactly what the assignment asks for. Here are some key words that often come up in test assignments.

    Categorize or *Classify:* Sort facts or ideas into groups.

    Compare or *Contrast:* Point out similarities (compare) or differences (contrast).

    Defend: Give evidence to show why a view is correct.

    Define: Tell what something is or means.

    Describe: Create a word picture with details and examples.

    Discuss: State your ideas about what something means.

    Evaluate: Give your opinion, with support, on whether an idea is good or bad, right or wrong.

    Explain: Make something clear by giving reasons, examples, or steps.

    Summarize: State main points, or retell important parts of a story or article.

- **Plan how you'll use your time.** Set aside a certain amount of time at the beginning to plan your paper and at the end to read through it and catch any errors.
- **Write a strong opening** to catch your reader's attention. Be sure it specifically addresses the topic.
- **Use specific facts and details** to develop your ideas.
- **Take time to plan an interesting conclusion.** Don't just stop writing because the time is up. Think about how you want to end your test assignment.

Models

NARRATIVE WRITING

Narrative writing tells a story, with a beginning, a middle, and an end. It describes events and the order in which they occur.

> Three years ago, my life changed completely. That's when my little sister Allie was born. When I first went to the hospital to see her, she was tiny and cute and screamed louder than all the other babies. That should have given me a clue. Allie wanted attention, now!
>
> At first, Allie slept all the time–during the day. She did that so she could cry at night. Mom was so sleepy on some mornings that she would give me cereal without a bowl! Luckily, Allie soon learned how to smile and coo. She learned really fast that smiling could get her anything she wanted–crackers, apple juice, toys. We became pals right away.
>
> Now Allie is three and follows me all over. I teach her new things, like salsa steps and songs. Allie still loves attention, and I love giving it to her.

Why is it good? Here's how the author uses the six traits of good writing to make the model enjoyable to read.

Focus/Ideas Details support the main idea that Allie loves attention.

Organization Events in order; connectors between paragraphs make passage of time clear (*three years ago, at first, now*)

Voice Writer's personality evident through details, style (*my life changed completely, I love giving it to her*)

Word Choice Exact nouns (*hospital, salsa*), strong verbs (*screamed, coo*), vivid adjectives (*tiny, sleepy*)

Sentences Lively, varied sentences with distinct rhythm

Conventions No errors

DESCRIPTIVE WRITING

Descriptive writing tells readers about a person, place, or thing. It uses sensory language that helps readers imagine what the subject looks, sounds, and feels like.

> The lagoon in our town is a wonderful recreation place. Bigger than a pond but smaller than a lake, the lagoon is just right for summer or winter fun.
>
> In summer, children feed the geese that swim there. Babies squeal with delight as the white birds paddle eagerly after chunks of bread. The banks under the big old trees provide a quiet spot for fishing. Sometimes I sit on the twisted tree roots and watch canoers paddle by.
>
> In winter, kids of all ages put on their skates and glide over the ice. On the banks, someone makes a fragrant cedar fire in the stone pit, and shivering skaters crowd around. In late afternoon, as the sun sets, the ice and the snow-covered trees take on a pink glow.
>
> Our town is lucky. Our lagoon provides an escape to nature in any season.

Why is it good? Here's how the author uses the six traits of good writing to make the model vivid and enjoyable to read.

Focus/Ideas Specific details that bring the lagoon into focus

Organization Organized by season with clear connecting words between paragraphs; strong beginning and ending

Voice Clear communication of enjoyment; enthusiasm for place

Word Choice Vivid verbs and modifiers that appeal to sight (*paddle, twisted, glide, snow-covered, pink*), hearing (*squeal*), smell (*fragrant cedar fire*), and feeling (*shivering*).

Sentences Interest through variation in sentence type and length

Conventions No errors

PERSUASIVE WRITING

Persuasive writing gives the writer's opinion. It also supports that opinion, giving the reasons the writer feels the way he or she does. Persuasive writing aims to convince readers to agree with the writer.

> Mountain climbing would provide a fun, healthful, and educational opportunity for our class. It doesn't have to be Mt. Everest. Let's be realistic! We can climb a mountain in Vermont.
>
> A mountain-climbing trip would be like an extended field trip! It would be fun to travel, meet new people, and take a break from the classroom routine.
>
> Mountain climbing also provides excellent health benefits. We would get a great physical workout. Even better, our minds would be challenged as we follow directions, stay alert, and pull ourselves up rocky paths. Reaching the summit would give us a great feeling of accomplishment.
>
> Best of all, mountain climbing is a learning experience that requires teamwork. Without communication and cooperation, someone could get lost or injured. This teamwork would carry over to the classroom.
>
> I hope you will agree that this trip would be a terrific boost to improve our performance at school.

Why is it good? Here's how the author uses the six traits of good writing to make the model persuasive and enjoyable to read.

Focus/Ideas Argument focused on clear main idea; good support

Organization Topic sentences within essay give reasons in order; most important reason signaled with *Best of all*

Voice Writer involved with topic and knowledgeable about it

Word Choice Persuasive words with emotional appeal (*healthful, educational, excellent, benefits, terrific boost*)

Sentences Various lengths and structures; smooth connectors (*Even better*)

Conventions No errors

EXPOSITORY WRITING

Expository writing gives information about a topic. It usually expresses its main idea in a topic sentence. Details develop that main idea.

> All plants go through a cycle in which they grow and reproduce. The cycle starts when insects such as bees carry pollen into the flower of a grown plant. They pollinate the flower so the plant can reproduce, and at this point a fruit begins to form. This fruit can be anything that contains seeds, such as a nut or berry. Each seed contains a baby plant called an embryo. The seed gets buried in the ground-it falls by itself or someone plants it. Then the embryo starts to grow. Soon the tiny plant puts out roots into the soil and a stem and leaves above the ground. Now we begin to see the plant we recognize. It will make its own flowers and begin the growing cycle again. In many flowers and vegetable plants, this whole cycle occurs in one year.

Why is it good? Here's how the author uses the six traits of good writing to make the model informative and enjoyable to read.

Focus/Ideas Clear main idea; all detail sentences develop it

Organization Strong topic sentence; cycle steps presented in proper order; connectors help express passage of time (*when, at this point, soon*)

Voice Natural and friendly but does not intrude into explanation

Word Choice Precise, accurate words to explain process (*pollinate, embryo, cycle*)

Sentences Good variety; excellent flow of ideas

Conventions No errors

The Writing Process

There are five helpful steps that you can use when you write: Prewrite, Draft, Edit, Revise, and Publish. This section will tell you more about each step.

1. PREWRITE: THINK BEFORE YOU WRITE

Give yourself a chance to think about and plan your writing before you actually put sentences on paper. Time you spend prewriting is time well spent.

- **Choose a topic.** Brainstorm a list of ideas. These ideas might come from books, magazines, or newspapers, or from experiences you or people you know have had.
- **Determine your purpose and audience.** Your purpose might be to express your feelings, to describe or explain something, to give or get information, to persuade your reader of something, or to tell a story. Your audience might be classmates, the editor of the local paper, or a friend who moved away.
- **Narrow your topic.** To focus on an idea specific enough to deal with, you might write down questions, create a web or cluster, or logically group words dealing with the topic.
- **Collect useful details about your topic.** Look in books, interview people, list points you want to make, or observe how things look, sound, smell, taste, and feel.
- **Organize your information.** Depending on your purpose for writing, you might use time order, spatial order, opinions backed by facts, or order of importance.

> **Prewriting Strategy**
> **Ask Yourself Questions**
>
> Asking yourself questions like these is a good way to help yourself choose and focus on a topic:
> - How much do I know about this topic?
> - Will this topic interest other people?
> - What do I think is the most interesting thing about this topic?
> - Is there too much information to explain?

2. DRAFT: PUT YOUR IDEAS ON PAPER

Once you have a plan, you can start to write. Try some of these strategies to get started.

- **Set a goal.** Decide how much you will write without stopping, right now.
- **Look at your notes.** Find the first thing you want to discuss.
- **Start with your main idea.** Put it in a sentence that is direct and interesting. Then support it with details.
- **Push ahead.** Write down all your ideas. Don't worry about perfect spelling or punctuation. If you change your mind about something, don't cross it out—just start a new sentence. You'll have time to correct errors later.

Drafting Strategy
Make A Strong Start

Good starting sentences capture readers' attention and make them want to read more. Your first sentence should introduce your topic and use strong, interesting words.

- I like cello music. *(weak start)*
- When I hear the sound of the cello, as mellow and sweet as honey, I feel like a cat curled up by a fireplace. *(strong start)*

What makes the second sentence so much stronger? It clearly states the writer's main idea, includes vivid details, and lets the writer's voice shine through.

3. REVISE: GO BACK AND MAKE CHANGES

Now that you have your ideas on paper, shape your rough draft into something more clear and concise. Reread your draft, looking for obvious errors, such as unclear sentences. You might also discuss your draft with other students or your teacher.

When you revise, you may make some or all of the following changes:
- **Add** missing words or ideas.
- **Take out** unnecessary words, sentences, or paragraphs.
- **Move** words, sentences, or paragraphs around. If you write on a computer, the Cut and Paste functions on a word processor make this easy.
- **Substitute** strong words or ideas for weaker ones. Strong, vivid language is exciting to read. (for example, *finch, spring, eggplant* instead of *bird, move, vegetable*)

Revising Strategy
Ask Yourself Questions

These questions might help you revise your work:
- Did I say what I wanted to say?
- Are my details in the best possible order?
- Do I have a beginning, middle, and end?
- Does each paragraph have a topic sentence and stick to one idea?
- Are there extra or inexact words I need to cut?

4. EDIT: POLISH YOUR WRITING

Once you have revised your draft, proofread it. To proofread is to look carefully at what you've written in order to catch mistakes in grammar, punctuation, and spelling. The proofreader's marks on page 236 will help you mark the changes that need to be made. Use the questions below as a proofreading checklist.
- Do the subjects and verbs agree?
- Did I keep the correct verb tense throughout?

- Is each sentence correctly punctuated?
- Have I avoided fragments and run-on sentences?
- Did I capitalize the first word of each sentence, as well as proper nouns?
- Did I check the spelling of unfamiliar words?

Once you have corrected all the mistakes you found, proofread your writing a final time.

> **Editing Strategy**
> **Check Carefully**
>
> If you write using a computer, you probably have spell-checking and grammar-checking tools. Use them with care. Computers also make errors. Keep a grammar book and dictionary handy.

5. PUBLISH: LET YOUR WORK SHINE

There are many ways of presenting your work, but most of your writing will be done on paper for your teacher to read. Your teacher probably has special rules on how to present your writing. Know what those rules are, and follow them.

> **Publishing Strategy**
> **Look Your Best**
>
> Your writing should always be easy to read. Leave space at the edges of the paper and indent at the start of each paragraph. If you write by hand, write neatly. If you use a computer, use a font that is easy to read.

Spelling Dictionary

Parts of a Dictionary Entry

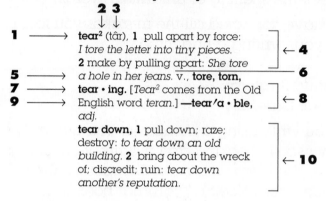

2 3

1 ——→ **tear**² (târ), **1** pull apart by force: *I tore the letter into tiny pieces.* **2** make by pulling apart: *She tore a hole in her jeans.* v., **tore, torn,**

5 ——→

7 ——→ **tear • ing.** [*Tear*² comes from the Old

9 ——→ English word *teran.*] **—tear′a • ble,** *adj.*

tear down, 1 pull down; raze; destroy: *to tear down an old building.* **2** bring about the wreck of; discredit; ruin: *tear down another's reputation.*

←— **4**

——— **6**

←— **8**

←— **10**

1 Entry word
2 Homograph number
3 Pronunciation
4 Definitions
5 Illustrative sentence or phrase
6 Part-of-speech label
7 Inflected forms
8 Etymology
9 Run-on entry
10 Idiom

Full Pronunciation Key

a	hat, cap	**i**	it, pin	**p**	paper, cup	**v**	very, save
ā	age, face	**ī**	ice, five	**r**	run, try	**w**	will, woman
ä	father, far			**s**	say, yes	**y**	young, yet
âr	care, hair	**j**	jam, enjoy	**sh**	she, rush	**z**	zero, breeze
		k	kind, seek	**t**	tell, it	**zh**	measure,
b	bad, rob	**l**	land, coal	**th**	thin, both		seizure
ch	child, much	**m**	me, am	**ᴛH**	then, smooth		
d	did, red	**n**	no, in			**ə**	represents:
		ng	long, bring	**u**	cup, cutter		a in about
e	let, best			**u̇**	pull, put		e in taken
ē	equal, be	**o**	hot, rock	**ü**	rule, move		i in pencil
ėr	term, learn	**ō**	open, go				o in lemon
		ȯ	all, saw				u in circus
f	fat, if	**ô**	order, store				
g	go, bag	**oi**	oil, voice				
h	he, how	**ou**	house, out				

Spellings of English Sounds*

Symbol	Spellings	Symbol	Spellings
a	at, plaid, half, laugh	ng	long, ink, handkerchief, tongue
ā	able, aid, say, age, eight, they, break, vein, gauge, crepe, beret	o	odd, honest
ä	father, ah, calm, heart, bazaar, yacht, sergeant	ō	open, oak, toe, own, home, oh, folk, though, bureau, sew, brooch, soul
âr	dare, aerial, fair, prayer, where, pear, their, they're	ȯ	all, author, awful, broad, bought, walk, taught, cough, Utah, Arkansas
b	bad, rabbit	ô	order, board, floor, tore
ch	child, watch, future, question	oi	oil, boy
d	did, add, filled	ou	out, owl, bough, hour
e	end, said, any, bread, says, heifer, leopard, friend, bury	p	pay, happy
		r	run, carry, wrong, rhythm
ē	equal, eat, eel, happy, cities, vehicle, ceiling, receive, key, these, believe, machine, liter, people	s	say, miss, cent, scent, dance, tense, sword, pizza, listen
		sh	she, machine, sure, ocean, special, tension, mission, nation
ėr	stern, earth, urge, first, word, journey	t	tell, button, two, Thomas, stopped, doubt, receipt, pizza
f	fat, effort, laugh, phrase	th	thin
g	go, egg, guest, ghost, league	ŦH	then, breathe
gz	example, exhaust	u	up, oven, trouble, does, flood
h	he, who, jai alai, Gila monster	u̇	full, good, wolf, should
hw	wheat	ü	food, junior, rule, blue, who, move, threw, soup, through, shoe, two, fruit, lieutenant
i	it, England, ear, hymn, been, sieve, women, busy, build, weird		
		v	very, have, of, Stephen
ī	I, ice, lie, sky, type, rye, eye, island, high, eider, aisle, height, buy, coyote	w	will, quick
		y	yes, opinion
		yü	use, few, cue, view, vacuum
j	jam, gem, exaggerate, schedule, badger, bridge, soldier, large, allegiance	z	zero, has, buzz, scissors, xylophone
k	coat, kind, back, echo, ache, quit, account, antique, excite, acquire	zh	measure, garage, division
		ə	alone, complete, moment, authority, bargain, April, cautious, circus, pageant, physician, oxygen, dungeon, tortoise
l	land, tell		
m	me, common, climb, solemn, palm		
n	no, manner, knife, gnaw, pneumonia		

*Not all English spellings of these sounds are included in this list.

A

a·bol·ish (ə bol′ish), do away with completely; put an end to: *Many people wish that nations would abolish war.* v.

ab·surd (ab sėrd′), plainly not true or sensible; foolish; ridiculous: *The idea that the number 13 brings bad luck is absurd.* adj. [*Absurd* comes from Latin *absurdus,* meaning "out of tune, senseless."] —**ab·surd′ly,** adv.

ac·cept (ak sept′), 1 take what is offered or given to one; consent to take: *She accepted the job.* 2 say yes to an invitation, offer, etc.: *They asked me to go along and I accepted.* v.

ac·ci·dent (ak′sə dənt), something harmful or unlucky that happens. *an automobile accident.* n., pl. **ac·ci·dents.**

ac·com·pa·ny (ə kum′pə nē), go along with: *May we accompany you on your walk?* v.

ac·cu·mu·late (ə kyü′myə lāt), collect little by little; pile up; gather: *They accumulated enough money to buy a car. Dust had accumulated in the empty house.* v., **ac·cu·mu·lat·ed, ac·cu·mu·lat·ing.**

ac·cur·ate (ak′yər it), without errors or mistakes; precisely correct; exact: *an accurate report, an accurate watch.* adj. [*Accurate* comes from Latin *accuratum,* meaning "done with care."]

ac·cuse (ə kyüz′), charge with having done something wrong or with having broken the law: *The driver was accused of speeding.* v., **ac·cused, ac·cus·ing.**

a·cre (ā′kər), a unit of area equal to 160 square rods or 43,560 square feet (4047 square meters), used to measure land. n.

a·cre·age (ā′kər ij), number of acres. n.

ac·tion (ak′shən), 1 process of acting; doing something: *The quick action of the firemen saved the building from being burned down. The situation called for immediate action.* 2 something done; act: *Helping a small child to cross the street was a kind action.* n.

ac·tu·al·ly (ak′chü ə lē), really; in fact: *Are you actually going to camp this summer or just wishing to go?* adv.

a·cute tri·an·gle (ə kyüt trī′ang′əl), a triangle with three acute angles.

a·dapt (ə dapt′), 1 make fit or suitable; adjust: *Can you adapt your way of working to the new job?* 2 change so as to make suitable for a different use: *The story was adapted for the movies from a novel by Jane Austen.* v. —**a·dapt′er, a·dap′tor,** n.

ad·just (ə just′), change to make fit: *These desks and seats can be adjusted to the height of any child.* v.

ad·mi·ra·tion (ad′mə rā′shən), a feeling of wonder, pleasure, and approval: *The beauty of the singing excited admiration.* n.

ad·mire (ad mīr′), 1 regard with wonder, pleasure, or satisfaction: *We admired the beautiful painting.* 2 think highly of; respect: *I admire your courage.* v., **ad·mired, ad·mir·ing.**

ad·mit (ad mit′), say (something) is real or true; acknowledge: *She admits now that she made a mistake. His opponent had to admit defeat.* v., **ad·mit·ted, ad·mit·ting.**

a·dopt (ə dopt′), take as one's own choice; accept: *We adopted all the ideas our friend suggested.* v., **a·dopt·ed, a·dopt·ing.**

ad·ven·ture (ad ven′chər), a bold and difficult undertaking, usually exciting and dangerous. n.

ad·ven·tur·ous (ad ven′chər əs), 1 fond of adventures; ready to take risks; daring: *a bold, adventurous explorer.* 2 full of risk; dangerous: *An expedition to the North Pole is an adventurous undertaking.* adj.

a·fraid (ə frād′), 1 feeling fear; frightened: *afraid of the dark.* 2 sorry to have to say: *I'm afraid you are wrong about that.* adj.

a·gain (ə gen′), another time; once more: *Come again to play. Say that again.* adv.

a·gainst (ə genst′), in the opposite direction to, so as to meet; upon or toward: *Rain beat against the window.* prep.

a·ghast (ə gast′), struck with surprise or horror; filled with terror: *I was aghast when I saw the destruction caused by the earthquake.* adj.

accident

an automobile **accident**

action (def. 1)

a·gree·a·ble (ə grē′ə bəl), giving pleasure; pleasing: *She had an agreeable manner. adj.*

ag·ri·cul·ture (ag′rə kul′chər), science or art of cultivating the soil, including the production of crops and the raising of livestock; farming. *n.*

a·head (ə hed′), in front; before: *Walk ahead of me. adv.*

air pol·lu·tion (âr′ pə lü′shən), the contamination of the air by waste gases from industry, fuel exhaust, and atomic fallout.

a·jar (ə jär′), slightly open: *Please leave the door ajar. adj.*

Al·a·bam·a (al′ə bam′ə), one of the south central states of the United States. *Abbreviation:* Ala. or AL *Capital:* Montgomery. *n.*

A·las·ka (ə las′kə), one of the Pacific states of the United States, in the NW part of North America. *Abbreviation:* Alas. or AK *Capital:* Juneau.

al·ien (ā′lyən), **1** person who is not a citizen of the country in which he or she lives. **2** creature from another planet or from outer space. *n., pl.* **al·iens.**

al·ler·gic (ə lėr′jik), having an allergy: *Some people who are allergic to eggs cannot eat them without breaking into a rash. adj.*

al·li·ga·tor (al′ə gā′tər), a large reptile with a rather thick skin, related and similar to the crocodile but having a shorter and flatter head. Alligators live in the rivers and marshes of the warm parts of America and China. *n.* [*Alligator* comes from Spanish *el lagarto*, meaning "the lizard."]

al·lit·e·ra·tion (ə lit′e rā′shən), repetition of the same sound or letter in a group of words or a line of poetry. *n.*

al·low (ə lou′), let (someone) do something; permit (something) to be done or happen: *Swimming is not allowed at this beach. v.,* **al·lowed, al·low·ing.**

all right (ȯl′ rīt′), **1** in a satisfactory way: *The engine seemed to be working all right.* **2** in good health: *The doctor says I am all right.*

a lot (ə lot′), a large number of persons or things considered as a group. *n.*

a·loud (ə loud′), loud enough to be heard; not in a whisper: *The book I was reading was so funny I laughed aloud. The teacher read the story aloud to the class. adv.*

al·read·y (ȯl red′ē), before this time; by this time; even now: *You are half an hour late already. adv.*

al·though or **al·tho** (ȯl ᴛʜō), in spite of the fact that; though: *Although it rained all morning, they went on the hike. conj.*

al·ways (ȯl′wāz or ȯl′wiz), at all times; every time: *Night always follows day. adv.*

am·a·teur (am′ə chər or am′ə tər), person who does something for pleasure, not for money or as a profession: *Only amateurs are allowed to compete in this tournament. n.*

am·bi·tious (am bish′əs), having or guided by ambition; desiring strongly: *She is ambitious to get through high school in three years. adj.*

am·bu·lance (am′byə ləns), an automobile equipped to carry sick, injured, or wounded persons. *n., pl.* **am·bu·lanc·es.**

a·mong (ə mung′), surrounded by: *a house among the trees. prep.*

a·mount (ə mount′), the total of two or more numbers taken together; sum: *What is the amount of the bill for the groceries? n.*

a·muse (ə myüz′), cause to laugh or smile: *The clown's antics amused everyone. The joke was amusing. v.,* **a·mused, a·mus·ing.**

an·a·lyze (an′l īz), examine carefully and in detail: *analyze a situation. The newspaper analyzed the results of the election. v.,* **an·a·lyzed, an·a·lyz·ing.**

agriculture

alligator
an **alligator** near the river

					stands for
a	hat	ī	ice	u̇	put	ə stands for
ā	age	o	not	ü	rule	a in about
ä	far, calm	ō	open	ch	child	e in taken
âr	care	ȯ	saw	ng	long	i in pencil
e	let	ô	order	sh	she	o in lemon
ē	equal	oi	oil	th	thin	u in circus
ėr	term	ou	out	ᴛʜ	then	
i	it	u	cup	zh	measure	

A·na·sa·zi (ä′nə sä′zē), member of an American Indian tribe who once lived in pueblos in the southwestern United States. *n., pl.* **A·na·sa·zi** or **A·na·sa·zis.**

and (and; *unstressed* ənd *or* ən), as well as: *You can come and go in the car. conj.*

an·i·mal (an′ə məl), any living thing that is not a plant. A dog, a bird, a fish, a snake, a fly, and a worm are animals. *n., pl.* **an·i·mals.**

an·noy (ə noi′), make somewhat angry; disturb; trouble; vex: *The baby is always annoying me by pulling my hair. v.*

an·oth·er (ə nuᴛʜ′ər), **1** one more: *Have another glass of milk* (*adj.*). *I ate a candy bar and then asked for another* (*pron.*). **2** a different one: *Show me another kind of hat.* 1,2 *adj.*, 1 *pron.*

an·swer (an′sər), words spoken or written in return to a question: *The girl gave a quick answer. n.*

an·te·lope (an′tl ōp), any of certain hoofed mammals of Africa and Asia that are related to the goat and cow but resemble the deer in appearance, grace, and speed. *n.*

an·to·nym (an′tə nim), word that means the opposite of another word. "Hot" is the antonym of "cold." *n.*

an·y·thing (en′ē thing), any thing: *Do you have anything to eat? pron.*

a·part·ment (ə pärt′mənt), room or group of rooms to live in; flat. *n.*

ape (āp), **1** any large, tailless monkey with long arms, able to stand almost erect and walk on two feet. Chimpanzees, gorillas, orangutans, and gibbons are apes. **2** imitate; mimic: *They aped the mannerisms of their favorite TV stars.* 1 *n.* 2 *v.*

ap·pear (ə pir′), seem; look as if: *The apple appeared sound on the outside, but it was rotten inside. v.*

ap·plause (ə plȯz′), approval shown by clapping the hands, shouting, etc.: *Applause for the singer's good performance rang out from the audience. n.*

ap·pre·ci·a·tion (ə prē′shē ā′shən), a valuing highly; sympathetic understanding: *She has no appreciation of modern art. n.*

ap·prox·i·mate (ə prok′sə mit), nearly correct: *The approximate length of a meter is 40 inches; the exact length is 39.37 inches. adj.*

ar·gue (är′gyü), discuss with someone who disagrees: *He argued with his sister about who should wash the dishes. v.,* **ar·gued, ar·gu·ing.**

ar·gu·ment (är′gyə mənt), **1** discussion by persons who disagree; dispute: *She won the argument by producing facts to prove her point.* **2** reason or reasons offered for or against something: *His arguments in favor of a new school building are very convincing. n.*

Ar·i·zo·na (ar′ə zō′nə), one of the southwestern states of the United States. *Abbreviation:* Ariz. or AZ *Capital:* Phoenix. *n.*

Ar·kan·sas (är′kən sȯ), one of the south central states of the United States. *Abbreviation:* Ark. or AR *Capital:* Little Rock. *n.*

arm (ärm), the part of a person's body between the shoulder and the hand. *n.*

ar·my (är′mē), a large, organized group of soldiers trained and armed for war. *n.*

ar·rest (ə rest′), seize by authority of the law; take to jail or court: *A policeman arrested the woman for shoplifting. v.,* **ar·rest·ed, ar·rest·ing.**

ar·row (ar′ō), a slender, pointed shaft or stick which is shot from a bow. *n.*

as·cent (ə sent′), **1** a going up; upward movement; rising: *The sudden ascent of the elevator made us dizzy.* **2** a climbing: *The ascent of Mount Everest is difficult. n.*

a·shore (ə shôr′), to the shore; to land: *The ship's passengers went ashore. adv.*

as·phalt (as′fȯlt), a mixture of a tarlike substance with crushed rock or sand. Asphalt is used in surfacing roads. *n.*

as·sent (ə sent′), express agreement; consent; agree: *Everyone assented to the plan. v.*

as·sign·ment (ə sīn′mənt), something assigned, especially a piece of work to be done: *Today's assignment in arithmetic consists of ten examples. n.*

as·tro·labe (as′trə lāb), an astronomical instrument formerly used for measuring the altitude of the sun or stars. It has been replaced by the sextant. *n.*

army

an **army** of soldiers

asphalt

a road of **asphalt**

ath·lete (ath/lēt/), person trained in exercises of physical strength, speed, and skill. Baseball players, runners, boxers, and swimmers are athletes. *n*. [*Athlete* is from Latin *athleta*, and can be traced back to Greek *athlon*, meaning "a prize, a contest."]

at·om (at/əm), the smallest whole bit of an element. *n*.

a·tri·um (ā/trē əm), either of the two chambers of the heart that receive blood from the veins and force it into a ventricle. *n*.

at·tend·ance (ə ten/dəns), act of being present at a place; an attending: *Our class had perfect attendance today. n*.

at·trac·tion (ə trak/shən), thing that delights or attracts people: *The elephants were the chief attraction at the circus. n*.

au·di·ence (ò/dē əns), people gathered in a place to hear or see: *The audience at the theater enjoyed the play. n*.

au·thor·i·ty (ə thôr/ə tē), 1 power to enforce obedience; right to command or act: *Parents have authority over their children. The police have the authority to arrest speeding drivers.* 2 person or group who has such power or right. *n*.

au·thor·ize (ò/thə rīz/), 1 give power or right to: *The committee authorized her to proceed.* 2 give formal approval to; approve: *Congress authorized the spending of money for a new post-office building. v.*, **au·thor·ized, au·thor·iz·ing.**

a·vail·a·ble (ə vā/lə bəl), able to be used: *She is not available for the job; she is out of town. adj.*

av·a·lanche (av/ə lanch), a large mass of snow and ice, or of dirt and rocks, rapidly sliding or falling down the side of a mountain. *n*.

av·er·age (av/ər ij), number obtained by dividing the sum of two or more addends by the number of addends. *n*.

a·ware (ə wâr/), having knowledge; realizing; conscious: *I was too sleepy to be aware how cold it was. She was not aware of her danger. adj.*

athlete
an **athlete** running

B

ba·by-sit (bā/bē sit), take care of a child or children while the parents are away for a while. *v.*, **ba·by-sat, ba·by-sit·ting.**

back·bone (bak/bōn/), the main bone along the middle of the back. The backbone is made up of many separate bones. *n*.

bal·ance (bal/əns), steady condition or position: *I lost my balance and fell off the ladder. n*.

Bal·ti·more (bòl/tə môr/), city in N Maryland, near Chesapeake Bay. *n*.

ban·jo (ban/jō), a musical instrument having four or five strings, played by plucking the strings with the fingers or a pick. *n., pl.* **ban·jos** or **ban·joes.** [*Banjo* is probably of Bantu origin.]

bank·rupt (bang/krupt), unable to pay one's debts. *adj*.

ban·quet (bang/kwit), a large meal with many courses, prepared for a special occasion or for many people; feast: *a wedding banquet. n*.

bar·gain (bär/gən), 1 agreement to trade or exchange; deal: *You can't back out on our bargain.* 2 something offered for sale cheap or bought cheap: *This hat is a bargain:* 1,2 *n*.
  bargain for, be ready for; expect: *I hadn't bargained for rain and have left my umbrella at home.*
  strike a bargain, make or reach an agreement: *They finally struck a bargain: a mitt for two baseballs and a bat.*

a	hat	ī	ice	u̇	put	ə stands for	
ā	age	o	not	ü	rule	a	in about
ä	far, calm	ō	open	ch	child	e	in taken
âr	care	ò	saw	ng	long	i	in pencil
e	let	ô	order	sh	she	o	in lemon
ē	equal	oi	oil	th	thin	u	in circus
ėr	term	ou	out	ᴛʜ	then		
i	it	u	cup	zh	measure		

251

bar graph (bär′ graf′), graph representing different quantities by rectangles of different lengths.

bat¹ (bat), **1** a stout wooden stick or club, used to hit the ball in baseball, cricket, etc. **2** hit with a bat; hit: *She bats well. I batted the balloon with my hand.* 1 *n.*, 2 *v.*, **bat·ted, bat·ting.**

bat² (bat), a flying mammal with a mouselike body and wings made of thin skin that are supported by the long, slim bones of the forelimbs. *Bats fly at night. n.*

bat·ter·y (bat′ər ē), container holding materials that produce electricity by chemical action; a single electric cell: *Most flashlights work on two batteries. n., pl.* **bat·ter·ies.**

bay¹ (bā), part of a sea or lake extending into the land. A bay is usually smaller than a gulf and larger than a cove. *n.*

bay² (bā), a long, deep barking, especially by a large dog: *The hunters heard the distant bay of the hounds. n.*

beard (bird), the hair growing on a man's chin and cheeks. *n.*

beau·ti·ful (byü′tə fəl), very pleasing to see or hear; delighting the mind or senses. *adj.*

be·cause (bi kòz′), for the reason that; since: *Because we were late, we ran the whole way home. conj.*

bee·tle (bē′tl), insect that has its front pair of wings modified as hard, shiny cases that cover the delicate rear pair of wings when at rest. *n.*

be·fore (bi fôr′), earlier than: *Come before five o'clock. prep.*

be·lief (bi lēf′), what is held to be true or real; thing believed; opinion: *Our beliefs are very similar to those of our parents. n., pl.* **be·liefs.**

be·lieve (bi lēv′), think (something) is true or real: *Who doesn't believe that the earth is round? v.*

be·long (bi lông′), to be a member of: *She belongs to the Girl Scouts. v.*

bench (bench), a long seat, usually of wood or stone. *n., pl.* **bench·es.**

be·tray (bi trā′), be unfaithful to: *She betrayed her promise. v.*

be·ware (bi wâr′), be on one's guard against; be careful: *Beware! there is a deep hole here. You must beware of swimming in a strong current. v.*

bi·cy·clist (bī′sik′list), person who rides a bicycle: *The bicyclist's helmet saved her from serious injury. The bicyclists' club meets Thursday. n.*

big (big), **1** great in amount or size; large: *a big room, a big book. An elephant is bigger than a horse. Our dog is the biggest on our block.* **2** grown up: *You are a big girl now. adj.,* **big·ger, big·gest.**

bill (bil), a proposed law presented to a lawmaking body for its approval: *This bill for the elderly will be voted on by the Senate today. n.*

bi·o·de·grad·a·ble (bī′ō di grā′də bəl), capable of being broken down by the action of bacteria: *a biodegradable detergent. adj.*

blank (blangk), **1** space left empty or to be filled in: *Leave a blank if you can't answer the question.* **2** not written or printed on: *blank paper.* 1 *n.*, 2 *adj.*

blind·fold (blīnd′fōld′), thing covering the eyes: *I put on the blindfold. n.*

blond or **blonde** (blond), **1** light in color: *blond hair, blond furniture.* **2** having yellow or light-brown hair and usually blue or gray eyes and fair skin. 1 *adj.*, 2 *n.*

blood (blud), the red liquid in the veins, arteries, and capillaries of vertebrates; the red liquid that flows from a cut. Blood is circulated by the heart, carrying oxygen and digested food to all parts of the body and carrying away waste materials. *n.*

bloom·ers (blü′mərz), **1** loose trousers, gathered at the knee, formerly worn by women and girls for physical training. **2** underwear made like these. *n. pl.* [*Bloomers* were named for Amelia J. Bloomer, 1818-1894, an American magazine publisher who popularized the use of this type of trousers.]

blue·print (blü′print′), **1** a photographic print that shows white outlines on a blue background. The process of making blueprints is used to copy original drawings of building plans, maps, etc. **2** a detailed plan for doing anything. *n.*

beetle

bloomers (def. 1)

old-fashioned **bloomers**

board (bôrd), a broad, thin piece of wood for use in building, etc.: *We used boards 10 inches wide, 1 inch thick, and 3 feet long for shelves in our new bookcase.* n.

board game (bôrd′ gām′), a game such as checkers in which pieces are moved from one section of a board to another.

board·walk (bôrd′wòk′), a wide sidewalk usually made of boards, along the beach at a shore resort. n.

boast (bōst), speak too highly of oneself or what one owns; brag: *He boasts about his grades.* v.

bomb (bom), container filled with an explosive. A bomb is set off by a fuse, a timing device, or by the force with which it hits something. n. [*Bomb* comes from Italian *bomba*, which can be traced back to Greek *bombos*, meaning "a booming sound."]

bon·jour (bòn zhür′), FRENCH. good day; good morning. *interj.*

book·shelf (bùk′shelf′), shelf for holding books. n., pl. **book·shelves.**

booth (büth), a covered stall or similar place where goods are sold or shown at a fair, market, convention, etc. n.

bored (bôrd), made weary by tiresome talk or by being dull. *I am bored by this book.* adj.

boul·der (bōl′dər), a large rock, rounded or worn by the action of water and weather. n.

bounce (bouns), **1** spring into the air like a ball: *The baby likes to bounce up and down on the bed.* **2** cause to bounce: *Bounce the ball to me.* v., **bounced, bounc·ing.**
bounce back, begin again, especially with enthusiasm.

bound (bound), **1** usually, **bounds,** *pl.* a limiting line; boundary; limit: *Keep your hopes within bounds.* **2 bounds,** *pl.* area included within boundaries. 1,2 n.
out of bounds, outside the area allowed by rules, custom, or law: *I kicked the ball out of bounds.*

bowl·ing (bō′ling), game played indoors, in which balls are rolled down an alley at bottle-shaped wooden pins; tenpins. n.

brain (brān), the part of the central nervous system in humans and other vertebrates that is enclosed in the skull or head and consists of a soft mass of nerve cells and nerve fibers. The brain controls almost all the functions of the body and with it we can learn, think, and remember. n.
rack one's brains, try very hard to think: *He racked his brains for his friend's phone number, but he couldn't remember it.*

brain·storm (brān′stôrm′), INFORMAL. a sudden idea or inspiration. n.

brake (brāk), anything used to slow or stop the motion of a wheel or vehicle by pressing or rubbing against. n., pl. **brakes.**

breast·stroke (brest′strōk′), stroke in swimming in which the swimmer lies face downward, draws both arms at one time from in front of the head to the sides, and kicks like a frog. n.

breath (breth), air drawn into and forced out of the lungs. n.

breathe (brēᴛʜ), draw air into the lungs and force it out. One breathes through the nose or through the mouth. v., **breathed, breath·ing.**

breeze (brēz), a light, gentle wind. n.

bridge (brij), something built over a river, road, or railroad so that people can get across. n.

brisk (brisk), keen; sharp: *A brisk wind was blowing from the north.* adj.

broom (brüm *or* brùm), brush with a long handle for sweeping. n.

buck·a·roo (buk′ə rü′ *or* buk′ə rü′), cowboy. n., pl. **buck·a·roos.** [*Buckaroo* apparently comes from a west African word *buckra*, meaning "white man," with the ending from Spanish *vaquero*, meaning "cowboy."]

boulder

bowling
indoor sport of **bowling**

a	hat	**ī**	ice	**ù**	put	**ə** stands for	
ā	age	**o**	not	**ü**	rule	**a**	in about
ä	far, calm	**ō**	open	**ch**	child	**e**	in taken
âr	care	**ò**	saw	**ng**	long	**i**	in pencil
e	let	**ô**	order	**sh**	she	**o**	in lemon
ē	equal	**oi**	oil	**th**	thin	**u**	in circus
ėr	term	**ou**	out	**ᴛʜ**	then		
i	it	**u**	cup	**zh**	measure		

buff (buf), to polish; shine: *I buffed my shoes to make them shine. v.*

buf·fa·lo (buf′ə lō), the bison of North America. *n.*

built (bilt), past tense and past participle of **build**. *The bird built a nest. It was built of twigs. v.*

bul·le·tin board (bul′ə tən bôrd′), board on which notices are posted.

bur·glar (bėr′glər), person who breaks into a house or other building, usually at night, to steal. *n.*

bus (bus), **1** a large motor vehicle with seats inside and formerly also on the roof. Buses are used to carry many passengers between fixed stations along a certain route. **2** take or go by bus: *The city bused the children to school.* 1 *n.,* 2 *v.*

bush (bush), woody plant smaller than a tree, often with many separate branches starting from or near the ground. Some bushes are used as hedges; others are cultivated for their fruit. *n., pl.* **bush·es.**

buy (bī), get by paying a price; purchase: *You can buy a pencil for ten cents. v.,* **bought** (bôt), **buy·ing.**

by (bī), at the side or edge of; near; beside: *The garden is by the house. Sit by me. prep.*

c

cab·i·net (kab′ə nit), **1** piece of furniture with shelves or drawers. **2** Also, **Cabinet.** group of advisers chosen by the head of a nation, usually to head departments of the government. The Attorney General is a member of the Cabinet of the President of the United States. *n.*

caf·e·ter·i·a (kaf′ə tir′ē ə), restaurant where people serve themselves. *n., pl.* **caf·e·ter·i·as.**

cal·a·boose (kal′ə bus), INFORMAL. a jail; prison. *n.* [*Calaboose* comes from Spanish *calabozo,* meaning "dungeon."]

cal·en·dar (kal′ən dər), table showing the months, weeks, and days of the year. A calendar shows the day of the week on which each day of the month falls. *The calendar shows that Memorial Day will fall on a Monday. n.*

Cal·i·for·nia (kal′ə fôr′nyə), one of the Pacific states of the United States. *Abbreviation:* Calif. or CA *Capital:* Sacramento. *n.*

calf (kaf), a young cow or bull. *n., pl.* **calves.**

cam·paign (kam pān′), series of connected activities to do or get something: *Our town had a campaign to raise money for a new hospital. n.*

can·cel (kan′səl), put an end to, set aside, or withdraw; do away with; stop: *The teacher canceled his order for the books. She canceled her appointment with the doctor. v.,* **can·celed, can·cel·ing** or **can·celled, can·cel·ling.**

can't (kant), cannot or can not.

cap·i·tal·ize (kap′ə tə līz), write or print with a capital letter: *You always capitalize the first letter of your name. v.*

cap·tain (kap′tən), commander of a ship. *n.*

car·a·mel (kar′ə məl or kär′məl), chewy candy flavored with sugar browned over heat. *n.*

ca·reer (kə rir′), way of living; occupation or profession: *I plan to make law my career. n.*

care·ful (kâr′fəl), showing care; done with thought or effort: *She did careful work. adj.* —**care′ful·ly,** *adv.*

carpools (kär′ pülz′), arrangements made by groups of persons to take turns driving to and from places: *The parents formed carpools to take their children to school. n.*

car wash·ing (kär′ wäsh′ing or kär wȯ′shing), cleaning the exterior of cars: *Our club pays for its party by holding a car washing. n.*

cas·se·role (kas′ə rōl′), **1** a covered baking dish in which food can be both cooked and served. **2** food cooked and served in such a dish. *n.*

cat (kat), **1** a small, furry, flesh-eating mammal, often kept as a pet or for catching mice and rats. **2** SLANG. fellow; person. *n.* —**cat′like′,** *adj.* **let the cat out of the bag,** tell a secret: *It was supposed to be a surprise party, but he let the cat out of the bag.*

caught (kȯt), past tense and past participle of **catch**. *I caught the ball. The mouse was caught in a trap. v.*

cat (def.1)

the family's **cat**

cau·li·flow·er (kȯ′lə flou′ər), vegetable having a solid, white head with a few leaves around it. It is related to the cabbage. *n.*

cel·e·brate (sel′ə brāt), **1** observe (a special time or day) with the proper ceremonies or festivities: *We celebrated her birthday with cake, ice cream, and presents.* **2** INFORMAL. have a gay time: *When the children saw the snow, they celebrated. v.,* **cel·e·brat·ed, cel·e·brat·ing.**

cen·ti·me·ter (sen′tə mē′tər), ¹⁄₁₀₀ of a meter; .3937 inch. *n.*

century (sen′chər ē), period of 100 years. *n., pl.* **cen·tur·ies.**

cer·e·al (sir′ē əl), food made from grain. Oatmeal and corn meal are cereals. *n.* [*Cereal* comes from Latin *Cerealem,* meaning "of *Ceres,*" the Roman goddess of agriculture.]

cer·e·bel·lum (ser′ə bel′əm), the part of the brain that controls the coordination of the muscles. *n.*

ce·re·brum (sə rē′brəm *or* ser′ə brəm), the part of the human brain that controls thought and voluntary muscular movements. *n.*

chan·nel (chan′l), the bed of a stream, river, etc.: *Rivers cut their own channels to the sea. n.*

char·ac·ter (kar′ik tər), person or animal in a play, poem, story, or book: *His favorite character in Charlotte's Web is Wilbur, the pig. n., pl.* **char·ac·ters.**

cheer·y (chir′ē), cheerful; pleasant; bright; gay: *a cheery smile. adj.,* **cheer·i·er, cheer·i·est.**

cheese (chēz), a solid food made from the curds of milk. Most cheeses are molded into a shape and are often covered with a rind. *n.*

chef (shef), a head cook: *the chef at a large restaurant. n., pl.* **chefs.**

Cher·o·kee (cher′ə kē), member of a tribe of American Indians of the southern Appalachians, now living mostly in Oklahoma. *n., pl.* **Cher·o·kee** *or* **Cher·o·kees.**

chest·nut (ches′nut), reddish-brown. *adj.*

chief (chēf), head of a group; person highest in rank or authority; leader: *a police chief. n.*

child (chīld), a young boy or girl: *a child's game. n., pl.* **chil·dren.**

child·ish (chīl′dish), not suitable for a grown person; weak; silly: *Crying for things you can't have is childish. adj.*

chil·dren (chil′drən), plural of **child**: *We looked at the children's artwork. n.*

chim·ney (chim′nē), **1** an upright structure of brick or stone, connected with a fireplace, furnace, etc., to make a draft and carry away smoke. **2** part of this that rises above a roof: *We could see the town's chimneys from afar. n.*

chip·munk (chip′mungk), a small, striped, North American rodent related to the squirrel; ground squirrel. Chipmunks live in burrows in the ground. *n.*

chlo·rine (klôr′ēn′), a greenish-yellow, bad-smelling, poisonous gas. Chlorine is very irritating to the nose, throat, and lungs. It is used in bleaching and disinfecting, and in making plastics, explosives, and dyes. *n.*

choice (chois), power or chance to choose: *I have my choice between a radio and a camera for my birthday. n.*

choke (chōk), stop the breath of (an animal or person) by squeezing or blocking up the throat: *They were choking from the smoke. v.,* **choked, chok·ing.**

choose (chüz), pick out; select from a number: *to choose a book, to choose wisely. v.,* **chose** (chōz), **cho·sen** (chō′zən), **choos·ing.**

chop (chop), cut by hitting with something sharp: *I chopped wood all morning. v.,* **chopped, chop·ping.**

channel

Cherokee
a **Cherokee** in his tribal clothing

a	hat	**ī**	ice	**u̇**	put	**ə** stands for	
ā	age	**o**	not	**ü**	rule	**a**	in about
ä	far, calm	**ō**	open	**ch**	child	**e**	in taken
âr	care	**ȯ**	saw	**ng**	long	**i**	in pencil
e	let	**ô**	order	**sh**	she	**o**	in lemon
ē	equal	**oi**	oil	**th**	thin	**u**	in circus
ėr	term	**ou**	out	**ᵺ**	then		
i	it	**u**	cup	**zh**	measure		

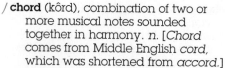

/ **chord** (kôrd), combination of two or more musical notes sounded together in harmony. *n.* [*Chord* comes from Middle English *cord*, which was shortened from *accord*.]

cho·rus (kôr′əs), group of singers who sing together, such as a choir: *Our school chorus gave a concert at the town hall. n.*

Christ·mas (kris′məs), the yearly celebration of the birth of Christ; December 25. *n.*

Cin·cin·nat·i (sin′sə nat′ē), city in SW Ohio, on the Ohio River. *n.*

cir·cle graph (sér′kəl graf′), a drawing that compares the parts of a quantity with the whole quantity.

cir·cuit (sér′kit), the path along which electric current moves. *n.*

cir·cus (sér′kəs), a traveling show of acrobats, clowns, horses, riders, and wild animals. The performers who give the show and the performances they give are both called the circus. *n.*

chorus

a **chorus** of young voices

civ·il (siv′əl), of a citizen or citizens: *civil duties. adj.*

ci·vil·ian (sə vil′yən), of civilians; not of the armed forces: *civilian clothes. adj.*

civ·i·li·za·tion (siv′ə lə zā′shən), **1** civilized condition; advanced stage in social development. **2** a civilizing or a becoming civilized: *The civilization of a primitive society is a gradual process which takes centuries.* **3** nations and peoples that have reached advanced stages in social development: *All civilization should be aroused against war. n.*

civ·i·lized (siv′ə līzd), showing culture and good manners; refined: *civilized behavior, a civilized attitude. adj.*

climber

a rock **climber**

claim (klām), demand as one's own or one's right: *The settlers claimed the land beyond the river as theirs. Does anyone claim this pencil? v.*

clas·si·fy (klas′ə fī), arrange in classes or groups; group according to some system: *Botanists have attempted to classify all plants. v.,* **clas·si·fied, clas·si·fy·ing.**

clear·ance (klir′əns), a clear space; distance between things that pass by each other without touching: *There was only a foot of clearance between the top of the truck and the roof of the tunnel. n.*

cliff (klif), steep slopes of rock, clay, etc. *n., pl.* **cliffs.**

cli·mate (klī′mit), the kind of weather a place has. Climate includes conditions of heat and cold, moisture and dryness, clearness and cloudiness, wind and calm. *n.*

climb·er (klī′mər), person or thing that climbs. *n.*

close-up (klōs′up′), **1** picture taken with a camera at close range. **2** a close view. *n.*

cloth (klòth), material made from wool, cotton, silk, rayon, or other fiber, by weaving, knitting, or rolling and pressing. *n.*

clothes (klōz *or* klōᴛʜz), coverings for a person's body: *I bought some new clothes for my trip. n. pl.*

clothes·line (klōz′līn′), rope or wire to hang clothes on to dry or air them. *n.*

cloth·ing (clō′ᴛʜing), clothes. *n.*

col·laps·i·ble (kə lap′sə bel), made so that it can be folded or pushed together: *a collapsible table. adj.*

col·lect (kə lekt′), **1** bring or come together; gather together: *We collected sticks of wood to make a fire. A crowd soon collected at the scene of the accident.* **2** gather together for a set: *I collect stamps as a hobby. v.*

co·lo·ni·al (kə lō′nē əl), of the thirteen British colonies which became the United States of America. *adj.*

col·o·nize (kol′ə nīz) establish a colony or colonies in: *The English colonized New England. v.,* **col·o·nized, col·o·niz·ing.**

co·me·di·an (kə mē′dē ən), person who amuses others with funny talk and actions. *n., pl.* **co·me·di·ans.**

com·e·dy (kom′ə dē), an amusing play or show having a happy ending. *n., pl.* **com·e·dies.**

com·fort·a·ble (kum′fər tə bəl), **1** giving comfort: *A soft, warm bed is comfortable.* **2** in comfort; at ease: *We felt comfortable in the warm house after a cold day outdoors. adj.*

com·mon name (kom′ən nām′), the name by which a plant or animal is generally known. *Tiger is the common name of a species of cat.*

com·mo·tion (kə mō′shən), violent movement; confusion; disturbance; tumult. *n.*

com·pa·ny (kum′pə nē), group of people, especially a group joined together for some purpose: *a company of actors, the Ford Motor Company. n., pl.* **com·pa·nies.**

com·pare (kem pâr′), find out or point out how persons or things are alike and how they are different: *I compared my answers with the teacher's and found I had made a mistake. v.,* **com·pared, com·par·ing.**

com·pete (kəm pēt′), try hard to win or gain something wanted by others; be rivals; contend: *She competed against many fine athletes for the gold medal. It is difficult for a small grocery store to compete with a supermarket. v.,* **com·pet·ed, com·pet·ing.**

com·pe·ti·tion (kom′pə tish′ən), **1** a trying hard to win or gain something wanted by others; rivalry: *competition among stores for customers.* **2** contest: *She won first place in the swimming competition. n.*

com·plain (kəm plān′), say that something is wrong; find fault: *We complained that the room was too cold. v.* —**com·plain′er,** *n.*

com·pli·cat·ed (kom′plə kā′tid), hard to understand; involved; complex: *These directions are too complicated. adj.*

com·pli·ment (kom′plə mənt), something good said about one; something said in praise of one's work: *She received many compliments on her science project. n.*

com·pose (kəm pōz′), **1** make up; form: *The ocean is composed of salt water.* **2** put together. *v.,* **com·posed, com·pos·ing.**

com·po·si·tion (kom′pə zish′ən), **1** the makeup of anything; what is in it: *The composition of this candy includes sugar, chocolate, and milk.* **2** a putting together of a whole. *n.*

com·pro·mise (kom′prə mīz), settle a quarrel or difference of opinion by agreeing that each will give up a part of what he demands: *A good politician knows how to compromise. n.*

com·put·er (kəm pyü′tər), an electronic machine that can store, recall, or process information. Computers keep files, solve mathematical problems, play games, and control the operations of other machines. *n.*

con·clu·sion (kən klü′zhən), decision or opinion reached by reasoning; inference: *Researchers came to the conclusion that the disease was caused by a virus. n.*

con·duc·tor (kən duk′tər), a material that transmits heat or electricity. *n.*

Con·fed·er·a·cy (kən fed′ər ə sē), group of eleven southern states that seceded from the United States in 1860 and 1861. *n.*

con·fer·ence (kon′fər əns), **1** meeting of interested persons to discuss a particular subject: *A conference was called to discuss the fuel shortage.* **2** act of consulting together: *The teacher was in conference with parents after school. n., pl.* **con·fer·ences.**

con·fi·dent (kon′fə dənt), having confidence; firmly believing; certain; sure: *I feel confident that our team will win. adj.*

con·fi·dent·ly (kon′fə dənt lē), in a confident manner. *adv.*

con·flict (kon′flikt), active opposition of persons or ideas; clash: *A conflict of opinion arose over the need for a new highway. n.*

Con·gress (kong′gris), the national lawmaking body of the United States, consisting of the Senate and House of Representatives, with members elected from every state. *n.*

con·science (kon′shəns), sense of right and wrong; ideas and feelings within you that tell you when you are doing right and warn you of what is wrong. *n.*

computer

a	hat	**ī**	ice	**u̇**	put	**ə stands for**	
ā	age	**o**	not	**ü**	rule	**a**	in about
ä	far, calm	**ō**	open	**ch**	child	**e**	in token
âr	care	**ȯ**	saw	**ng**	long	**i**	in pencil
e	let	**ô**	order	**sh**	she	**o**	in lemon
ē	equal	**oi**	oil	**th**	thin	**u**	in circus
ėr	term	**ou**	out	**ᵺ**	then		
i	it	**u**	cup	**zh**	measure		

con·scious (kon′shəs), 1 having experience; aware; knowing: *I was conscious of a sharp pain.* 2 able to feel or perceive; awake: *About five minutes after fainting he became conscious again. adj.*

con·ser·va·tion (kon′sər vā′shən), a preserving from harm or decay; protecting from loss or from being used up: *The conservation of our mineral resources is important because they can never be replaced. n.*

con·stant (kon′stənt), 1 going on without stopping: *Three days of constant rain caused flooding.* 2 continually happening; repeated again and again: *a constant ticking sound.* 1,2, *adj.*

con·ta·gious (kən tā′jəs), 1 spreading by contact; catching: *Mumps is a contagious disease.* 2 easily spreading from one person to another: *Yawning is often contagious. adj.*

con·tent·ed (kən ten′tid), satisfied; pleased; easy in mind. *adj.*

con·test (kon′test *for 1;* kən test′ *for 2),* 1 trial of skill to see which can win. A game or race is a contest; so is a debate. 2 fight for; struggle for: *The soldiers contested every inch of ground.* 1 *n.,* 2 *v.*

contestant

contestants racing

con·test·ant (kən tes′tənt), person who contests; person who takes part in a contest: *My sister was a contestant in the 100-yard dash. n.*

con·tin·ue (kən tin′yü), keep up, keep on, go on with: *The rain continued all day. v.,* **con·tin·ued, con·tin·u·ing.**

con·trol (kən trōl′), individual or group serving as a standard of comparison for testing the results of a scientific experiment performed on a similar individual or group. *n.*

con·ver·sa·tion (kon′vər sā′shən), friendly talk; exchange of thoughts by talking informally together. *n.*

con·vert·i·ble (kən ver′tə bəl), automobile with a folding top. *n.*

corn (kôrn), kind of grain that grows on large ears. *n.*

crane (def. 1)

A **crane** lifts heavy objects.

cor·re·spond·ent (kôr′ə spon′dənt), 1 person who exchanges letters with another: *My cousin and I are correspondents.* 2 person employed by a newspaper, magazine, radio or television network, etc., to send news from a particular place or region: *reports from correspondents in China and Great Britain. n.*

cos·tume (kos′tüm *or* kos′tyüm), 1 way of dressing, including the way the hair is worn, kind of jewelry worn, etc.: *a hunting costume. The kimono is part of the national costume of Japan.* 2 dress belonging to another time or place, worn on the stage, at masquerades, etc.: *The actors wore colonial costumes. n., pl.* **cos·tumes.**

couch (kouch), a long seat, usually upholstered and having a back and arms; sofa. *n.*

could've (kúd′əv), could have.

cour·age (ker′ij), a meeting danger without fear; bravery; fearlessness: *The pioneers faced the hardships of the westward trek with courage. n.*

cou·ra·geous (kə rā′jəs), full of courage; brave; fearless. *adj.*

course (kôrs), direction taken: *Our course was straight to the north. n.*

cour·te·ous (ker′tē əs), thoughtful of others; polite: *The clerks are always courteous at this store. adj.* **—cour′te·ous·ly,** *adv.*

cour·te·sy (ker′tə sē), polite behavior; thoughtfulness for others: *It is a sign of courtesy to give one's seat to an old person on a crowded bus. n.*

cous·in (kuz′n), son or daughter of one's uncle or aunt. First cousins have the same grandparents; second cousins have the same great-grandparents. *We took care of my cousin's dog. I stayed at my cousins' house. n.*

cow·boy (kou′boi′), man whose work is looking after cattle on a ranch. *n., pl.* **cow·boys.**

crane (krān), 1 machine with a long, swinging arm, for lifting and moving heavy weights. 2 a large wading bird with long legs, neck, and bill. 3 stretch (the neck) as a crane does, in order to see better: *The little girl craned her neck to see the parade over the heads of the crowd.* 1,2 *n.,* 3 *v.*

crawl (krôl), creep on hands and knees: *We crawled through a hole in the fence. v.*

cre·ate (krē āt′), make a thing which has not been made before; cause to be; bring into being; make: *Composers create music. v.,* **cre·at·ed, cre·at·ing.**

cre·a·tive (krē ā′tiv), having the power to create; inventive: *a creative person. adj.* **—cre·a′tive·ly,** *adv.*

crea·ture (krē'chər), any living person or animal. n.

crew (krü), **1** the sailors who work aboard a ship. **2** the group of persons who fly and work on an aircraft. **3** any group of people working or acting together: *a crew of loggers, a railroad maintenance crew.* n.

crime (krīm), a harmful or grave offense against the law. Theft, kidnaping, murder, and arson are crimes. n.

crisp (krisp), hard and thin; breaking easily with a snap: *Dry toast and fresh celery are crisp.* adj.

cross·walk (krȯs'wȯk'), area marked with lines, used by pedestrians in crossing a street. n.

cuff (kuf), **1** band of material attached to a sleeve and worn around the wrist. **2** turned-up fold around the bottom of trousers. n., pl. **cuffs.**

cup·cake (kup'kāk'), a small cake baked in a pan shaped like a cup. n.

curl (kėrl), **1** twist into ringlets; roll into coils: *curl someone's hair. My hair curls naturally.* **2** a curled lock of hair. 1 v., 2 n.

cur·rent (kėr'ənt), the smooth flow of electric charges from one place to another. n.

cur·tain (kėrt'n), cloth hung at windows or in doors for protection or ornament. n.

cus·tom·ar·y u·nits (kus'tə mer'ē yü'nits), a system for measuring length in *inches, feet, yards,* and *miles;* capacity in *cups, pints, quarts,* and *gallons;* weight in *ounces, pounds,* and *tons;* temperature in *degrees Fahrenheit.*

cute (kyüt), INFORMAL **1** pretty and dear: *a cute baby.* **2** handsome; good-looking. adj., **cut·er, cut·est.**

cyl·in·der (sil'ən dər), **1** a solid bounded by two equal, parallel circles and by a curved surface. **2** the piston chamber of an automobile engine. n.

cym·bal (sim'bəl), one of a pair of brass plates, used as a musical instrument. When cymbals are struck together, they make a loud, ringing sound. n.

D

Dad (dad) INFORMAL. father: *I visited Dad's office.* n.

dair·y (dâr'ē), store or company that sells milk, cream, butter, and cheese. n.

dam (dam), wall built to hold back the water of a stream or any flowing water: *There was a flood when the dam burst.* n.

dan·ger·ous (dān'jər əs), likely to cause harm; not safe; risky: *Shooting off firecrackers can be dangerous.* adj.

da·ta (dā'tə or dat'ə), facts from which conclusions can be drawn; things known or admitted; information: *Names, ages, grades, and other data about the class are written in the teacher's notebook.* n. pl.

daugh·ter (dȯ'tər), a female child. A girl or woman is the daughter of her father and mother. n.

day·light (dā'līt'), light of day: *It is easier to read by daylight than by lamplight.* n.

dear (dir), much loved; precious: *His sister was very dear to him.* adj.

de·cide (di sīd'), make up one's mind. *She decided to become a doctor.* v., **de·cid·ed, de·cid·ing.**

dec·i·me·ter (des'ə mē'tər), measure of length equal to ⅒ of a meter, or 3.937 inches. n.

de·clare (di klâr') announce publicly or formally; make known: *Congress has the power to declare war.* v., **de·clared, de·clar·ing.**

dec·o·ra·tion (dek'ə rā'shən), thing used to decorate; ornament: *We put up pictures and other decorations in the classroom.* n.

dam
The **dam** holds back water.

a	hat	**ī**	ice	**u̇**	put	**ə** stands for	
ā	age	**o**	not	**ü**	rule	**a**	in about
ä	far, calm	**ō**	open	**ch**	child	**e**	in taken
âr	care	**ȯ**	saw	**ng**	long	**i**	in pencil
e	let	**ô**	order	**sh**	she	**o**	in lemon
ē	equal	**oi**	oil	**th**	thin	**u**	in circus
ėr	term	**ou**	out	**ŦH**	then		
i	it	**u**	cup	**zh**	measure		

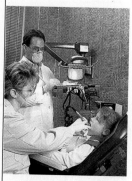

dentist

dentist taking care of teeth

desert (def. 1)

a barren **desert**

de·fend·ant (di fen′dənt), person accused or sued in a court of law: *The defendant is charged with theft. n.*

de·fi·ant (di fī′ənt), showing defiance; openly resisting: *She told us in a defiant manner that she was against our plans. adj.* —**de·fi·ant·ly**, *adv.*

de·gree (di grē′), rank or title given by a college or university to a student whose work fulfills certain requirements, or to a noted person as an honor: *a bachelor's degree, a master's degree. n.*

dense (dens), closely packed together; thick: *a dense forest, a dense fog. adj.*

den·tist (den′tist), doctor whose work is the care of teeth. A dentist fills cavities in teeth, cleans, straightens, or extracts them, and supplies artificial teeth. *n.*

de·par·ture (di pär′chər), act of going away: *The airplane's departure was delayed. n.*

des·ert (dez′ərt), **1** a dry, barren region that is usually sandy and without trees. The Sahara Desert is a great desert in northern Africa. **2** not inhabited or cultivated; wild: *They were shipwrecked on a desert island.* **1** *n.,* **2** *adj.*

des·sert (di zėrt′), course of pie, cake, ice cream, cheese, fruit, etc., served at the end of a meal. *n.* [*Dessert* came into English about 300 years ago from French *dessert,* and can be traced back to Latin *dis-,* meaning "not," and *servire,* meaning "serve."]

de·stroy (di stroi′), break to pieces; make useless; ruin; spoil: *A tornado destroyed the farmhouse. v.,* **de·stroyed, de·stroy·ing.**

de·struc·tive (di struk′tiv), destroying; causing destruction. *n.*

De·troit (di troit′), city in SE Michigan. *n.*

dia·mond (dī′mənd *or* dī′ə mənd), **1** a colorless or tinted precious stone, formed of pure carbon in crystals. **2** figure shaped like this: ◊. **3** (in baseball) the area bounded by home plate and the three bases; infield. *n.*

di·a·phragm (dī′ə fram), a partition of muscles and tendons separating the cavity of the chest from the cavity of the abdomen. *n.*

did·n't (did′nt), did not.

dif·fer·ent (dif′ər ənt), **1** not the same; separate; distinct: *I saw her three different times today.* **2** not like others or most others; unusual: *Our teacher is quite different; he never gives us homework. adj.* —**dif′fer·ent·ly**, *adv.*

din·er (dī′nər), **1** person who is eating dinner. **2** a railroad car in which meals are served. **3** a small eating place that often looks like such a car. *n.*

din·ner (din′ər), the main meal of the day: *In the city we have dinner at night, but in the country we have dinner at noon. n.*

di·rect (də rekt′ *or* dī rekt′), **1** have authority or control over; manage or guide: *The teacher directs the work of the class.* **2** order; command: *The policeman directed the traffic to stop.* **3** tell or show the way: *Can you direct me to the airport?* **4** point or aim: *We should be directing our efforts to the problem at hand. v.*

di·rec·tion (də rek′shən *or* dī rek′shən), **1** a directing; managing or guiding: *The school is under the direction of the principal.* **2** order; command: *It was her direction that I prepare a report. n.*

di·rec·tor (də rek′tər *or* dī rek′tər), person who directs; manager. A person who directs the performance of a play, a motion picture, or a television or radio show is called a director. *n.*

dis·a·bil·i·ty (dis′ə bil′ə tē), something that disables: *Deafness is a disability for a musician. Her physical disability did not hamper her success in playing soccer. n.,* pl. **dis·a·bil·i·ties.**

dis·ad·van·tage (dis′əd van′tij), unfavorable condition: *There are many disadvantages in not having public transportation. n.,* pl. **dis·ad·van·tag·es.**

dis·a·gree (dis′ə grē′), **1** fail to agree; be different: *Your account of the accident disagrees with hers.* **2** have unlike opinions; differ: *Doctors sometimes disagree about the proper method of treating a patient. v.,* **dis·a·greed, dis·a·gree·ing.**

dis·ap·point (dis′ə point′), fail to satisfy or please; leave wanting or expecting something: *The circus disappointed me because there were no elephants.* v.

dis·ap·prove (dis′ə prüv′), have or express an opinion against; show dislike: *Parents often disapprove of rough games in the house.* v., **dis·ap·proved, dis·ap·proving.**

dis·cov·er (dis kuv′ər), see or learn of for the first time; find out: *discover a new drug, discover a secret.* v., **dis·cov·ered, dis·cov·er·ing.**

dis·loy·al (dis loi′əl), not loyal; unfaithful: *a disloyal friend, a disloyal act.* adj. —**dis·loy′al·ly,** *adv.*

dis·may (dis mā′), sudden loss of courage because of fear of danger: *They were filled with dismay when they saw the rattlesnake.* n.

dis·o·bey (dis′ə bā′), refuse to obey; fail to obey: *The student who disobeyed the teacher was punished.* v.

dis·or·der (dis ôr′dər), lack of order; confusion: *Our whole house was in disorder after the birthday party.* n.

doc·tor (dok′tər), person trained in treating diseases or injuries. Physicians, surgeons, dentists, and veterinarians are doctors. *I took my doctor's advice.* n.

does·n't (duz′nt), does not.

dom·i·nant (dom′ə nənt), most powerful or influential; controlling; ruling; governing: *She was a dominant figure in local politics.* adj.

dom·i·neer (dom′ə nir′), rule or assert one's authority or opinions in an arrogant way: *The oldest child in a family may sometimes domineer over the younger children.* v.

don·key (dong′kē), a small animal somewhat like a horse but with longer ears and a shorter mane. n., pl. **don·keys.**

don't (dōnt), do not.

dough (dō), INFORMAL. money. n. [*Dough* comes from Old English *dāg.*]

down·town (doun′toun′), to or in the central or main business section of a town or city: *My parents went downtown shopping (adv.). Her office is in downtown Chicago (adj.).* adv., adj.

draw·bridge (drȯ′brij′), bridge that can be entirely or partly lifted, lowered, or moved to one side. In old castles drawbridges were lifted to keep out enemies. A drawbridge over a river is lifted to let boats pass. n.

drawl (drȯl), a slow way of talking by drawing out the vowels; speech of someone who drawls: *a southern drawl, a soft-spoken drawl.* n. [*Drawl* apparently comes from Dutch *dralen,* meaning "linger, delay."]

dream (drēm), **1** images passing through the mind during sleep: *I had a bad dream last night.* **2** imagine mentally during sleep. 1, n. 2, v, **dreamed** or **dreamt, dreaming.**

dreamt (dremt), dreamed; a past tense and a past participle of **dream,** v.

dress (dres), an outer garment worn by women and girls. n., pl. **dress·es.**

drew (drü), past tense of **draw.** *He drew a picture of his mother.* v.

drought (drout), a long period of dry weather; continued lack of rain: *a drought caused the stream to dry up.* n., pl. **droughts.**

drown (droun), die under water or other liquid because of lack of air to breathe: *We almost drowned when our sailboat suddenly overturned.* v.

Du·luth (də lüth′), city in E Minnesota, on Lake Superior. n.

dun·ga·rees (dung′gə rēz′), trousers, work clothes, or overalls made of a coarse cotton cloth. n. pl.

donkey
riding a **donkey**

drawbridge
a **drawbridge** in operation

a	hat	**ī**	ice	**u̇**	put		**ə** stands for	
ā	age	**o**	not	**ü**	rule	**a**	in about	
ä	far, calm	**ō**	open	**ch**	child	**e**	in taken	
âr	care	**ȯ**	saw	**ng**	long	**i**	in pencil	
e	let	**ô**	order	**sh**	she	**o**	in lemon	
ē	equal	**oi**	oil	**th**	thin	**u**	in circus	
ėr	term	**ou**	out	**ᴛH**	then			
i	it	**u**	cup	**zh**	measure			

E

each oth·er (ēch′ uⷮH′ər), **1** each one the other one: *They struck each other.* **2** one another: *They struck at each other.*

ear·ly (ėr′lē), **1** near the beginning; in the first part: *The sun was not hot earlier in the day.* **2** before the usual or expected time: *Please come early* (adv.). *We had an early dinner* (adj.). 1,2 *adv.,* 2 *adj.,* **ear·li·er, ear·li·est.**

ear·rings (ir′ringz), ornaments for the ear. *n. pl.*

earth·quake (ėrth′kwāk′), a shaking or sliding of a portion of the earth's crust. It is caused by the sudden movement of masses of rock along a fault or by changes in the size and shape of masses of rock far beneath the earth's surface. Earthquakes are often related to volcanic activity. *n.*

earthquake

homes damaged by an **earthquake**

eas·y (ē′zē), not hard to do or get: *Today's arithmetic lesson was easier than yesterday's. This was the easiest test I ever took. adj.,* **eas·i·er, eas·i·est.**

eat·en (ēt′n), past participle of **eat.** *Have you eaten your dinner? v.*

ech·o (ek′ō), the repetition of a sound. You hear an echo when a sound you make bounces back from a distant hill or wall so that you hear it again. *n., pl.* **ech·oes.**

ed·u·cate (ej′ə kāt), develop in knowledge or skill by teaching, training, or study; teach: *The job of teachers is to educate people. v.,* **ed·u·cat·ed, ed·u·cat·ing.**

ed·u·ca·tion (ej′ə kā′shən), development in knowledge or skill by teaching, training, or study: *In the United States, public schools offer an education to all children. n.*

election

voting in the **election**

eer·ie (ir′ē), causing fear because of strangeness or weirdness: *a dark and eerie old house. adj.,* **eer·i·er, eer·i·est.**

ei·ther (ē′ⷮHər *or* ī′ⷮHər), one or the other of two: *You may read either book* (adj.). *Choose either of the candy bars* (pron.). *Either come in or go out* (conj.). *adj., pron., conj.*

e·lect (i lekt′), choose or select for an office by voting: *We elect our class officers every autumn. v.*

e·lec·tion (i lek′shən), a choosing or selecting for an office by vote: *In our city we have an election for mayor every four years. n.*

e·lec·tric·i·ty (i lek′tris′ə tē), form of energy which can produce light, heat, motion, and magnetic force. *n.*

e·lec·tron (i lek′tron), a negatively charged atomic particle. *n.*

el·e·ment (el′ə mənt), one of the 109 basic substances of matter. *n., pl.* **el·e·ments.**

el·e·va·tion (el′ə vā′shən), height above the earth's surface: *The airplane flew at an elevation of 20,000 feet. n.*

el·e·va·tor (el′ə vā′tər), **1** something which raises or lifts up. **2** a moving platform or cage to carry people and things up and down in a building, mine, etc. *n.*

E·man·ci·pa·tion Proc·la·ma·tion (i man′sə pā′shən prok′lə mā′shən), announcement issued by Abraham Lincoln on January 1, 1863, freeing all persons held as slaves in any state armed against the United States.

em·bar·go (em bär′gō), **1** an order of a government forbidding ships to enter or leave its ports. **2** any restriction put on commerce by law. *n., pl.* **em·bar·goes.**

em·bar·rassed (em bar′əst), made uneasy and ashamed; made self-conscious. *I was embarrassed by her questions. adj.*

e·mer·gen·cy (i mėr′jən sē), a sudden need for immediate action: *I keep a box of tools in my car for use in an emergency. n.*

e·mo·tion·al (i mō′shə nəl), of the emotions: *His constant fears show that he is suffering from a serious emotional disorder. adj.*

em·per·or (em′pər ər), man who is the ruler of an empire. *n.* [*Emperor* came into English about 700 years ago from French *empereor,* which came from Latin *imperator,* originally meaning "commander."]

em·ploy·er (em ploi′ər), person or firm that employs one or more persons. *n.*

emp·ty (emp′tē), with nothing or no one in it: *an empty house. The birds had gone and their nest was empty. adj.*

en·dan·gered spe·cies (en dān′jərd spē′shēz), a group of animals or plants that are liable to become extinct. *Giant condors are an endangered species.*

en·er·gy (en′ər jē), capacity for doing work, such as lifting or moving an object. Light, heat, and electricity are different forms of energy: *A steam engine changes heat into mechanical energy.* n.

e·nough (i nuf′), as much or as many as needed or wanted; sufficient: *Buy enough food for the picnic. Are there enough seats for all?* adj.

en·roll (en rōl′), **1** write in a list; register: *The secretary enrolled our names.* **2** enlist: *He enrolled in the navy.* v., **en·rolled, en·rolling.**

en·thrall (en thrôl′), **1** hold captive by beauty or interest; fascinate; charm. **2** make a slave of; enslave: *The captive peoples were enthralled by their conquerors.* v., **en·thralled, en·thrall·ing.**

en·vi·ron·ment (en vī′rən mənt), all the surrounding things, conditions, and influences affecting the growth of living things: *A child's character is greatly influenced by the environment at home. A plant will often grow differently in a different environment.* n.

e·quip·ment (i kwip′mənt), what a person or thing is equipped with; outfit; furnishings; supplies: *camping equipment.* n.

es·cape plan (e skāp′ plan′), a plan for getting out of a building or area in an emergency.

e·soph·a·gus (ē sof′ə gəs), passage for food from the throat to the stomach; gullet. n.

es·pe·cial·ly (e spesh′ə lē), more than others; specially; particularly; chiefly: *This book is designed especially for students.* adv.

es·ti·mate (es′tə māt), make calculations not requiring exact answers. v., **es·ti·mat·ed, es·ti·mat·ing.**

et·y·mol·o·gy (et′ə mol′ə jē), **1** the derivation of a word. **2** account or explanation of the origin and history of a word. **3** the study dealing with the origin and history of words. n., pl. **et·y·mol·o·gies.**

eve·ning (ēv′ning), the last part of day and early part of night; time between sunset and bedtime. n.

eve·ry·bod·y (ev′rē bud′ē or ev′rē bod′ē), every person; everyone: *Everybody likes the new principal.* pron.

eve·ry·one (ev′rē wun or ev′rē wən), each one; everybody: *Everyone in the class is here.* pron.

eve·ry·thing (ev′rē thing), every thing; all things: *She did everything she could to help her friend.* pron.

e·vil (ē′vəl), **1** causing harm; bad; wrong; wicked: *an evil life, an evil character, an evil plan.* **2** bad or evil quality; wickedness: *Their thoughts were full of evil.* 1 adj., 2 n.

ex·act (eg zakt′), without any mistake; correct; accurate; precise: *an exact measurement, the exact amount.* adj.

ex·ag·ge·rate (eg zaj′ə rāt′), make too large; say or think something is greater than it is; go beyond the truth: *The little boy exaggerated when he said there were a million cats in the backyard.* v., **ex·ag·ge·rat·ed, ex·ag·ge·rat·ing.**

ex·am·ine (eg zam′ən), look at closely and carefully: *The doctor examined the wound.* v., **ex·am·ined, ex·am·in·ing.**

ex·cel·lent (ek′sə lənt), of unusually good quality; better than others; superior: *Excellent work deserves high praise.* adj.

ex·cept (ek sept′), **1** leaving out; other than: *He works every day except Sunday.* **2** only; but: *I would have had a perfect score except I missed the last question.* 1 prep., 2 conj.

ex·cit·ed (ek sī′tid), stirred up; aroused: *The excited mob rushed into the mayor's office.* adj.

endangered species
The condor is an
endangered species

							stands for
a	hat	ī	ice	u̇	put	ə	
ā	age	o	not	ü	rule	a	in about
ä	far, calm	ō	open	ch	child	e	in taken
âr	care	ȯ	saw	ng	long	i	in pencil
e	let	ô	order	sh	she	o	in lemon
ē	equal	oi	oil	th	thin	u	in circus
ėr	term	ou	out	ŦH	then		
i	it	u	cup	zh	measure		

ex·cit·ing (ek sī′ting), causing excitement; arousing; stirring: *We read an exciting story about pirates and buried treasure. adj.*

ex·claim (ek sklām′), speak suddenly in surprise or strong feeling; cry out: *"Here you are at last!" exclaimed her mother. v.,* **ex·claimed, ex·claim·ing.**

ex·ec·u·tive branch (eg zek′yə tiv branch′), person, group, or branch of government that has the power to put laws into effect; *the President and his Cabinet.*

ex·hale (eks hāl′), breathe out: *We exhale air from our lungs. v.,* **ex·haled, ex·hal·ing.**

ex·hib·it (eg zib′it), an exhibiting; public showing: *The village art exhibit drew 10,000 visitors. n.*

ex·ist (eg zist′), have life; live: *A person cannot exist without air. v.,* **ex·ist·ed, ex·ist·ing.**

ex·pe·di·tion (ek′spə dish′ən), **1** journey for some special purpose, such as exploration, scientific study, or for military purposes. **2** the people, ships, etc., making such a journey. *n.*

ex·per·i·ence (ek spir′ē əns), knowledge or skill gained by seeing, doing, or living through things; practice: *Have you had any experience in this kind of work? n.*

ex·per·i·ment (ek sper′ə mənt), trial or test to find out something: *a chemistry experiment. Scientists test out theories by experiments. n.*

ex·plode (ek splōd′), burst with a loud noise; blow up: *The building was destroyed when the defective boiler exploded. v.,* **ex·plod·ed, ex·plod·ing.**

ex·ploit (ek sploit′), make unfair or selfish use of: *Nations exploited their colonies, taking as much wealth out of them as they could. v.,* **ex·ploit·ed, ex·ploit·ing.**

ex·plo·ra·tion (ek′splə rā′shən), a traveling in little-known lands or seas for the purpose of discovery. *n.*

eye·brows (ī′brouz), the hair that grows along the bony ridge just above each eye. *n. pl.*

eye·lash·es (ī′lash′əz), the hairs on the edge of each eyelid. *n. pl.*

Ferris wheel

a ride on the **Ferris wheel**

F

fac·to·ry (fak′tər ē), building or group of buildings where things are made with machines, or by hand. *n., pl.* **fac·to·ries.**

fac·tu·al (fak′chü əl), concerned with fact; consisting of facts: *I kept a detailed factual account of the trip in my diary. adj.* —**fac′tu·al·ly,** *adv.*

faint (fānt), lose consciousness temporarily. *v.*

faith·ful (fāth′fəl), **1** worthy of trust; loyal: *a faithful friend.* **2** true to fact; accurate: *The witness gave a faithful account of what happened.* **1,2** *adj.,* —**faith′ful·ly,** *adv.*

fa·mous (fā′məs), very well known; much talked about or written about; noted: *The famous singer was greeted by a large crowd. adj.*

fan (fan), instrument or device that stirs the air in order to cool a room or a person. One kind of fan can be folded or spread out into part of a circle. Another kind has revolving blades that are turned by a motor. *n.*

fan·ta·sy (fan′tə sē), play of the mind; product of the imagination; fancy. Many stories, such as *Gulliver's Travels* and *Alice in Wonderland,* are fantasies. *n., pl.* **fan·ta·sies.**

fas·ci·nate (fas′n āt), attract very strongly; charm: *He was fascinated by the movement of the dancers. v.,* **fas·ci·nat·ed, fas·ci·nat·ing.**

fas·ten (fas′n), tie, lock or make hold together in any way; fix firmly in place: *fasten a seat belt. v.*

fa·vor·ite (fā′vər it), liked better than others: *What is your favorite flower? adj.*

Feb·ru·ar·y (feb′rü er′ē or feb′yü er′ē), the second month of the year. It has 28 days except in leap years, when it has 29. *n.*

Fer·ris wheel (fer′is hwēl′), a large, revolving wheel with hanging seats, used in carnivals, amusement parks, fairs, etc. [The *Ferris wheel* was named for George W. G. Ferris, 1859-1896, an American engineer who invented it.]

fifth (fifth), next after the fourth; last in a series of 5. *adj., n.*

fight (fīt), **1** a violent struggle; combat; contest: *A fight ends when one side gives up.* **2** take part in a violent struggle, quarrel, etc.; have a fight: *When people fight, they hit one another. Soldiers fight by shooting with guns. Countries fight with armies.* **1** *n.,* **2** *v.,* **fought** (fôt), **fight·ing.**

fi·nal·ly (fī/nl ē), at the end; at last. *adv.*

fin·ished (fin/isht), ended or completed. *adj.*

fire·place (fīr/plās/), place built to hold a fire. Indoor fireplaces are usually made of brick or stone, with a chimney leading up through the roof. *n.*

first aid (fėrst/ ād/), emergency treatment given to an injured or sick person before a doctor sees the person.

fish (fish), animal with a backbone that lives in the water and has gills instead of lungs for breathing. Fish are usually covered with scales and have fins for swimming. Some fishes lay eggs in the water; others produce living young. *n.*

flag¹ (flag), **1** piece of cloth with a pattern or picture on it that stands for some country, city, etc.: *the flag of the United States.* **2** stop or signal (a person, train, etc.), especially by waving a flag: *The train was flagged at the bridge.* **3** communicate by a flag: *flag a message.* **1** *n.,* **2,3** *v.,* **flagged, flag·ging.**

flag² (flag), iris with blue, purple, yellow, or white flowers and sword-shaped leaves. *n.*

flash·light (flash/līt/), a portable electric light, operated by batteries. *n.*

flex·i·ble (flek/sə bəl), easily bent; not stiff; bending without breaking: *Leather, rubber, and wire are flexible. adj.*

flood (flud), a great flow of water over what is usually dry land: *The heavy rains caused a serious flood in the riverside district. n.*

flour·ish (flėr/ish), grow or develop with vigor; do well; thrive: *Your radishes are flourishing. Our newspaper business flourished. v.*

fluo·res·cent (flù res/nt or flü/ə res/nt), able to give off light by fluorescence. Fluorescent substances glow in the dark when exposed to X rays. *adj.*

foe (fō), enemy. *n., pl.* **foes.**

fol·low (fol/ō), go or come after: *We followed our scout leader through the forest. v.,* **fol·lowed, fol·low·ing.**

fol·low·ing (fol/ō ing), next after: *If that was Sunday, then the following day must have been Monday. adj.*

foot (fùt), **1** the end part of a leg. **2** unit of length equal to 12 inches. **3** feet [=] 1 yard. *n., pl.* **feet** (fēt). **on foot,** standing or walking. **put one's foot down,** make up one's mind and act firmly. **under foot,** in the way.

fore·cast (fôr/kast/), statement of what is coming; prophecy; prediction: *weather forecast. n.*

for·tu·nate (fôr/chə nit), having good luck; lucky: *You are fortunate in having such a fine family. adj.* —**for/tu·nate·ly,** *adv.*

fos·sil (fos/əl), the hardened remains or traces of an animal or plant of a former age. Fossils of ferns are found in coal. *n.*

fossil fuels (fyü/əlz), fuels that formed over millions of years from the remains of small living things.

foun·da·tion (foun dā/shən), **1** part on which the other parts rest for support; base: *the foundation of a house.* **2** basis: *This report has no foundation in fact. n.*

foun·tain (foun/tən), **1** water flowing or rising into the air in a spray. **2** place to get a drink: *a drinking fountain, a soda fountain. n.*

fra·grance (frā/grəns), a sweet smell; pleasing odor: *the fragrance of perfume. n., pl.* **fra·granc·es.**

free·dom (frē/dəm), **1** condition of being free. **2** power to do, say, or think as one pleases; liberty. *n.*

fireplace
log in the **fireplace**

fluorescent
a **fluorescent** image

a	hat	**ī**	ice	**ù**	put	**ə** stands for	
ā	age	**o**	not	**ü**	rule	**a**	in about
ä	far, calm	**ō**	open	**ch**	child	**e**	in taken
âr	care	**ò**	saw	**ng**	long	**i**	in pencil
e	let	**ô**	order	**sh**	she	**o**	in lemon
ē	equal	**oi**	oil	**th**	thin	**u**	in circus
ėr	term	**ou**	out	**ŦH**	then		
i	it	**u**	cup	**zh**	measure		

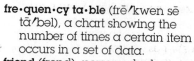

fre·quen·cy ta·ble (frē′kwen sē tā′bəl), a chart showing the number of times a certain item occurs in a set of data.

friend (frend), person who knows and likes another: *She and I are friends. I borrowed my friend's hat.* n., pl. **friends.**

fright·ening (frīt′ning), causing fright; making afraid. *Thunder and lightning are often frightening.* adj.

front-end dig·its (frunt′end′ dij′its), The digits in numbers that have the greatest place value.

fron·tier (frun tir′), the farthest part of a settled country, where the wilds begin. n.

frost·bite (fróst′bīt′), injury to a part of the body caused by freezing. n.

fro·zen (frō′zn), 1 hardened by cold; turned into ice: *frozen sherbet.* 2 preserved by being subjected to low temperatures: *frozen foods.* adj.

fur·ni·ture (fér′nə chər), movable articles needed in a room or house. Beds, chairs, tables, and desks are furniture. n.

fuse (fyüz), a safety device that melts and opens a circuit when too much current is flowing. n., pl. **fus·es.**

fu·ture (fyü′chər), time to come; what is to come; what will be: *You cannot change the past, but you can do better in the future.* n.

frozen (def. 1)

a **frozen** mass of ice

G

gar·bage (gär′bij), scraps of food to be thrown away. n.

gen·er·al (jen′ər əl), 1 of all; for all; from all: *A government takes care of the general welfare.* 2 not detailed: *The teacher gave us general instructions.* adj.

gen·e·ra·tor (jen′ə rā′tər), a device that uses a magnet to change mechanical energy into electricity. n.

ge·nus (jē′nəs), group of related animals or plants ranking below a family and above a species. n.

ge·og·ra·phy (jē og′rə fē), study of the earth's surface, climate, continents, countries, peoples, industries, and products. n.

Geor·gia (jôr′jə), one of the southeastern states of the United States. *Abbreviation:* Ga. or GA *Capital:* Atlanta. n.

graceful

a **graceful** dancer's performance

get (get), come to have; obtain: *I am getting a new video game for my birthday.* v., **got** (got), **got** or **got·ten** (got′n), **get·ting.**

ghet·to (get′ō), part of a city where any racial group or nationality lives. n., pl. **ghet·tos.**

ghost (gōst), spirit of a dead person, supposed to appear to living people as a pale, dim, shadowy form. *The ghost of the murdered servant was said to haunt the house.* n.

gill (gil), part of the body of a fish, tadpole, or crab by which it breathes in water. Oxygen passes in and carbon dioxide passes out through the thin walls of the gills. n., pl. **gills.**

glass·ware (glas′wâr′), articles made of glass. n.

glide (glīd), move along smoothly, evenly, and easily. v., **glid·ed, glid·ing.**

glis·ten (glis′n), shine with a twinkling light, sparkle: *The stars glistened in the sky.* v., **glis·tened, glis·ten·ing.**

globe (glōb), sphere with a map of the earth or sky on it. n.

goal·ie (gō′lē), player who tries to keep the ball or puck from crossing the goal in soccer and some other games. n.

gov·ern·ment (guv′ərn mənt), 1 the ruling of a country, state, district, etc. 2 person or persons ruling a country, state, district, etc., at any time. 3 system of ruling: *The United States has a democratic form of government.* n.

grab (grab), seize suddenly; snatch: *I grabbed the child before she fell.* v., **grabbed, grab·bing.**

grace·ful (grās′fəl), beautiful in form, movement, or manner; pleasing; agreeable: *a graceful dancer.* adj.

grade (grād), 1 division of elementary school or high school, arranged according to the pupils' progress and covering a year's work: *the seventh grade.* 2 number or letter that shows how well one has done: *Her grade in English is B.* 3 give a grade to. 1,2 n., pl. **grades;** 3 v., **grad·ed, grad·ing.**

grain (grān), the seed of wheat, corn, oats, and similar cereal grasses. n.

grand·fa·ther (grand′fä′ᵺər), father of one's father or mother: *my grandfather's watch.* n.

grand·moth·er (grand'muᴛʜ'ər), mother of one's mother or father: *my grandmother's ring.* n.

grand·par·ent (grand'pâr'ənt), grandfather or grandmother. n.

grasp (grasp), seize and hold fast by closing the fingers around: *I grasped the tree limb to keep from falling.* v.

grav·i·ty (grav'ə tē), the natural force that causes objects to move or tend to move toward the center of the earth. Gravity causes objects to have weight. n.

gro·cer·y (grō'sər ē), 1 store that sells food and household supplies. 2 groceries, pl. articles of food and household supplies sold by a grocer. n., pl. **gro·cer·ies.**

growl (groul), 1 a deep, low, angry sound; deep, warning snarl. 2 complain angrily; grumble: *The sailors growled about the poor food.* 3 an angry complaint; grumble. 4 rumble: *Thunder growled in the distance.* 5 a rumble. 1,3,5 n., 2,4 v. —**growl'er,** n. —**growl'ing·ly,** adv.

guard (gärd), person or group that guards. A soldier or group of soldiers guarding a person or place is a guard. n.

gui·tar (gə tär'), a musical instrument usually having six strings, played with the fingers or with a pick. n.

H

hab·i·tat (hab'ə tat), place where an animal or plant naturally lives or grows: *The jungle is the habitat of monkeys.* n. [*Habitat* comes from Latin *habitat,* meaning "it inhabits," and can be traced back to *habere,* meaning "to have, hold."]

hair·cut (hâr'kut'), act or manner of cutting the hair. n.

Hal·low·een (hal'ō ēn'), evening of October 31. It is observed especially by children, who wear costumes and ask for treats from door to door. n.

halves (havz), two equal parts: *Two halves make a whole.* n.

ham·burg·er (ham'bėr'gər), sandwich made with ground beef, usually in a roll or bun. n. [*Hamburger* comes from German *Hamburger,* meaning "of Hamburg."]

hand·ker·chief (hang'kər chif), a small, soft square of cloth used for wiping the nose and face. n., pl. **hand·ker·chiefs.**

hand·writ·ing (hand'rī'ting), manner or style of writing: *He recognized his mother's handwriting on the envelope.* n.

hang·er (hang'ər), thing on which something else is hung: *a coat hanger.* n.

hap·pen (hap'ən), come about, take place: *Both events happened on the same day.* v., **hap·pened, hap·pen·ing.**

hap·pi·ly (hap'ə lē), 1 in a happy manner: *The cousins played happily together.* 2 by luck; with good fortune: *Happily, I found my lost wallet.* adv.

hap·pi·ness (hap'ē nis), a being happy; gladness. n.

hard·ware (härd'wâr'), 1 articles made from metal. Locks, hinges, nails, screws, etc., are hardware. 2 the mechanical parts of a computer system. n.

har·mo·ny (här'mə nē), agreement of feeling, ideas, or actions; getting on well together: *The two brothers lived and worked in perfect harmony.* n.

Ha·wai·i (hə wī'ē), state of the United States in the N Pacific, consisting of the Hawaiian Islands. *Abbreviation:* HI *Capital:* Honolulu. n.

guitar

halves
halves of an orange

a	hat	ī	ice	u̇	put		ə stands for
ā	age	o	not	ü	rule	a	in about
ä	far, calm	ō	open	ch	child	e	in taken
âr	care	ȯ	saw	ng	long	i	in pencil
e	let	ô	order	sh	she	o	in lemon
ē	equal	oi	oil	th	thin	u	in circus
ėr	term	ou	out	ᴛʜ	then		
i	it	u	cup	zh	measure		

head·ache (hed′āk′), pain in the head. n.

health (helth), 1 a state of being well; freedom from sickness: *Rest is important to your health.* 2 condition of body or mind: *be in excellent health. n. [Health* is from Old English *hǣlth,* which comes from *hāl,* meaning "whole."]

heard (hėrd), past tense and past participle of **hear.** *I heard the noise. The sound was heard a mile away. v.*

heav·y (hev′ē), hard to lift or carry; of great weight: *a heavy load. adj.*

hec·tic (hek′tik), very exciting; feverish: *The children had a hectic time getting to school after the big snowstorm. adj.*

hel·met (hel′mit), covering made of steel, leather, plastic, or some other sturdy material, worn to protect the head. n.

her·it·age (her′ə tij), what is handed down from one generation to the next; inheritance: *The heritage of freedom is precious to Americans. n.*

her·o (hir′ō), a person admired for bravery, great deeds, or noble qualities: *Daniel Boone and Clara Barton are American heroes. n., pl.* **her·oes.**

hex·a·gon (hek′sə gon), a plane figure with six angles and six sides. n.

hide·out (hīd′out′), place for hiding or being alone. n.

high school (hī′ skül′), school attended after elementary school or junior high school; secondary school. High school consists of grades 9 through 12 or 10 through 12.

hi·lar·i·ous (hə lâr′ē əs), very merry; very funny; noisy and cheerful: *a hilarious tale, a hilarious party. adj.* —**hi·lar′i·ous·ly,** *adv.*

hire (hīr), pay for the use of (a thing) or the work or services of (a person): *They hired a car and a driver. The florist wants to hire someone to deliver flowers. v.,* **hired, hir·ing.**

his·to·ric (hi stôr′ik), famous or important in history: *Plymouth Rock and Bunker Hill are historic spots. adj.*

horseback

demonstration on **horseback**

home run (hōm′ run′), a hit in baseball which allows the batter to round the bases without a stop and reach home plate to score a run.

home·spun (hōm′spun′), not polished; plain; simple: *homespun manners. adj.*

home·work (hōm′wėrk′), lesson to be studied or prepared outside the classroom. n.

hon·or·a·ble (on′ər ə bəl), having or showing a sense of what is right and proper; honest; upright: *It is not honorable to lie or cheat. adj.*

hoof (hůf or hüf), a hard, horny covering on the feet of horses, cattle, sheep, pigs, and some other animals. n., pl. **hoofs** or **hooves** (hůfs or hüvz).

hor·ri·ble (hôr′ə bəl), 1 causing horror; terrible; dreadful; frightful; shocking: *a horrible crime, a horrible disease.* 2 extremely unpleasant: *a horrible noise. adj.*

horse·back (hôrs′bak′), on the back of a horse: *ride horseback. adv.*

hot dog (hot′ dog′), 1 INFORMAL. sandwich made with a hot frankfurter enclosed in a bun. 2 INFORMAL. frankfurter.

hound (hound), 1 dog of any of various breeds, most of which hunt by scent and have large, drooping ears and short hair. 2 any dog. 3 urge on; nag: *The children hounded their parents to buy a swimming pool.* 1,2 *n.,* 3 *v.*

House of Rep·re·sent·a·tives (hous′ əv rep′ri zen′tə tivz), the lower house of Congress or of the legislature of certain states of the United States.

house·work (hous′wėrk′), work to be done in housekeeping, such as washing, ironing, cleaning, and cooking. n.

Hous·ton (hyü′stən), city in SE Texas. n.

hu·mor (hyü′mər), ability to see or show the funny or amusing side of things: *A sense of humor helps one overcome many problems. n.*

hu·mor·ous (hyü′mər əs), full of humor; funny; amusing: *We all laughed at the humorous story. adj.*

hun·dred (hun′drəd), ten times ten; 100. There are one hundred cents in a dollar. *n., adj.*

hus·tle (hus′əl), to hurry: *Mother hustled the baby to bed. v.,* **hus·tled, hus·tling.**

hy·dro·e·lec·tric pow·er (hī/drō i lek/trik pou/ər), electricity generated by moving water.

hy·dro·gen (hī/drə jən), a colorless, odorless gas that burns easily. Hydrogen is a chemical element that weighs less than any other element. It combines with oxygen to form water and is present in most organic compounds. *n.*

hy·per·bo·le (hī pėr/bə lē), an exaggerated statement used for effect and not meant to be taken literally. EXAMPLE: *Waves high as mountains broke over the reef n.* [*Hyperbole* can be traced back to Greek *hyper,* meaning "above, over, beyond," and *ballein,* meaning "to throw."]

hy·poth·e·sis (hī poth/ə sis), something assumed because it seems likely to be a true explanation; theory: *Let us act on the hypothesis that he is honest. n., pl.* **hy·poth·e·ses.**

I

ice·berg (īs/bėrg/), a large mass of ice, detached from a glacier and floating in the sea. About 90 percent of its mass is below the surface of the water. *n.* [*Iceberg* comes from Dutch *ijsberg,* meaning "ice mountain."]

i·ci·cle (ī/si kəl), a pointed, hanging stick of ice formed by the freezing of dripping water. *n., pl.* **i·ci·cles.** [*Icicle* is from Middle English *isykle,* which comes from Old English *is,* meaning "ice," and *gicel,* meaning "icicle."]

id·i·om (id/ē əm), phrase or expression whose meaning cannot be understood from the ordinary meanings of the words in it. "Hold one's tongue" is an English idiom meaning "keep still." *n.*

ig·loo (ig/lü), an Eskimo hut shaped like a dome, often built of blocks of hard snow. *n., pl.* **ig·loos.** [*Igloo* comes from Eskimo *igdlu,* meaning "house."]

I'll (īl), **1** I shall. **2** I will.

Il·li·nois (il/ə noi/ *or* il/ə noiz/), one of the north central states of the United States. *Abbreviation:* Ill. or IL *Capital:* Springfield. *n.*

il·lu·mi·nate (i lü/mə nāt), **1** light up; make bright: *The room was illuminated by four large lamps.* **2** make clear; explain: *Our teacher could illuminate almost any subject we studied.* **3** decorate with lights. *v.,* **il·lu·mi·nat·ed, il·lu·mi·nat·ing.**

il·lus·tra·tion (il/ə strā/shən), picture, diagram, or map used to explain or decorate something. *n., pl.* **il·lus·tra·tions.**

il·lus·tra·tor (il/ə strā/tər), artist who makes pictures to be used as illustrations. *n.*

I'm (īm), I am.

i·mag·i·na·tion (i maj/ə nā/shən), power of forming pictures or images in the mind of things not present to the senses: *The poet had imagination. n.*

i·mag·ine (i maj/ən), picture in one's mind; form an image or idea of: *The girl likes to imagine herself a doctor. v.,* **i·mag·ined, i·mag·in·ing.**

im·pair (im pâr/), make worse; damage; harm; weaken: *Poor eating habits impaired his health. v.*

im·pet·u·ous (im pech/ü əs), acting or done with sudden or rash energy; hasty: *He was so angry that he made an impetuous decision. adj.* —**im·pet/u·ous·ly,** *adv.*

inch (inch), unit of length, ¹⁄₁₂ of a foot. *n.*

in·cin·er·a·tor (in sin/ə rā/tər), furnace or other device for burning trash and other things to ashes. *n.*

igloo
an **igloo** at night

							stands for
a	hat	ī	ice	u̇	put	ə	
ā	age	o	not	ü	rule	a	in about
ä	far, calm	ō	open	ch	child	e	in taken
âr	care	ȯ	saw	ng	long	i	in pencil
e	let	ô	order	sh	she	o	in lemon
ē	equal	oi	oil	th	thin	u	in circus
ėr	term	ou	out	ᵺ	then		
i	it	u	cup	zh	measure		

in·de·struct·i·ble (in/di struk/tə bəl), not able to be destroyed. *adj.*

In·di·an·a (in/dē an/ə), one of the north central states of the United States. *Abbreviation:* Ind. or IN *Capital:* Indianapolis. *n.*

in·di·go (in/də gō), 1 a blue dye formerly obtained from various plants, but now usually made artificially. 2 plant from which indigo was made. *n.*

in·dus·try (in/də strē), any branch of business, trade, or manufacture: *Industries dealing with steel, copper, coal, and construction employ millions of people. n., pl.* **in·dus·tries.**

industry

the steel **industry**

in·flate (in flāt/), increase (prices or amount of currency) beyond the normal amount. *v.,* **in·flat·ed, in·flat·ing.**

in·fla·tion (in flā/shən), a sharp increase in prices resulting from too great an expansion in paper money or bank credit. *n.*

in·for·ma·tion (in/fər mā/shən), 1 knowledge given or received concerning some fact or circumstance; news: *We have just received information of the astronauts' safe landing.* 2 things known; facts; data: *A dictionary contains much information about words. n.*

in·hale (in hāl/), draw (air, gas, fragrance, tobacco smoke, etc.) into the lungs; breathe in. *v.,* **in·haled, in·hal·ing.**

in-line skates (in/līn skāts/), a kind of roller skate having the wheels or rollers aligned rather than side by side in pairs.

in·no·cent (in/ə sənt), doing no wrong or evil; free from sin or wrong; not guilty: *In the United States a person is innocent until proved guilty. adj.*

in·spire (in spīr/), fill with a thought or feeling; influence: *A chance to try again inspired her with hope. v.,* **in·spired, in·spir·ing.**

in·struct (in strukt/), 1 give knowledge to; show how to do; teach; train; educate: *Our teacher instructs us in reading.* 2 give directions to; order: *The doctor instructed him to go to bed.* 3 inform; tell: *The family lawyer instructed them that the contract would be signed Monday. v.*

invertebrate

slippery, crawling

invertebrates

in·struc·tion (in struk/shən), 1 a teaching or educating. 2 knowledge or teaching given; lesson. *n.*

in·stru·ment (in/strə mənt), device for producing musical sounds: *A violin, cello, and piano were the instruments in the trio. n., pl.* **in·stru·ments.**

in·su·la·tor (in/sə lā/tər), a material that does not conduct heat or electricity well. *n., pl.* **in·su·la·tors.**

in·ter·cep·tion (in/tər sep/shən), an intercepting or a being intercepted. *n.*

in·ter·ga·lac·tic (in/tər gə lak/ tik), situated or taking place between galaxies: *intergalactic space. adj.*

in·to (in/tü; *before consonants often* in/tə), to the inside of; toward and inside: *Come into the house. We drove into the city. I will look into the matter. prep.*

in·vent (in vent/), 1 make up for the first time; think out (something new): *Alexander Graham Bell invented the telephone.* 2 make up; think up: *Since they had no good reason for being late, they invented an excuse. v.*

in·ven·tion (in ven/shən), 1 a making something new: *the invention of gunpowder.* 2 thing invented: *TV is a modern invention. n.*

in·ver·te·brate (in vėr/tə brit or in vėr/tə brāt), animal without a backbone. Worms and insects are invertebrates; fishes and mammals are vertebrates. *n., pl.* **in·ver·te·brates.**

in·vis·i·ble (in viz/ə bəl), not visible; not capable of being seen: *Thought is invisible. Germs are invisible to the naked eye. adj.*

Ir·o·quois (ir/ə kwoi/), member of a powerful confederacy of American Indian tribes called the Five Nations, formerly living mostly in what is now New York State. *n. pl.* **Ir·o·quois.**

is·land (ī/lənd), body of land smaller than a continent and completely surrounded by water: *To reach the island you go by boat. n.*

i·tin·e·rar·y (ī tin/ə rer/ē), 1 route of travel; plan of travel. 2 record of travel. *n., pl.* **i·tin·e·rar·ies.**

its (its), of it; belonging to it: *The dog wagged its tail. adj.*

it's (its), 1 it is: *It's my turn.* 2 it has: *It's been a beautiful day.*

I've (īv), I have.

J

jeal·ous (jel'əs), full of envy; envious: *She is jealous of her sister's good grades. adj.*

jel·ly·fish (jel'ē fish'), any of a group of sea animals without backbones, with a body formed of a mass of almost clear jellylike tissue. Most jellyfish have long, trailing tentacles that may bear stinging cells. *n.*

jew·el (jü'əl), a precious stone. *n.*

jew·el·ry (jü'əl rē), 1 ornaments set with precious stones: *She keeps her jewelry in a small box.* 2 ring, bracelet, necklace, or other ornament to be worn. *n.*

jour·nal (jėr'nl), a daily record of events or occurrences. A diary is a journal of what a person does, thinks, feels, and notices. *n.*

jour·nal·ist (jėr'nl ist), person whose work is writing for, editing, managing, or publishing a newspaper or magazine. *n.*

jour·ney (jėr'nē), a traveling from one place to another; trip: *a journey around the world. n.*

joy·ful (joi'fəl), glad; happy: *a joyful heart. adj.*

joy·ous (joi'əs), joyful; glad; gay: *a joyous song, a joyous person. adj.*

judge (juj), a public official appointed or elected to hear and decide cases in a court of law. *n.*

jud·i·cial branch (jü dish'əl branch'), the branch of government in charge of deciding whether laws have been broken and what the laws mean.

Ju·neau (jü'nō), capital of Alaska, in the SE part. *n.*

jun·gle (jung'gəl), wild land overgrown with bushes, vines, and trees. Jungles are hot and humid regions with many kinds of plants and wild animals. *n.*

jun·ior (jü'nyər), 1 student in the third year of high school or college. 2 of these students: *the junior class.* 1 *n.,* 2 *adj.*

jus·tice (jus'tis), 1 just conduct; fair dealing: *The judge had a sense of justice.* 2 a judge. The Supreme Court has nine justices. *n., pl.* **jus·tic·es.**

K

Ken·tuck·y (kən tuk'ē), one of the south central states of the United States. *Abbreviation:* Ky. or KY *Capital:* Frankfort. *n.*

kick·stand (kik'stand'), a metal rod or other device attached to a bicycle or motorcycle that holds the vehicle upright when not in use. *n.*

ki·lom·e·ter (kə lom'ə tər *or* kil'ə mē'tər), unit of length equal to 1000 meters, or 3280.8 feet. *n.*

ki·mo·no (kə mō'nə), a loose outer garment held in place by a sash, worn by Japanese men and women. *n.*

kin·der·gar·ten (kin'dər gärt'n), school or class for children from about 4 to 6 years old that educates them by games, toys, and pleasant occupations. *n.* [*Kindergarten* is from German *Kindergarten,* which comes from *Kinder,* meaning "children," and *Garten,* meaning "garden."]

king·dom (king'dəm), one of the three divisions of the natural world; the animal kingdom, the vegetable kingdom, or the mineral kingdom. *n.*

kiss (kis), touch with the lips as a sign of love, greeting, or respect: *She gave her grandchildren many kisses. n., pl.* **kiss·es.**

knap·sack (nap'sak'), a canvas or leather bag with two shoulder straps, used for carrying clothes, equipment, etc., on the back; backpack. *n.*

knead (nēd), press or mix together (dough or clay) into a soft mass: *A baker kneads dough. v.*

jewel
The ruby is a beautiful **jewel**

kimono
silk **kimono** with sash

a	hat	**ī**	ice	**u̇**	put	**ə** *stands for*	
ā	age	**o**	not	**ü**	rule	**a**	in about
ä	far, calm	**ō**	open	**ch**	child	**e**	in taken
âr	care	**ȯ**	saw	**ng**	long	**i**	in pencil
e	let	**ô**	order	**sh**	she	**o**	in lemon
ē	equal	**oi**	oil	**th**	thin	**u**	in circus
ėr	term	**ou**	out	**ᵵH**	then		
i	it	**u**	cup	**zh**	measure		

knew (nü *or* nyü), past tense of **know**. *She knew the right answer.* v.

knick·knack (nik′nak′), a pleasing trinket; ornament. n., pl. **knick·knacks**.

knit (nit), make clothing by looping yarn or thread together with long needles, or by machinery which forms loops instead of weaving. v., **knit·ted** or **knit, knit·ting**.

knock-knock joke (nok′nok′ jōk′), a joke in the form of a dialogue: *"Knock-knock." "Who's there?" "Arthur." "Arthur who?" "Arthur any more at home like you?"*

know (nō), have knowledge: *I know from experience how to drive on icy roads.* v., **knew, known** (nōn), **know·ing**.

know·ing·ly (nō′ing lē), **1** in a knowing way. **2** on purpose: *I would not knowingly hurt anyone.* adv.

knowl·edge (nol′ij), what one knows: *a gardener's knowledge of flowers.* n.

knowl·edge·a·ble (nol′i jə bəl), well-informed, especially about a particular subject. adj.

known (nōn), recognized; well-known: *a known fact, a person of known ability.* adj.

L

la·bel (lā′bəl), slip of paper or other material attached to anything and marked to show what or whose it is, or where it is to go: *Can you read the label on the bottle?* n.

la·bor un·ions (lā′bər yü′nyenz), groups of workers joined together to protect and promote their interests by dealing as groups with their employers; unions.

la·crosse (lə krós′), game played on a field with a ball and long-handled, loosely strung rackets by two teams, usually of 10 players each. The players carry the ball in the rackets, trying to send it into the other team's goal. n.

land·fill (land′fil′), place where garbage and other refuse are buried and covered with dirt in order to build up low-lying or wet land. n., pl. **land·fills**.

lacross

exciting game of **lacrosse**

land·form (land′fôrm′), a physical feature of the earth's surface. Plains, plateaus, hills, and mountains are landforms. n., pl. **land·forms**.

lan·guid (lang′gwid), **1** feeling weak; without energy; drooping: *A hot, sticky day makes a person languid.* **2** without interest or enthusiasm; indifferent. adj. —**lan′guid·ly**, adv.

lar·i·at (lar′ē ət), a long rope with a noose at the end, used for catching horses and cattle; lasso. n. [*Lariat* comes from Spanish *la reata*, meaning "the rope."]

las·so (las′ō *or* la sü′), **1** a long rope with a running noose at one end, used for catching horses and cattle; lariat. **2** catch with a lasso. 1 n., pl. **las·sos** or **las·soes**; 2 v. [*Lasso* is from Spanish *lazo*, which came from Latin *laqueus*, meaning "a noose."]

laugh·ter (laf′tər), **1** sound of laughing: *Laughter filled the room.* **2** action of laughing: *The clown's antics brought forth laughter from the children.* n.

launch (lónch), push out or put forth into the air: *launch a plane from an aircraft carrier. The satellite was launched in a rocket.* v.

laun·dry (lón′drē), clothes, tablecloths, towels, etc., washed or to be washed. n.

lawn mow·ing (lón′mō′ing), cutting the grass with a lawn-mower and taking care of the lawn: *I earn a lot of money every summer lawn mowing.*

leaf (lēf), one of the thin, usually flat, green parts of a tree or other plant that grow on the stem or grow up from the roots. n., pl. **leaves** (lēvz).

ledge (lej), a narrow shelf: *a window ledge.* n.

leg·end (lej′ənd), story coming down from the past, which may be based on actual people and events but is not regarded as historically true: *The stories about King Arthur and his knights of the Round Table are legends.* n.

leg·is·la·tive branch (lej′ə slā′tiv branch′), the part of the government that has the power to make laws for a state or country.

length (lengkth *or* length), how long a thing is; what a thing measures from end to end; the longest way a thing can be measured: *the length of a room, an animal eight inches in length. n.*

les·son plan (les′n plan′), a written outline of topics and materials to be used in teaching a lesson.

let's (lets), let us.

lib·er·ty (lib′ər tē), **1** condition of being free; freedom; independence. **2** right or power to do as one pleases; power or opportunity to do something: *liberty of speech. n., pl.* **lib·er·ties.**

li·brar·y (lī′brer′ē), room or building where a collection of books, magazines, films, and recordings is kept for public use and borrowing. *n., pl.* **li·brar·ies.**

life (līf) **1** a living or being alive. **2** time of being alive. **3** a living being; person: *Many lives were lost in the flood. n., pl.* **lives.**

life span (līf′ span′), the length of time something can be expected to live. *The average life span of a tiger is twenty years.*

light¹ (līt), pale in color; approaching white: *light hair, light blue. adj.,* **light·er, light·est.**

light² (līt), easy to carry; not heavy: *a light load. adj.,* **light·er, light·est.**

light·ly (līt′lē), quickly; easily: *She jumped lightly aside. adv.*

light·ning (līt′ning), flash of light in the sky caused by a discharge of electricity between clouds, or between a cloud and the earth's surface. The sound that it makes is thunder. *n.*

lis·ten (lis′n), try to hear; attend with the ears so as to hear: *She is listening to her favorite radio station. v.,* **lis·tened, lis·ten·ing.**

Lit·tle Rock (lit′əl rok′), capital of Arkansas, in the central part.

liv·ing room (liv′ing rüm′), room for general family use; sitting room.

loaf (lōf), bread shaped and baked as one piece: *My mother baked six loaves of bread. n., pl.* **loaves** (lōvz).

lob·ster (lob′stər), **1** a large shellfish having five pairs of legs, with large claws on the front pair. Its shell turns a bright red when boiled. **2** its flesh; used as food *n.*

lodge (loj), a place to live in; a house, especially a small or temporary house: *My aunt rents a lodge in the mountains for the summer. n.*

lone·ly (lōn′lē), feeling oneself alone and longing for company or friends: *He was lonely while his brother was away. adj.*

long·horn (lông′hôrn′), one of a breed of cattle with very long horns, formerly common in the southwestern United States. *n.*

long·house (lông′hous′), a large, rectangular dwelling of certain North American Indians, especially the Iroquois. Many families lived together in one longhouse.

Los An·ge·les (lòs an′jə ləs *or* lòs an′jə lēz′), the principal city in S California and the second largest city in the United States.

Lou·i·si·an·a (lü ē′zē an′ə), one of the south central states of the United States. *Abbreviation:* La. *or* LA *Capital:* Baton Rouge. *n.* [*Louisiana* comes from French *Louisiane,* originally the name of the entire Mississippi valley. The French explorer La Salle named it in honor of his king, *Louis* XIV.]

loy·al (loi′əl), true and faithful to love, promise, or duty. *adj.* —**loy′al·ly,** *adv.*

luck·i·ly (luk′ə lē), by good luck; fortunately. *adv.*

lu·nar (lü′nər), **1** of the moon. **2** like the moon: *the lunar surface of the dark desert at night. adj.*

lightning
an evening show of
lightning

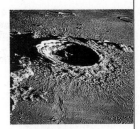

lunar (def. 1)
the **lunar** surface

a	hat	**ī**	ice	**u̇**	put		**ə** stands for	
ā	age	**o**	not	**ü**	rule	**a**	in about	
ä	far, calm	**ō**	open	**ch**	child	**e**	in taken	
âr	care	**ȯ**	saw	**ng**	long	**i**	in pencil	
e	let	**ô**	order	**sh**	she	**o**	in lemon	
ē	equal	**oi**	oil	**th**	thin	**u**	in circus	
ėr	term	**ou**	out	**ŦH**	then			
i	it	**u**	cup	**zh**	measure			

M

ma·chine (mə shēn′), arrangement of fixed and moving parts for doing work, each part having some special function: *Washing machines make housework easier.* n.

made (mād), past tense and past participle of **make**. *The cook made the cake. It was made of flour, milk, butter, eggs, and sugar.* v.

mag·ni·fy (mag′nə fī), cause to look larger than real size: *The mirror magnified the features of his face.* v., **mag·ni·fied, mag·ni·fy·ing.**

mail·box (māl′boks′), a private box to which mail is delivered. n.

main (mān), most important; largest: *the main dish at dinner, the main street of town.* adj.

main·land (mān′land′ or mān′lənd), the main part of a continent or country, apart from outlying islands and peninsulas. n.

ma·jes·tic (mə jes′tik), of or having majesty; grand; noble; dignified; stately. adj.

ma·jor (mā′jər), more important; larger; greater: *Take the major share of the profits.* adj.

make (māk), bring into being; put together; build; form; shape: *make a new coat, make a fire, make jelly.* v., **made, mak·ing.**

man·ag·er (man′ə jər), person who manages, especially one who manages a business: *She is the manager of the department store.* n.

mane (mān), the long, heavy hair growing on the back of or around the neck of a horse, lion, etc. n.

map·mak·er (map′māk′ər), person who creates maps. n., pl. **map·mak·ers.**

mar·gar·ine (mär′jər ən or mär′jə rēn′), substitute for butter, made from cottonseed oil, soybean oil, or other vegetable oils. n.

mar·vel (mär′vəl), something wonderful; astonishing thing: *The airplane is one of the marvels of science.* n., pl. **mar·vels.**

mar·vel·ous (mär′və ləs), excellent; splendid: fine: *a marvelous time.* adj.

mass pro·duc·tion (mas′prə duk′chən), the making of goods in large quantities, especially by machinery.

mass production
mass production of aluminum sheets

match (mach), a short, slender piece of wood or pasteboard tipped with a mixture that catches fire when rubbed on a rough or specially prepared surface. n., pl. **match·es.**

ma·ter·i·al (mə tir′ē əl), what a thing is made from or done with: *dress materials, building materials, writing materials.* n., pl. **ma·ter·i·als.**

mat·i·nee (mat′n ā′), a dramatic or musical performance held in the afternoon. n., pl. **mat·i·nees.**

may·be (mā′bē), it may be; possibly; perhaps: *Maybe you'll have better luck next time.* adv.

mead·ow (med′ō), piece of grassy land, especially one used for growing hay or as a pasture. n.

mean (mēn), **1** have as its thought; signify; import; denote: *What does this word mean?* **2** intend to say or indicate: *"Keep out! That means you!"* v. **meant** (ment), **mean·ing.**

meas·ure (mezh′ər), find the size or amount of (anything); find out how long, wide, deep, large, much, etc., (a thing) is: *We measured the room and found it was 20 feet long and 15 feet wide.* v., **meas·ured, meas·ur·ing.**

me·chan·ic (mə kan′ik), worker skilled with tools, especially one who repairs machines: *an automobile mechanic.* n.

meet (mēt), a meeting; a gathering: *an athletic meet.* n.

mem·or·y (mem′ər ē), person, thing, or event that is remembered: *I was so young when we moved that our old house is only a vague memory.* n, pl. **mem·or·ies.** [*Memory* came into English about 600 years ago from French *memorie*, and can be traced back to Latin *memor*, meaning "mindful."]

Mem·phis (mem′fis), city in SW Tennessee, on the Mississippi. n.

met·al (met′l), a group of elements that are usually solid at room temperature, are shiny, and conduct heat and electricity well. n., pl. **met·als.**

me·ter (mē′tər), the basic unit of length in the metric system. A meter is equal to 39.37 inches. n. Also, **metre.**

met·ric units (met′rik yü′nits), a system for measuring length in *millimeters, centimeters, decimeters, meters,* and *kilometers;* capacity in *milliliters* and *liters;* mass in *grams* and *kilograms;* temperature in *degrees Celsius.*

Mi·am·i (mī am′ē), city in SE Florida, famous as a winter resort. *n.*

Mich·i·gan (mish′ə gən), one of the north central states of the United States. *Abbreviation:* Mich. or MI *Capital:* Lansing. *n.*

mid·night (mid′nit′), twelve o'clock at night; the middle of the night. *n.*

mid·stream (mid′strēm′), middle of a stream. *n.*

mid·way (mid′wā′), in the middle; halfway. *adv., adj.*

mid·week (mid′wēk′), the middle of the week. *n.*

Mid·west·ern (mid′wes′tərn), Middle Western. *adj.*

mid·year (mid′yir′), happening in the middle of the year. *adj.*

mightn't (mīt′nt), might not. *v.*

mil·dew (mil′dü *or* mil′dyü), kind of fungus producing a whitish coating or discoloration on plants, paper, clothes, etc., during damp weather. *n.*

mile (mīl), unit of distance equal to 5280 feet. *n.*

mile·age (mī′lij), length, extent, or distance in miles: *The mileage of a railroad is its total number of miles of roadbed. n.*

mil·li·me·ter (mil′ə mē′tər), unit of length equal to 1/1000 of a meter. *n.*

mil·lion·aire (mil′yə nâr′) a very wealthy person. *n.*

min·i·a·ture (min′ē ə chùr *or* min′ə chər), **1** anything represented on a small scale: *In the museum there is a miniature of the* Mayflower. **2** done or made on a very small scale; tiny: *miniature furniture for a dollhouse.* 1 *n.,* 2 *adj.* [*Miniature* comes from Italian *miniatura,* meaning "picture in an illuminated manuscript," and can be traced back to Latin *miniare,* meaning "to paint red."]

min·ute[1] (min′it), one of the 60 equal periods of time that make up an hour; sixty seconds. *n.*

mi·nute[2] (mī nüt′ *or* mī nyüt′), very small; tiny: *a minute speck of dust. n.*

mis·er·a·ble (miz′ər ə bəl), very unhappy or unfortunate; wretched: *The sick child was miserable. adj.*

mis·sile (mis′əl), a self-propelled rocket or bomb, such as a guided missile. *n., pl.* **mis·siles.**

mis·tle·toe (mis′əl tō), plant with small, waxy, white berries that grows as a parasite on trees. It is used as a Christmas decoration. *n.*

mis·un·der·stand·ing (mis′un′dər stan′ding), wrong understanding; failure to understand; mistake as to meaning. *n.*

moist (moist), slightly wet; damp. *adj.*

mois·ten (moi′sn), make or become moist: *His eyes moistened with tears. v.* —**mois′·ten·er,** *n.*

mol·e·cule (mol′ə kyül), two or more atoms joined chemically. *n.*

mol·lusk (mol′əsk), a large group of animals having soft bodies not composed of segments, and usually covered with a hard shell. Snails, mussels, oysters, clams, and octopuses are mollusks. *n., pl.* **mol·lusks.**

Mom (mom), INFORMAL. Mother: *I love Mom's meatloaf. n.*

mo·nop·o·ly (mə nop′ə lē), the exclusive control of a commodity or service: *The only milk company in town has a monopoly on milk delivery. n.*

month (munth), one of the 12 parts into which the year is divided. September, April, June, and November have 30 days; February has 28 days except in leap years, when it has 29; all the other months have 31 days. *n., pl.* **months.**

mollusk
Clams are **mollusks.**

a	hat	**ī**	ice	**ù**	put	**ə stands for**	
ā	age	**o**	not	**ü**	rule	**a**	in about
ä	far, calm	**ō**	open	**ch**	child	**e**	in taken
âr	care	**ȯ**	saw	**ng**	long	**i**	in pencil
e	let	**ô**	order	**sh**	she	**o**	in lemon
ē	equal	**oi**	oil	**th**	thin	**u**	in circus
ėr	term	**ou**	out	**ᴛʜ**	then		
i	it	**u**	cup	**zh**	measure		

naturalist
Naturalists discover something new.

nomad
a **nomad** and his camel

morn·ing (môr′ning), the early part of the day, ending at noon. *n., pl.* **morn·ings.**

mo·squi·to (mə skē′tō), any of various small, slender insects with two wings. The female bites and sucks blood from people and animals, causing itching. One kind of mosquito transmits malaria; another transmits yellow fever. *n., pl.* **mo·squi·toes** or **mo·squi·tos.** [*Mosquito* is from Spanish *mosquito,* meaning "little fly," which came from Latin *musca,* meaning "fly."]

mur·mur (mér′mər), a soft, low, sound that rises and falls and goes on without breaks: *the murmur of a stream, the murmur of voices in a room. n.*

mu·se·um (myü zē′əm), a building or rooms where a collection of objects illustrating science, ancient life, art, history, or other subjects is kept and displayed. *n.* [*Museum* was borrowed from Latin *museum,* which came from Greek *mouseion,* meaning "seat of the Muses."]

mu·sic (myü′zik), **1** art of putting sounds together in beautiful, pleasing, or interesting arrangements. **2** beautiful, pleasing, or interesting arrangements of sounds. *n.*

mus·tang (mus′tang), a small, wild or half-wild horse of the North American plains. *n.* [*Mustang* comes from Spanish *mestengo,* meaning "untamed."]

mys·te·ri·ous (mi stir′ē əs), full of mystery; hard to explain or understand; secret; hidden. *adj.*

mys·ter·y (mis′tər ē), **1** something that is not explained or understood: *the mystery of the migration of birds.* **2** novel or story, about a mysterious event or events which are not explained until the end. *n., pl.* **mys·ter·ies.**

N

na·tion (nā′shən), people occupying the same country, united under the same government, and usually speaking the same language: *The President appealed to the nation for support of his policies. n.*

nat·u·ral·ist (nach′ər ə list), person who makes a study of animals and plants. *n.*

nat·u·ral re·sourc·es (nach′ər əl rē′sôrs əz), materials supplied by nature. Minerals, forests, and water power are natural resources.

naugh·ty (nȯ′ tē), **1** bad; not obedient: *a naughty child.* **2** somewhat improper: *a naughty joke. adj.*

nav·i·ga·tion (nav′ə gā′shən), act or process of navigating. *n.*

near (nir), close; not far: *They found the nearest drugstore. adj.,* **near·er, near·est.**

near·by (nir′bī′), near; close at hand: *a nearby house (adj.). They went nearby to visit (adv.). adj., adv.*

nec·es·sar·y (nes′ə ser′ē), needed; having to be done: *a necessary repair. adj.*

neck·lace (nek′lis), string of jewels, gold, silver, beads, etc., worn around the neck as an ornament. *n.*

need (nēd), be in want of; be unable to do without; lack: *I need a new hat. Plants need water. v.*

nerv·ous (nér′vəs), **1** having easily excited nerves; jumpy: *a nervous, impatient person.* **2** easily excited or upset; restless, uneasy, or timid: *Are you nervous about staying alone at night? adj.*

neu·tron (nü′tron), a particle with no charge in the nucleus of an atom. *n.*

no one (nō′ wun′), no person; nobody.

nois·y (noi′zē), **1** making much noise: *a noisy crowd, a noisy machine.* **2** full of noise: *a noisy street, the noisy city. adj.*

no·mad (nō′mad), member of a tribe which moves from place to place to have food or pasture for its cattle: *Many Arabs are nomads. n.*

non·met·al (non met′l), element with properties opposite those of metals. *n., pl.* **non·met·als.**

non·re·new·a·ble re·sourc·es (non′ri nü′ə bəl rē′ sôrs əz), resources that cannot be replaced once they are used up.

north (nôrth), direction to which a compass needle points; direction to the right as one faces the setting sun. *n.*

north·ern (nôr/ᴛʜərn), of or in the north: *northern countries. adj.*

note·book (nōt/bùk/), book in which to write notes of things to be learned or remembered. *n.*

noth·ing (nuth/ing), not anything; no thing: *Nothing arrived by mail. pron.*

nour·ish (nėr/ish), make grow, or keep alive and well, with food; feed; nurture: *Milk is all we need to nourish our small baby. v.*

no·where (no/hwâr), in no place; at no place; to no place. *adv.*

nu·cle·ar energy (nü/klē ər en/ər jē), energy released when atoms split or join.

nu·cle·us (nü/klē əs), the central part of an atom. *n., pl.* **nu·cle·i** (nü/klē ī), **nu·cle·us·es.**

numb (num), having lost the power of feeling or moving: *My fingers are numb with cold. adj.*

nur·ture (nėr/chər), bring up; care for; foster; rear; train: *Parents nurture their children. v.*

O

o·be·di·ent (ō bē/ dē ənt), doing what one is told: *The obedient dog came when it was called. adj.* —**o·be/di·ent·ly,** *adv.*

ob·serv·ant (əb zėr/vənt), quick to notice; watchful: *If you are observant in the fields and woods, you will find many flowers that others fail to notice. adj.*

ob·ser·va·tion (ob/zər vā/shən), act of watching for some special purpose; study: *The observation of nature is important in science. n.*

ob·sta·cle (ob/stə kəl), something that stands in the way or stops progress; hindrance: *A fallen tree was an obstacle to traffic. He overcame the obstacle of blindness and became a musician. n.*

ob·tuse tri·an·gle (əb tüs/ trī/ang/gəl or əb tyüs/ trī/ang/gəl), a triangle with one obtuse angle.

oc·ca·sion (ə kā/zhən), a cause; reason: *The dog that was the occasion of the quarrel had run away. n.*

oc·cu·pant (ok/yə pənt), **1** one that occupies: *The occupants of the car stepped out as I approached.* **2** person in actual possession of a house, estate, office, etc. *n.*

oc·cur (ə kėr/), take place; happen: *Storms often occur in winter. v.,* **oc·curred, oc·cur·ring.**

oc·ta·gon (ok/ tə gon) an eight-sided polygon. *n.*

Oc·to·ber (ok tō/bər), the tenth month of the year. It has 31 days. *n.* [*October* comes from Latin *octo* meaning "eight," from the order of the Roman calendar.]

of (ov *or* uv; *unstressed* əv), belonging to: *a friend of my childhood, the news of the day, the driver of the car. prep.*

off (ȯf), **1** from the usual or correct position, condition, etc.: *I took off my hat.* **2** from; away from: *I jumped off the step. We are miles off the road.* **3** in full; wholly: *She clears off her desk.* 1,3 *adv.,* 2 *prep.*

one (wun), the first and lowest whole number; the number 1. *n.*

on·o·mat·o·poe·ia (on/ə mat/ə pē/ə), formation of a name or word by imitating the sound associated with the thing designated, as in *buzz, hum, slap, splash. n.*

o·pen (ō/pən), make not closed or shut: *I opened the window. She opened her mouth. v.,* **o·pened, o·pen·ing.**

op·po·nent (ə pō/nənt), person who is on the other side in a fight, game, or discussion: *She defeated her opponent in the election. n.*

op·por·tu·ni·ty (op/ər tü/nə tē or op/ər tyü/nə tē), a good chance; favorable time. *n. pl.* **op·por·tu·ni·ties.**

or·ches·tra (ôr/kə strə), group of musicians playing together on various stringed, wind, and percussion instruments. *n.*

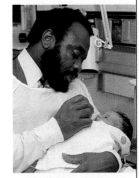
nourish
nourishing the newborn

orchestra
orchestra entertains the audience

a	hat	**ī**	ice	**ù**	put	**ə** stands for	
ā	age	**o**	not	**ü**	rule	**a**	in about
ä	far, calm	**ō**	open	**ch**	child	**e**	in taken
âr	care	**ȯ**	saw	**ng**	long	**i**	in pencil
e	let	**ô**	order	**sh**	she	**o**	in lemon
ē	equal	**oi**	oil	**th**	thin	**u**	in circus
ėr	term	**ou**	out	**ᴛʜ**	then		
i	it	**u**	cup	**zh**	measure		

O·re·gon (ôr′ə gon *or* ôr′ə gən), one of the Pacific states of the United States. *Abbreviation:* Ore., Oreg., or OR *Capital:* Salem. *n.*

or·gan·i·za·tion (ôr′gə nə zā′shən), group of persons united for some purpose. Churches, clubs, and political parties are organizations. *n.*

or·gan·ize (ôr′gə nīz), put into working order; get together and arrange: *We helped our teacher organize a trip to the city zoo. v.,* **or·gan·ized, or·gan·iz·ing.**

our (our), of us; belonging to us: *We need our coats now. adj.*

out·side (out′sīd′) space that is beyond or not inside. *n.*

o·ver·ride (ō′vər rīd′), prevail over: *The new rule overrides all previous ones. v.,* **o·ver·rode** (ō′vər·rōd′), **o·ver·rid·den** (ō′vər rid′n), **o·ver·rid·ing.**

own·er (ō′nər), one who owns: *Who is the owner of this dog? n.*

ox·y·gen (ok′sə jən), a colorless, odorless gas that forms about one fifth of the atmosphere. Animals and plants cannot live, and fire will not burn, without oxygen. *n.*

oys·ter (oi′stər), shellfish having a rough, irregular shell in two halves. Oysters are found in shallow water along seacoasts. Many kinds are good to eat and some kinds yield pearls. *n.*

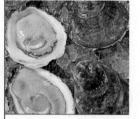

oyster

oysters in their shells

P

pad (pad), soft mass used for comfort, protection, or stuffing; cushion: *We should wear knee pads when roller-skating. n., pl.* **pads.**

pa·ja·mas (pə jä′məz *or* pə jam′əz), garments to sleep or lounge in consisting of a shirt and loose trousers. *n.pl.*

part (pärt), something less than the whole; not all: *He ate part of an apple. n.*

part-time (pärt′tim′), for part of the usual time: *A part-time job helped her finish college. adj.*

par·tial (pär′shəl), not complete; not total: *My parents made a partial payment on our new car. adj.*

par·tic·i·pant (pär tis′ə pənt), person who shares or participates. *n.*

par·ti·cle (pär′tə kəl), a very little bit: *a dust particle in my eye. n.*

par·tic·u·lar (pər tik′yə lər), **1** apart from others; considered separately; single: *That particular chair is already sold.* **2** different from others; unusual; special: *This vacation was of particular importance to her, for she was going to Brazil. He is a particular friend of mine. adj.*

par·tridge (pär′trij), any of several game birds of the United States, such as the quail or bobwhite. *n.*

pass (pas), **1** to go by; move past: *The parade passed.* **2** to hand from one to another: *Please pass the butter.* **3** to move the ball from one player to another: *She passed the soccer ball.* **4** a moving of the ball to another player: *He caught two passes in the game.* **5** a free ticket: *1-3 v.,* **pass·es, passed, pass·ing;** *4, 5 n., pl.,* **pass·es.**
pass out, 1 give out; distribute. **2** INFORMAL. faint; lose consciousness.

past (past), time gone by; time before; what has happened: *forget the past. History is a study of the past. n.*

pat·i·o (pat′ē ō), a terrace for outdoor eating and lounging. *n., pl.* **pat·i·os.**

pave·ment (pāv′mənt), a covering or surface for streets or sidewalks, made of asphalt, concrete, gravel or stones. *n.*

pea·nut but·ter (pē′nut′ but′ər), food made of roasted peanuts ground until soft and smooth. It is spread on bread, crackers, etc.

pe·des·tri·an (pə des′trē ən), person who goes on foot; walker: *The pedestrian's attention was not on the passing car. n.*

pen pal (pen′ pal′), person with whom one corresponds regularly, often in another country and without ever having met.

pen·ta·gon (pen′tə gon), a five-sided polygon. *n.*

peo·ple (pē′pəl), **1** men, women, and children; persons: *There were ten people present.* **2** body of citizens of a state; the public. *1,2 n., pl.* **peo·ple; peo·pled, peo·pling.**

per·cent·age (pər sen′ tij), **1** rate or proportion of each hundred; part of each hundred; percent: *What percentage of children were absent?* **2** part or proportion. *n.*

per·haps (pər haps´), it may be; maybe; possibly: *Perhaps a letter will come to you today. adv.*

per·son (pėr´sən), man, woman, or child; human being: *Any person who wishes may come to the fair. n.*

pet-sit·ter (pet´sit´ər), a person who takes care of pets while the owner is absent: *Being a pet-sitter is an easy way to make extra money in my neighborhood. n.*

Phil·a·del·phi·a (fil´ə del´fē ə), city in SE Pennsylvania, on the Delaware River. *n.* [*Philadelphia* can be traced back to Greek *philos,* meaning "loving," and *adelphos,* meaning "brother."]

pi·an·o (pē an´ō), a large musical instrument whose tones come from many wires. The wires are sounded by hammers that are worked by striking keys on a keyboard. *n., pl.* **pi·an·os.**

pic·ture (pik´chər), a drawing, painting, portrait, or photograph; print of any of these: *Our math books contain many pictures. n., pl.* **pic·tures.**

piece (pēs), one of the parts into which a thing is divided or broken; bit: *The cup broke in pieces. n.*
go to pieces, 1 fall apart; break up: *Another ship had gone to pieces on the rocks.* **2** break down; collapse: *When her business failed, she went completely to pieces.*
piece of one's mind, a scolding: *I gave them a piece of my mind for coming late again.*

pierce (pirs), make a hole in; bore into or through: *A nail pierced the tire of our car. v.*

pi·o·neer (pī´ə nir´), person who settles in a part of a country, preparing it for others: *The pioneers of the American West included trappers, explorers, and farming families. n.*

Pitts·burgh (pits´bėrg´), city in SW Pennsylvania, a center of the iron and steel industry. *n.*

plan·et (plan´it), one of the heavenly bodies (except comets and meteors) that move around the sun in nearly circular paths. Mercury, Venus, Earth, Mars, Jupiter, Saturn, Uranus, Neptune, and Pluto are planets. *n.*

plan·e·tar·i·um (plan´ə târ´ē əm), **1** apparatus that shows the movements of the sun, moon, planets, and stars by projecting lights on the inside of a dome. **2** room or building with such an apparatus. *n., pl.* **plan·e·tar·i·ums, plan·e·tar·i·a** (plan´ə târ´ē ə).

plant (plant), a living thing that has leaves, roots, and a soft stem, and is small in contrast with a tree or shrub: *a tomato plant, a houseplant. n.*

pla·teau (pla tō´), plain in the mountains or at a height considerably above sea level; large, high plain; tableland. *n., pl.* **pla·teaus** (pla tōz).

pleas·ant (plez´nt), that pleases; giving pleasure; agreeable: *a pleasant swim on a hot day. adj.*

please (plēz), **1** be agreeable to: *Toys please children.* **2** be agreeable: *Such a fine meal cannot fail to please. v.,* **pleased, pleas·ing.**
be pleased, be moved to pleasure; happy: *I was pleased with my new book.*

plumb·ing (plum´ing), the water pipes and fixtures in a building: *bathroom plumbing. n.*

poi·son (poi´zn), **1** substance very dangerous to life and health. Arsenic and lead are both poisons. **2** kill or harm by poison. **1** *n.,* **2** *v.*

pol·i·ti·cian (pol´ə tish´ən), person who gives much time to political affairs; person who is experienced in politics. *n.*

pol·i·tics (pol´ə tiks), management of political affairs; the science and art of government: *Our senior senator has been engaged in politics for many years. n. sing. or pl.*

planet

the **planet** Saturn

a	hat	**ī**	ice	**u̇**	put		**ə** stands for	
ā	age	**o**	not	**ü**	rule	**a**	in about	
ä	far, calm	**ō**	open	**ch**	child	**e**	in taken	
âr	care	**ȯ**	saw	**ng**	long	**i**	in pencil	
e	let	**ô**	order	**sh**	she	**o**	in lemon	
ē	equal	**oi**	oil	**th**	thin	**u**	in circus	
ėr	term	**ou**	out	**ᴛн**	then			
i	it	**u**	cup	**zh**	measure			

pol·lute (pə lüt′), make dirty; defile: *The water at the beach was polluted by refuse.* v., **pol·lut·ed, pol·lut·ing.**

pol·y·gon (pol′ē gon), a closed plane figure with three or more sides and angles. n.

pol·y·he·dron (pol′ē hē′drən), a solid figure made of flat surfaces called *faces.* Each face is a polygon. n.

pop·u·la·tion (pop′yə lā′shən), **1** people of a city, country, or district. **2** the number of people. n.

port·fo·li·o (pôrt fō′lē ō), a portable case for loose papers, drawings, etc.; briefcase. n., pl. **port·fo·li·os.**

Port·land (pôrt′lənd), **1** seaport in SW Maine. **2** seaport in NW Oregon. n.

pos·ses·sion (pə zesh′ən), **1** ownership: *On her 21st birthday she came into possession of 50 thousand dollars.* **2** thing possessed; property: *Please move your possessions from my room.* n.

pos·si·ble (pos′ə bəl), capable of being, being done, or happening: *It is possible to cure tuberculosis. Space travel is now possible.* adj.

post·pone (pōst pōn′), put off till later; put off to a later time; delay: *The picnic was postponed because of rain.* v., **post·poned, post·pon·ing.**

po·ta·to (pə tā′tō), a round or oval, hard, starchy vegetable with thin skin. Potatoes grow underground. n., pl. **po·ta·toes.**

pouch (pouch), bag or sack: *a tobacco pouch.* n., pl. **pouch·es.** —**pouch′like′,** adj.

pow·der (pou′dər), **1** a solid reduced to dust by pounding, crushing, or grinding. **2** some special kind of powder: *face powder, bath powder.* n.

prac·ti·cal (prak′tə kəl), useful: *An outdoor swimming pool is more practical in Florida than in Minnesota.* adj.

prac·tice (prak′tis), skill gained by experience or exercise: *They were out of practice at batting.* n.

prair·ie (prâr′ē), a large area of level or rolling land with grass but few or no trees. n.

prairie

pre·cious (presh′əs), **1** having great value; worth much; valuable. **2** much loved; dear: *a precious child.* 1,2 adj.

pre·cip·i·ta·tion (pri sip′ə tā′shən), something that is precipitated, such as rain, dew, or snow. n.

pre·cook (prē′kük′), cook completely or partially beforehand, for quick heating or final cooking later. v.

pred·a·tor (pred′ə tər), animal or person that preys upon. n.

pre·his·to·ric (prē′hi stôr′ik), of or belonging to times before histories were written: *Prehistoric peoples used stone tools.* adj.

prej·u·dice (prej′ə dis), opinion formed without taking time and care to judge fairly: *a prejudice against foreigners.* n.

pre·ma·ture (prē′mə chùr′, prē′mə tùr′, or prē′mə tyùr′), before the proper time; too soon: *Their arrival an hour before the party began was premature.* adj.

prep·a·ra·tion (prep′ə rā′shən), thing done to get ready: *He made thorough preparations for his trip by carefully planning routes.* n.

pre·pare (pri pâr′), make ready; get ready: *prepare lessons, prepare dinner.* v., **pre·pared, pre·par·ing.**

pre·pay (prē pā′), pay or pay for in advance. v., **pre·paid, pre·pay·ing.**

pre·re·cord (prē′ri kôrd′), record in advance for later use: *The television show was prerecorded on videotape.* v., **pre·re·cord·ed, pre·re·cord·ing.**

pre·school (prē′skül′), before the age of going to regular school, usually from infancy to the age of five or six: *preschool children.* adj.

pres·i·dent (prez′ə dənt, prez′dənt), **1** the chief officer of a company, corporation, college, society, club, etc. **2** Often, **President.** the highest executive officer of a republic. **3** the head of state in certain countries where the prime minister is chief executive. n.

pre·tend (pri tend′), make believe: *Let's pretend that we are grown-ups.* v.

pre·test (prē′test′, prē test′), **1** subject (students) to a preliminary test. **2** a pretesting; preliminary test. 1 v., 2 n.

pre·vent (pri vent′), keep from happening: *Rain prevented the game.* v.

prin·ci·pal (prin′sə pəl), the head of an elementary or middle school: *The principal's office is on the first floor*. *n*.

pris·on·er (priz′n ər), **1** person who is under arrest or held in a jail or prison. **2** person who is confined unwillingly, or who is not free to move. *n*.

prob·a·bly (prob′ə blē), more likely than not. *adv*.

prob·lem (prob′ləm), something to be worked out: *a problem in arithmetic*. *n*.

prod·uct (prod′əkt), thing produced; result of work or of growth: *factory products, farm products*. *n., pl.* **prod·ucts.**

pro·hib·it (prō hib′it), forbid by law or authority. *v*.

proj·ect (proj′ekt), a special assignment planned and carried out by a student, a group of students, or an entire class. *n*.

pro·tec·tion (prə tek′shən), thing or person that prevents damage: *A hat is protection from the sun*. *n*.

pro·ton (prō′ton), a positively charged particle in the nucleus of an atom. *n*.

proud (proud), **1** thinking well of oneself. **2** feeling or showing pleasure or satisfaction: *I am proud to call him my friend*. **3** having respect for oneself, one's position, or one's character: *The family was too proud to ask for charity*. *adj*.

pro·vide (prə vīd′), give what is needed or wanted; supply; furnish: *Sheep provide us with wool*. *v.,* **pro·vid·ed, pro·vid·ing.**

pueb·lo (pweb′lō), an American Indian village built of adobe and stone. There were once many pueblos in the southwestern United States. *n., pl.* **pueb·los.**

pump (pump), draw or force as if from a pump: *pumping one's bicycle pedals as fast as possible*. *v.,* **pumped, pump·ing.**

pump·kin (pump′kin *or* pung′kin), the large, roundish, orange-yellow fruit of a trailing vine, used for making pies, as a vegetable, and for jack-o'-lanterns. *n*.

pun (pun), a humorous use of a word where it can have different meanings; play on words. *n*.

punch line (punch′ līn′), the line or sentence in a story, play, or drama which makes or enforces the point.

pur·pose (pėr′pəs), **1** something one has in mind to get or do; plan; aim; intention. **2** object or end for which a thing is made, done, used, etc. *n*.

purse (pėrs), handbag. *n*.

py·thon (pī′thon), a very large snake of Asia, Africa, and Australia that is related to the boa and kills its prey by squeezing. *n*.

pueblo

a **pueblo** built of adobe

Q

quad·ri·lat·er·al (kwod′rə lat′ər əl), a four-sided polygon. *n*.

quar·rel (kwôr′əl), **1** an angry dispute; a fight with words: *The children had a quarrel over the division of the candy*. **2** fight with words; dispute or disagree angrily: *The two friends quarreled and now they don't speak to each other*. **3** cause for a dispute or disagreement; reason for breaking off friendly relations: *He picks quarrels*. **1,3** *n.,* **2** *v.,* **quar·reled, quar·rel·ing** *or* **quar·relled, quar·rel·ling.**

quar·ter (kwôr′tər), coin of the United States and Canada equal to 25 cents. Four quarters make one dollar. *n*.

ques·tion·naire (kwes′chə nâr′), a written or printed list of questions used to gather information, to obtain a sampling of opinion, etc. *n*.

python

							ə stands for	
a	hat	ī	ice	u̇	put		ə	in about
ā	age	o	not	ü	rule		e	in taken
ä	far, calm	ō	open	ch	child		i	in pencil
âr	care	ȯ	saw	ng	long		o	in lemon
e	let	ô	order	sh	she		u	in circus
ē	equal	oi	oil	th	thin			
ėr	term	ou	out	ᴛʜ	then			
i	it	u	cup	zh	measure			

R

rac·coon (ra kün′), a small, grayish, meat-eating mammal with a bushy, ringed tail, that lives mostly in wooded areas near water, and is active at night. *n.*

ra·di·a·tion (rā′dē ā′shən), particles or electromagnetic waves given off by the atoms and molecules of a radioactive substance as a result of nuclear decay. Radiation is harmful to living tissue. *n.*

ra·di·o (rā′dē ō), 1 apparatus for sending or receiving and making audible the sound signals sent in this way. 2 transmit or send out by radio. *1 n., pl.* **ra·di·os;** *2 v.,* **ra·di·oed, ra·di·o·ing.**

rail·road (rāl′rōd′), road or track with parallel steel rails on which the wheels of the cars go. Engines pull trains on railroads. *n., pl.* **rail·roads.**

raise (rāz), lift up; put up: *raise the flag. Children in school raise their hands to answer a question. v.,* **raised, rais·ing.**

ram (ram), 1 a male sheep. 2 butt against; strike head on; strike violently: *One ship rammed the other ship. 1 n., 2 v.,* **rammed, ram·ming.**

ranch (ranch), a large farm with grazing land, used for raising cattle, sheep, or horses. *n., pl.* **ranch·es.**

rat·tle·snake (rat′l snāk′), a poisonous American snake with a thick body and a broad, triangular head, that makes a rattling or buzzing noise with its tail. *n.*

re·ac·tion (rē ak′shən), action in response to some influence or force: *Our reaction to a joke is to laugh. The doctor observed carefully the patient's reactions to certain tests. n.*

re·al·ize (rē′ə līz), understand clearly; be fully aware of: *I realize how hard you worked. v.,* **re·al·ized, re·al·iz·ing.**

re·al·ly (rē′ə lē), 1 actually; truly; in fact: *Try to see things as they really are. 2 indeed: Oh, really? adv.*

rea·son·a·ble (rē′zn ə bəl), 1 according to reason; sensible; not foolish. 2 not asking too much; fair; just. *adj.*

re·as·sure (rē′ə shùr′), 1 restore to confidence: *The crew's calmness during the storm reassured the passengers.* 2 assure again or anew. *v.,* **re·as·sured, re·as·sur·ing.**

re·ceive (ri sēv′), take (something offered or sent): take into one's hands or possession: *receive gifts. v.*

re·cord (ri kôrd′ *for* 1; rek′ərd *for* 2), 1 set down in writing so as to keep for future use: *Listen to the speaker and record what she says.* 2 an official written account: *Our secretary kept good records of our meetings. 1 v., 2 n., pl.* **re·cords.**

re·cy·cle (rē sī′kəl), to process or treat (something) in order that it may be used again. Paper, aluminum, and glass products are commonly recycled. *v.,* **re·cy·cled, re·cy·cling.**

re·fer (ri fėr′), 1 send or direct for information, help, or action: *Our teacher refers us to many good books.* 2 hand over; submit: *Let's refer the dispute to the umpire.* 3 turn for information or help: *A person refers to a dictionary to find the meaning of words. v.,* **re·ferred, re·fer·ring.**

ref·er·ence point (ref′ər əns point′), When estimating, a number used for comparison with other numbers.

re·frig·e·ra·tor (ri frij′ə rā′tər), box, room, etc., that keeps foods and other items cool, usually by mechanical means. *n.*

rein·deer (rān′dir′), a kind of large deer with branching antlers that lives in northern regions. It is used to pull sleighs and also for meat, milk, and hides. *n., pl.* **rein·deer.** [*Reindeer* came into English about 600 years ago from Icelandic *hreindyri.*]

re·ject (ri jekt′), 1 refuse to take: *She rejected our help.* 2 throw away as useless or unsatisfactory: *Reject all apples with soft spots. v.*

re·jec·tion (ri jek′shən), a rejecting or a being rejected: *The inspector ordered the rejection of the faulty parts. n.*

re·mote control (rə mōt′ kon trōl′), control from a distance of a machine, operation, etc., usually by electrical impulses or radio signals: *Some model airplanes can be flown by remote control.*

recycle

A community **recycles** products.

reindeer

reindeer on a snowy mountain

re·new·a·ble re·sourc·es (ri nü′ə bəl ri sôrs′ez), resource that cannot be used up.

re·pair (ri pâr′), put in good condition again; mend: *He repairs shoes. v.*

re·peat (ri pēt′), **1** do or make again: *repeat an error.* **2** say again: *repeat a word for emphasis. v.*

rep·re·sent·a·tive (rep′ ri zen′tə tiv), person appointed or elected to act or speak for others. *n.*

re·quire·ment (ri kwīr′mənt), **1** a need; thing needed: *Patience is a requirement in teaching.* **2** a demand; thing demanded: *fulfill the requirements for graduation. n.*

re·search (ri sėrch′ *or* rē′sėrch′), **1** a careful hunting for facts or truth; inquiry; investigation: *cancer research.* **2** to hunt for facts or truth; inquire; investigate. 1 *n.*, 2 *v.*, **re·searched, re·search·ing.**

res·i·dent (rez′ə dənt), person living in a place permanently; dweller: *The residents of the town are proud of their new library. n.*

re·source (ri sôrs′ *or* rē′sôrs), any supply that will meet a need. We have resources of money, of knowledge, of strength, etc. *n.*

re·spect (ri spekt′), high regard; honor; esteem: *The children always showed great respect for their grandparents. n.*

re·spect·ful (ri spekt′fəl), showing respect; considerate and polite. *adj.* —**re·spect′ful·ly,** *adv.*

re·spec·tive·ly (ri spek′tiv lē), as regards each of several persons or things in turn or in the order mentioned: *Pat, José, and Kathy are 16, 18, and 20 years old, respectively. adv.*

re·spon·si·ble (ri spon′sə bəl), **1** obliged or expected to account for; accountable; answerable: *You are responsible for the care of your schoolbooks.* **2** deserving credit or blame: *Rain was responsible for the small attendance. adj.*

re·turn (ri tėrn′), go back; come back: *Return home at once. My cousin will return this summer. v.,* **re·turned, re·turn·ing.**

re·vers·i·ble (ri vėr′sə bəl), **1** able to be reversed; able to reverse. **2** (of a fabric, etc.) finished on both sides so that it can be worn with either side showing. *adj.*

rhythm (riŦH′əm), movement with a regular repetition of a beat, accent, rise and fall, or the like: *the rhythm of dancing, the rhythm of the tides, the rhythm of one's heartbeats. n.*

rice (rīs), the starchy grain of a kind of cereal grass, or the plant that it grows on. Rice is grown in warm climates and is an important food in India, China, and Japan. *n.*

rid·dle (rid′l), a puzzling question, statement, problem, etc. EXAMPLE: *When is a door not a door?* ANSWER: *When it is ajar. n.*

ridge (rij), a long, narrow chain of hills or mountains: *The Blue Ridge of the Appalachian Mountains is a magnificent sight. n.*

right (rīt), proper; suitable; fitting: *Learn to say the right thing at the right time. adj.*

right tri·an·gle (trī′ang′əl), a triangle with one right angle.

ring¹ (ring), **1** a circle: *You can tell the age of a tree by counting the number of rings in its wood; one ring grows every year. We danced in a ring.* **2** a thin circle of metal or other material: *a napkin ring, a wedding ring, a key ring. n.*

ring² (ring), give forth a clear sound, as a bell does: *Did the telephone ring? v.,* **rang** (rang), **rung** (rung), **ring·ing.**

rise (rīz), **1** get up from a lying, sitting, or kneeling position; stand up: *Please rise from your seat when you recite.* **2** a going up; a going higher: *a rise in prices. We watched the rise of the balloon.* 1 *v.,* **rose** (rōz), **ris·en** (riz′n), **ris·ing;** 2 *n.*

research (def. 1)
research in the laboratory

ridge
a mountain **ridge**

a	hat	**ī**	ice	**u̇**	put	**ə** *stands for*	
ā	age	**o**	not	**ü**	rule	**a**	in about
ä	far, calm	**ō**	open	**ch**	child	**e**	in taken
âr	care	**ȯ**	saw	**ng**	long	**i**	in pencil
e	let	**ô**	order	**sh**	she	**o**	in lemon
ē	equal	**oi**	oil	**th**	thin	**u**	in circus
ėr	term	**ou**	out	**ŦH**	then		
i	it	**u**	cup	**zh**	measure		

risk (risk), **1** chance of harm or loss; danger: *If you drive carefully, there is no risk of being fined.* **2** expose to the chance of harm or loss: *You risk your neck trying to climb that tree.* **3** take the risk of: *She risked defeat in running against the popular candidate.* 1 *n.,* 2,3 *v.*

road map (rōd´ map´), map for automobile travel, showing the roads in a region and the distances between cities and towns. *n., pl.* **road maps.**

rock·et (rok´it), **1** device consisting of a tube open at one end in which an explosive or fuel is rapidly burned. The fuel creates gases that escape from the open end and force the tube and whatever is attached to it upward or forward. **2** spacecraft, missile, etc., propelled by such a device. **3** go like a rocket; rise very fast; skyrocket: *rocket across the finish line in a race. The author rocketed to fame when her book was published.* 1,2 *n.,* 3 *v.*

rocket (def. 2)

ro·de·o (rō´dē ō *or* rō dā´ō), **1** a contest or exhibition of skill in roping cattle, riding horses and steers, etc. **2** (in the western United States) the driving of cattle together. *n., pl.* **ro·de·os.**

rol·ler skates (rō´lər skāts´), shoes or metal bases with four small wheels, used for skating on a floor, sidewalk, or other surface.

roof (rüf *or* rùf), the top covering of a building: *The roofs of all the houses had red tiles. n., pl.* **roofs.**

round·ing (roun´ding), expressing numbers to the nearest 10, 100, or 1,000. *In rounding to the nearest 10, 97 would become 100. v.*

round·up (round´up´), **1** act of driving or bringing cattle together from long distances. **2** the people and horses that do this. **3** any similar gathering: *a roundup of old friends. n., pl.* **round·ups.**

rum·bling (rum´bling), a deep, heavy, continuous sound: *We could hear the rumbling of the trains passing overhead. n.*

sampan

sampan on the water

S

sac·ri·fice (sak´rə fīs), **1** a giving up of one thing for another: *Our teacher does not approve of any sacrifice of studies to sports.* **2** give up: *sacrifice one's savings to help the homeless.* 1 *n.,* 2 *v.,* **sac·ri·ficed, sac·ri·fic·ing.**

sad·dle (sad´l), seat for a rider on a horse's back, on a bicycle, etc. *n.*

safe·ty (sāf´tē), a being safe; freedom from harm or danger: *A bank assures safety for your money. You can cross the street in safety when the green light is on. n.*

said (sed), past tense and past participle of **say.** *He said he would come. They had said "No" every time.*

sail·or (sā´lər), **1** person whose work is handling a boat or other vessel. **2** member of a ship's crew who is not an officer. *n.*

sam·pan (sam´pan), a type of small boat used in China and Japan. A sampan often has a single sail and a cabin made of mats. *n., pl.* **sam·pans.** [*Sampan* comes from Chinese *san pan.*]

sam·ple (sam´pəl), part of a group upon which an experiment or survey is conducted. *n.*

sand·wich (sand´wich), two or more slices of bread with meat, jelly, cheese, or some other filling between. *n.* [*Sandwich* was named for the fourth Earl of *Sandwich,* 1718–1792, a British official who supposedly invented it so that he would not have to leave a card game to eat.]

San Fran·cis·co (san´ frən sis´kō), large seaport in W California.

sat·is·fy (sat´i sfī), **1** give enough to; fulfill (desires, hopes, demands, etc.); put an end to (needs, wants, etc.): *He satisfied his hunger with a sandwich and milk.* **2** make contented; please: *Are you satisfied now? v.,* **sat·is·fied, sat·is·fy·ing.**

sau·sage (sò´sij), chopped pork, beef, or other meats, seasoned and usually stuffed into a very thin casing. *n.*

sax·o·phone (sak/sə fōn), a woodwind instrument having a curved metal body with keys for the fingers and a mouthpiece with a single reed. n. [Saxophone was formed in French from the name of its Belgian inventor, Adolphe Sax, 1814–1894, and Greek phōnē, meaning "sound."]

say (sā), 1 speak; utter: What did you say? "Thank you," she said. 2 put into words; express; declare: Say what you think. v., said, say·ing.

scar (skär), the mark left by a healed cut, wound, burn, or sore. n.

schol·ar (skol/ər), 1 a learned person; person having much knowledge: The professor was a famous scholar. 2 pupil at school; learner; a student who gets scholarship. n.

school¹ (skül), 1 place for teaching and learning: Children go to school to study. 2 of a school or schools: Our school playground is very large. 1 n., 2 adj.

school² (skül), a large number of the same kind of fish or water animals swimming together: a school of mackerel. n.

sci·en·tif·ic meth·od (sī/ən tif/ik meth/əd), an orderly method used in scientific research, generally consisting in identifying a problem, gathering the data, forming a hypothesis, performing experiments, interpreting the results, and drawing a conclusion.

sci·en·tif·ic name (sī/ən tif/ik nām/), the name, usually in Latin, by which a species of plants or animals is known by scientists. Tigris is the scientific name for tiger.

scoop (sküp), 1 tool like a small shovel, having a short handle and a deep, hollow part for dipping out things. 2 take up or out with a scoop, or as a scoop does: Scoop out a quart of grain. The children scooped up the snow with their hands to make snowballs. 1 n., 2 v.

scrub·ber (skrub/ər), a device for removing ashes from smoke. n., pl. **scrub·bers.**

scu·ba div·ing (skü/bə dī ving), a sport in which portable tanks of compressed air are strapped to a diver's back. A hose and mouthpiece with valves regulate the air. [Scuba is formed by using the first letters of the words self contained underwater breathing apparatus.]

sea·coast (sē/kōst/), land along the sea; coast: the seacoast of Maine. n.

se·cede (si sēd/), withdraw formally from an organization. v., **se·ced·ed, se·ced·ing.**

sec·re·tar·y (sek/rə ter/ē), a person who writes letters and keeps records for a person, company, or club: There are five secretaries in my mother's office. n., pl. **sec·re·tar·ies.**

sec·tion·al·ism (sek/shə nə liz/əm), too great regard for sectional interests; sectional prejudice or hatred. n.

seg·ment (seg/mənt), 1 (in geometry) part of a circle cut off by a straight line. 2 line segment. 3 divide into segments. 1,2 n., 3 v. [Segment comes from Latin segmentum and secare, meaning "to cut."]

se·lec·tion (si lek/shən), act of selecting; choice: His selection of a hat took a long time. The shop offered a very good selection of hats. n.

Sen·ate (sen/it), the upper house of Congress or of a state legislature. n.

sense (sens), 1 power of an organism to know what happens outside itself. Sight, hearing, touch, taste, and smell are senses. 2 understanding; judgment. n., pl. **sens·es.**

sen·si·ble (sen/sə bəl), having or showing good sense or judgment; wise: She is too sensible to do anything foolish. adj.

saxophone

seacoast
a splendid **seacoast**

a	hat	ī	ice	u̇	put	**ə stands for**	
ā	age	o	not	ü	rule	a	in about
ä	far, calm	ō	open	ch	child	e	in taken
âr	care	ȯ	saw	ng	long	i	in pencil
e	let	ô	order	sh	she	o	in lemon
ē	equal	oi	oil	th	thin	u	in circus
ėr	term	ou	out	ᴛʜ	then		
i	it	u	cup	zh	measure		

sen·ti·nel (sen′tə nəl), person stationed to keep watch and guard against surprise attacks. *n.* [*Sentinel* is from French *sentinelle,* which comes from Italian *sentinella,* and can be traced back to Latin *sentire,* meaning "to perceive, to feel."]

serv·ant (sér′vənt), person employed in a household, such as a cook or maid. *n.*

set·ting (set′ing), place, time, etc., of a play or story. *n.*

set·tle (set′l), **1** take up residence (in a new country or place): *settle in New York.* **2** establish colonies in; colonize: *The English settled New England. v.,* **set·tled, set·tling.**

sew·age (sü′ij), the waste matter that passes through sewers. *n.*

sham·poo (sham pü′), **1** wash (the hair, the scalp, a rug, etc.) with a soapy or oily preparation. **2** the preparation used in this way. *1 v., 2 n.* [*Shampoo* comes from Hindustani *chāmpō,* meaning "press, squeeze."]

share (shâr), **1** use together; enjoy together; have in common: *The sisters are sharing the same room.* **2** divide into parts, each taking a part: *The child shared his candy with his sister. v.,* **shared, shar·ing.**

shell (shel), **1** the hard outside covering of certain animals. Oysters, turtles, and beetles all have shells. **2** separate (grains of corn) from the cob. **3** fire cannon at; bombard with shells: *The enemy shelled the town.* 1 *n.,* 2,3 *v.*

shell out, INFORMAL. hand over (money); pay out: *We had to shell out five dollars for the movie.*

sher·bet (shér′bet), a frozen dessert made of fruit juice, sugar, and water or milk. *n.* [*Sherbet* is from Turkish *şerbet,* which came from Arabic *sharbat,* meaning "a drink."]

she's (shēz; *unstressed* shiz), **1** she is. **2** she has.

ship (ship), **1** any large vessel for travel on water, such as a steamship, frigate, or galley. **2** send or carry from one place to another by a ship, train, truck, etc.: *Did you ship it by express or by freight?* 1 *n.,* 2 *v.,* **shipped, ship·ping.**

ship·build·ing (ship′bil′ding), the designing or building of ships. *n.*

should've (shùd′əv), should have.

shriek (shrēk), a loud, sharp, shrill sound: *We heard the shriek of the engine's whistle. n.*

shrink (shringk), become smaller: *My wool sweater shrank when it was washed. When his influence shrank, his wealth also decreased. v.,* **shrank** (shrangk) or **shrunk** (shrungk), **shrunk** or **shrunken** (shrung′kən), **shrinking.**

shut·tle (shut′l), **1** move quickly to and fro. **2** bus, train, airplane, etc., that runs back and forth regularly over a short distance. 1 *v.,* **shut·tled, shut·tling;** 2 *n.*

side·burns (sid′bérnz′), whiskers in front of the ears, especially when the chin is shaved. *n. pl.* [*Sideburns* is a different form of *burnsides,* which were named for Ambrose E. Burnside, 1824–1881, a Union general in the Civil War, who wore such whiskers.]

side·walk (sīd′wok′), place to walk at the side of a street, usually paved. *n.*

sign (sīn), an inscribed board, space, etc., serving for advertisement, information, etc.: *See the sign over the door. The sign reads, "Keep off the grass." n.*

sig·nal (sig′nəl), **1** a sign giving notice, warning, or pointing out something: *A red light is a signal of danger. A siren is used as a fire signal. The raising of the flag was a signal to advance.* **2** make a signal or signals to: *She signaled the car to stop by raising her hand.* 1 *n.,* 2 *v.,* **sig·naled, sig·nal·ing** or **sig·nalled, sig·nal·ling.**

sig·na·ture (sig′nə chər), a person's name written by that person. *n.*

sil·ver·ware (sil′vər wâr′), silver things; utensils or dishes made of or plated with silver. *n.*

Sioux (sü), an American Indian tribe living on the plains of the northern United States and southern Canada. *n.*

si·ren (sī′rən), **1** kind of whistle that makes a loud, piercing sound: *We heard the sirens of the fire engines.* **2** (in Greek myths) any of a group of nymphs who, by their sweet singing, lured sailors to destruction upon the rocks. *n., pl.* **si·rens.**

silverware

silverware for the table

sis·ter (sis′tər), daughter of the same parents: *I borrowed my sister's sweater. n.*

skate·board (skāt′bôrd′), a narrow board resembling a surfboard, with roller-skate wheels attached to each end, used for gliding or moving on any hard surface. *n.*

skel·e·ton (skel′ə tən), **1** the framework of bones in a body that supports the muscles, organs, etc. **2** frame: *the steel skeleton of a building. n.*

skill·ful (skil′fəl), **1** having skill; expert: *a skillful surgeon.* **2** showing skill: *a skillful piece of bricklaying. adj.* Also, **skilful.** —**skill′ful·ly,** *adv.* —**skill′ful·ness,** *n.*

skin·ny (skin′ē), very thin; very lean. *adj.,* **skin·ni·er, skin·ni·est.**

skunk (skungk), a black, bushy-tailed mammal of North America, usually with white stripes along its back. It is about the size of a cat. When frightened, skunks squirt a spray with strong, unpleasant smell from glands near the tail. *n.*

slaugh·ter (slȯ′tər), **1** the killing of an animal or animals for food; butchering: *the slaughter of a steer, to fatten hogs for slaughter.* **2** brutal killing; much or needless killing: *The battle resulted in a frightful slaughter. n.*

slav·er·y (slā′vər ē), custom of owning slaves. Where slavery is permitted, certain people own other people. *n.*

slay (slā), kill with violence: *Jack slew the giant. v.,* **slew** (slü), **slain** (slān), **slay·ing. —slay′er,** *n.*

sleigh (slā), carriage or cart mounted on runners for use on ice or snow. In northern countries people use sleighs in the winter. *n.* [*Sleigh* comes from Dutch *slee.*]

slide (slīd), **1** to slip as when losing one's foothold: *The car slid into the ditch.* **2** a smooth surface for sliding on: *The frozen brook makes a good slide.* 1 *v.,* **slid** (slid), **slid·ing;** 2 *n.*

slope (slōp), any line, surface, land, etc., that goes up or down at an angle: *If you roll a ball up a slope, it will roll down again. n.*

small (smȯl), not large; little; not large as compared with other things of the same kind: *A cottage is a small house. adj.*

smear (smir), a mark or stain left by smearing: *There are smears of paint on the wallpaper. n.*

smith (smith), **1** worker in metal, especially iron. **2** blacksmith. *n.*

smoke de·tec·tor (smōk′ də tek′ tər), an alarm that sounds when there is too much smoke in an area.

snake·skin (snāk′skin′), leather made from the skin of a snake. *n.*

snow·ball (snō′bȯl), ball made of snow pressed together. *n.*

so·lar (sō′lər), of the sun: *solar energy, a solar eclipse. adj.*

solar energy (sō′lər en′ər jē), radiant energy from the sun.

sol·id waste (sol′id wāst′), garbage and trash that is buried in landfills.

solve (solv), find the answer to; clear up; explain: *The detective solved the mystery. He has solved all the problems in the lesson. v.,* **solved, solv·ing.**

some·one (sum′wun), some person; somebody: *Someone is coming. pron.*

some·thing (sum′thing), some thing; a particular thing not named or known: *I'm sure I've forgotten something. She has something on her mind. n.*

some·times (sum′tīmz), now and then; at times: *She comes to visit sometimes. adv.*

sor·ry (sor′ē or sôr′ē), feeling pity, regret, sympathy; sad: *I am sorry that you are sick. We are sorry that we cannot come to the party. adj.*

soup du jour (süp′ də zhür′), soup of the day.

South Car·o·li·na (south′ kar′ə lī′nə), one of the southeastern states of the United States. *Abbreviation:* S.C. or SC *Capital:* Columbia.

sleigh
sleigh pulled by horses

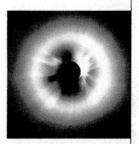

solar
total **solar** eclipse

a	hat	**ī**	ice	**ů**	put	**ə** stands for	
ā	age	**o**	not	**ü**	rule	**a**	in about
ä	far, calm	**ō**	open	**ch**	child	**e**	in taken
âr	care	**ȯ**	saw	**ng**	long	**i**	in pencil
e	let	**ô**	order	**sh**	she	**o**	in lemon
ē	equal	**oi**	oil	**th**	thin	**u**	in circus
ėr	term	**ou**	out	**ᴛʜ**	then		
i	it	**u**	cup	**zh**	measure		

sou·ve·nir (sü′və nir′ or sü′və nir), something given or kept for remembrance; a remembrance; keepsake. *n.*

spa·ghet·ti (spə get′ē), long, slender sticks made of a mixture of flour and water. Spaghetti is cooked by boiling in water. *n.*

spare (spâr), get along without; do without: *Mother couldn't spare the car, so father and I had to take the bus. v.,* **spared, spar·ing.**

spe·cies (spē′shēz), group of animals or plants that have certain characteristics in common and are able to interbreed. A species ranks next below a genus. The lion is one species of cat. *n.*

speech (spēch), a public talk: *We heard many speeches at the meeting. n., pl.* **speech·es.**

speed·om·e·ter (spē dom′ə tər), instrument to indicate the speed of an automobile or other vehicle, and often the distance traveled. *n.*

spi·der (spī′dər), a small animal with eight legs, no wings, and a body divided into two parts. Many spiders spin webs to catch insects for food. *n.*

spill (spil), let (liquid or loose matter) run or fall: *My father spilled a whole carton of milk. v.,* **spilled** or **spilt** (spilt), **spill·ing.**

spin (spin), **1** draw out and twist (cotton, flax, wool, etc.) into thread. **2** make (thread, yarn, etc.) by drawing out and twisting cotton, wool, flax, etc. *v.,* **spun** (spun), **spin·ning.**

spin·ach (spin′ich), the green leaves of a garden plant, cooked and eaten as a vegetable, or used uncooked in a salad. *n.*

splash·down (splash′doun′), the landing of a capsule or other spacecraft in the ocean after reentry. *n.*

spoil (spoil), damage or injure (something) so as to make it unfit or useless; ruin; destroy: *I spoiled two pieces of paper while trying to write a neat letter. The rain spoiled the picnic. v.*

sponge (spunj), a water animal having a tough, elastic skeleton with many pores. Most sponges live in large colonies on the bottom of the ocean, attached to stones, plants, etc. *n.*

stair·way (stâr′wā′), way up and down by stairs; a flight or flights of stairs: *the back stairway. n.*

starve (stärv), **1** die because of hunger. **2** suffer severely because of hunger. *v.,* **starved, starv·ing.**

stat·ue (stach′ü), image of a person or animal carved in stone or wood, cast in bronze, or modeled in clay or wax: *Nearly every city has a statue of some famous person. n.*

steam·boat (stēm′bōt′), boat moved by steam. *n.*

sting (sting), **1** to wound with a sharp-pointed part. **2** a wound caused by stinging: *The wasp sting began to swell.* **1** *v.,* **2** *n.*

stop (stop), **1** keep from moving, doing, or working: *I stopped the clock.* **2** stay; halt: *She stopped at the bank on her way home. v.,* **stopped, stop·ping.**

stran·ger (strān′jer), person not known, seen, or heard of before: *She is a stranger to us. n.*

strat·e·gy (strat′ə jē), the skillful planning and management of anything. *n., pl.* **strat·e·gies.**

strength·en (strengk′thən), make or grow stronger: *Exercise strengthens muscles. v.*

strike (strīk), **1** stop work to get better pay, shorter hours, etc.: *The coal miners struck when the company refused to improve safety conditions in the mines.* **2** such a stopping of work: *The workers were home for six weeks during the strike last year.* **1** *v.,* **struck** (struk), **struck** or **strick·en** (strik′ən), **strik·ing; 2** *n.*

strong (strông), having much force or power: *A strong person can lift heavy things. A strong wind blew down the trees. A strong nation has many able citizens and great resources. adj.,* **strong·er** (strông′gər), **strong·est** (strông′gist).

stu·dent (stüd′nt or styüd′nt), person who is studying in a school, college, or university: *That high school has 3000 students. n., pl.* **stu·dents.**

stum·ble (stum′bəl), trip by striking the foot against something: *He stumbled over the stool in the dark kitchen. v.,* **stum·bled, stum·bling.**

style (stīl), manner; method; way: *the Gothic style of architecture. She learned several styles of swimming. n.*

splashdown

the **splashdown** of Apollo 11

steamboat

steamboat moving down the river

sub·ject (sub′jikt), something thought about, discussed, investigated, etc.: *The subject for our composition was "An Exciting Moment."* n.

sub·ur·ban (sə bėr′bən), of a suburb; in a suburb: *We have excellent suburban train service.* adj.

suc·ceed (sək sēd′), turn out well; do well; have success: *Her plans succeeded.* v.

sug·gest (səg jest′), put forward; propose: *She suggested a swim, and we all agreed.* v.

sun·flow·er (sun′flou′ər), a tall plant related to the aster, having large yellow flowers with brown centers. Its seeds are used as food and to produce oil for cooking. n.

sun·set (sun′set′), the time when the sun last appears; the close of day. n.

sun·tan (sun′tan′), the reddish-brown color of a person's skin tanned by the sun or by a sunlamp. n.

sup·posed (sə pōzd′), accepted as true; considered as possible or probable; assumed: *The supposed beggar was really a prince.* adj.

Su·preme Court (sə prēm′ kôrt′), the highest court in the United States, which meets at Washington, D.C. It is made up of a chief justice and eight associate justices.

sur·face (sėr′fis), any face or side of a thing: *A cube has six surfaces.* n.

sur·ren·der (sə ren′dər), give up; give (oneself or itself) up; yield: *The town surrendered to the enemy. They surrendered themselves to bitter grief.* v.

sur·round (sə round′), form an enclosure around; encircle: *They surrounded the invalid with every comfort.* v.

sur·vey (sėr vā′), look over; view; examine: *The buyers surveyed the goods offered for sale.* v.

sur·vive (sėr vīv′), live longer than; remain alive after: *He survived his wife by three years. Only ten of the crew survived the shipwreck.* v., **sur·vived, sur·viv·ing.**

swear (swâr), make a solemn statement, appealing to God or some other sacred being or object; take an oath: *A witness at a trial is asked, "Do you swear to tell the truth, the whole truth, and nothing but the truth, so help you God?"* n.

swung (swung), past tense and past participle of **swing.** *She swung her arms as she walked. The door had swung open.* v.

sym·bol (sim′bəl), **1** something that stands for or represents something else. **2** one or two letters that stand for an element's name. n.

sym·pho·ny (sim′fə nē), symphony orchestra: *the Chicago Symphony.* n., pl. **sym·pho·nies.**

T

tal·ent (tal′ənt), a special natural ability: *She has talent for music.* n.

task (task), work to be done; piece of work: *His task is to set the table.* n.

taught (tòt), past tense and past participle of **teach.** *That professor taught my brother. She has taught arithmetic for many years.* v.

teach (tēch), **1** help to learn; show how to do; make understand: *He is teaching his dog tricks.* **2** give instruction to: *She teaches her classes well.* v., **taught, teach·ing.**

ted·dy bear or **Ted·dy bear** (ted′ē bâr′), a child's furry toy bear. [The word **teddy** comes from **Teddy,** a nickname for President Theodore Roosevelt. A cartoon of the time showed him refusing to shoot a bear cub when he was hunting. Soon, stuffed toy animals were being sold that came to be known as "teddy bears."]

tel·e·scope (tel′ə skōp), instrument for making distant objects appear nearer and larger. The stars are studied by means of telescopes. n. [*Telescope* comes from Greek *tēle,* meaning "far," and *skopein,* meaning "look at."]

telescope

a	hat	ī	ice	u̇	put	ə *stands for*	
ā	age	o	not	ü	rule	a	in about
ä	far, calm	ō	open	ch	child	e	in taken
âr	care	ȯ	saw	ng	long	i	in pencil
e	let	ô	order	sh	she	o	in lemon
ē	equal	oi	oil	th	thin	u	in circus
ėr	term	ou	out	ŦH	then		
i	it	u	cup	zh	measure		

tentacle

flexible **tentacles**

tem·per·a·ture (tem′pər ə chər), degree of heat or cold. The temperature of freezing water is 32 degrees Fahrenheit (0 degrees Celsius). *n.*

tense (tens), stretched tight; strained to stiffness: *a tense rope, a face tense with pain. adj.*

ten·sion (ten′shən), **1** a stretching. **2** a stretched condition: *The tension of the bow gives speed to the arrow. n.*

ten·ta·cle (ten′tə kəl), a long, slender, flexible growth on the head or around the mouth of an animal, used to touch, hold, or move; feeler. *n., pl.* **ten·ta·cles.**

te·pee (tē′pē), tent used by the American Indians of the Great Plains, made of hides sewn together and stretched over poles arranged in the shape of a cone. *n., pl.* **te·pees.**

ter·ri·ble (ter′ə bəl), **1** causing great fear; dreadful; awful: *a terrible storm.* **2** INFORMAL. extremely bad; unpleasant: *a terrible temper. adj.*

text·book (tekst′bùk′), book for regular study by pupils. Most books used in schools are textbooks. *n.*

Thanks·giv·ing (thangks giv′ing), day set apart as a holiday to give thanks for past blessings. In the United States, it is the fourth Thursday in November. *n.*

that's (ᴛʜats), that is.

their (ᴛʜâr), of them; belonging to them: *I like their house. adj.*

them·selves (ᴛʜem selvz′ *or* ᴛʜəm selvz′), **1** form of *they* or *them* used to make a statement stronger: *The teachers themselves said the test was too hard.* **2** form used instead of *them* in cases like: *They speak for themselves. They hurt themselves sledding down the hill.* **3** their normal or usual selves: *They are ill and are not themselves today. pron.*

then (ᴛʜen), next in time or place: *First comes spring, then summer. adv.*

the·or·y (thē′ər ē *or* thir′ē), an explanation based on observation and reasoning: *According to one scientific theory of life, the more complicated animals developed from the simpler ones. n.*

there (ᴛʜâr; *unstressed* ᴛʜər), to or into that place: *We are going there tomorrow. adv.*

there's (ᴛʜârz), there is.

there've (ᴛʜârv), there have.

the·sau·rus (thi sôr′əs), **1** dictionary in which synonyms, antonyms, and other related words are classified under certain headings. *n., pl.* **the·sau·rus·es, the·sau·ri** (thi sôr′ī). [*Thesaurus* comes from Latin *thesaurus,* meaning "treasure."]

they (ᴛʜā), the persons, animals, things, or ideas spoken about: *I had three books yesterday. Do you know where they are? They are on the table. pron.*

they're (ᴛʜâr), they are.

thief (thēf), person who steals, especially one who steals secretly and usually without using force: *A thief stole my bicycle. n., pl.* **thieves** (thēvz).

thor·ough·bred (ther′ō bred′), an animal of pure breed or stock. *n.*

though (ᴛʜō), in spite of the fact that: *Though it was pouring, no one went indoors. conj.*

thought (thot), past tense and past participle of **think.** *We thought it would snow yesterday. v.*

threw (thrü), past tense of **throw.** *She threw the ball to me. v.*

through (thrü), from end to end of; from side to side of; between the parts of; from beginning to end of: *march through a town, cut a tunnel through a mountain, drive through a snowstorm. prep.*

through·out (thrü out′), **1** all the way through; through all; in every part of: *The Fourth of July is celebrated throughout the United States.* **2** in every part: *The house is well built throughout.* **1** *prep.,* **2** *adv.*

thumb·tack (thum′tak′), tack with a broad, flat head, that can be pressed into a wall, board, etc., with the thumb. *n.*

ti·ny (tī′nē), very small; wee: *a tiny baby. adj.,* **ti·ni·er, ti·ni·est.**

to (tü; *unstressed* tù *or* tə), **1** in the direction of; toward a destination: *She came to work yesterday.* **2** as far as; until: *rotten to the core, faithful to the end.* **3** *To* is used with verbs. *I like to play the piano.* **4** *To* is used to show action toward. *Give the present to him. prep.*

to·bac·co (tə bak′ō), the prepared leaves of certain related plants, used for smoking or chewing or as snuff. *n.*

to·day or **to-day** (tə dā′), **1** this day; the present time: *Have you seen today's newspaper?* **2** on or during this day: *What are you doing today?* 1 *n.*, 2 *adv.*

to·ma·to (tə mā′tō or tə mä′tō), a juicy, red or yellow fruit, eaten as a vegetable. Tomatoes grow on a spreading plant. *n.*, *pl.* **to·ma·toes.** [*Tomato* is from Spanish *tomate*, which came from Nahuatl *tomatl*.]

tomb (tüm), grave, vault, mausoleum, etc., for a dead body, often above ground. *n.*

too (tü), **1** beyond what is desirable, proper, or right; more than enough: *I ate too much.* **2** in addition; also, besides. *adv.*

tooth·brush (tüth′brush′), small brush for cleaning the teeth. *n.*, *pl.* **tooth·brush·es.**

tor·na·do (tôr nā′dō), extremely violent and destructive whirlwind. Tornadoes extend down from a mass of dark clouds as twisting funnels and move over the land in a narrow path. *n.*, *pl.* **tor·na·does** or **tor·na·dos.**

tow·el (tou′əl), piece of cloth or paper for wiping and drying something wet. We have hand towels, face towels, and bath towels. *n.*

tra·che·a (trā′kē ə), the passage by which air is carried from the throat to the lungs; windpipe. *n.*, *pl.* **tra·che·ae** (trā′kē ē′), **tra·che·as.**

track (trak), a double, parallel line of metal rails for cars to run on: *railroad tracks.* *n.*

tract (trakt), stretch of land, water, etc.; area: *a tract of desert land.* *n.*

tra·di·tion (trə dish′ən), a belief, custom, or opinion handed down from parents to children: *The people of every country have many traditions.* *n.*, *pl.* **tra·di·tions.**

trait (trāt), quality of mind or character; distinguishing feature; characteristic: *Courage, love of fair play, and common sense are desirable traits.* *n.*, *pl.* **traits.**

trans·fer (tran sfėr′ or tran′sfėr′), change or move from one person or place to another; hand over: *The clerk was transferred to another department.* *v.*, **trans·ferred, trans·fer·ring.**

treas·ure (trezh′ər), wealth or riches stored up; valuable things: *The pirates buried their treasure along the coast.* *n.*

treas·ur·er (trezh′ər ər), person in charge of money. The treasurer of a club pays its bills. *n.*

treat·ment plant (trēt′mənt plant′), a place where waste matter or sewage is cleaned.

trick·ster (trik′stər), a cheat; deceiver. *n.*

tried (trīd), past tense and past participle of **try.** attempted; made an effort: *I tried to do the work. Have you tried calling again?* *v.*

tro·phy (trō′fē), any prize or cup awarded to a victorious person or team: *Our school basketball team has won many trophies.* *n.*, *pl.* **tro·phies.**

trunk (trungk), an enclosed compartment in an automobile for storing baggage, a spare tire, etc. *n.*

try (trī), **1** make an effort; attempt: *I tried to do the work.* **2** attempt to do or accomplish: *It seems easy until you try it.* *v.*, **tried, try·ing.**

tum·ble (tum′bəl), **1** perform leaps, springs and somersaults. **2** fall headlong: *I tumbled down the stairs.* **3** confusion; disorder: *Her desk was a complete tumble of papers.* 1,2 *v.*, **tum·bled, tum·bling;** 3 *n.*

tur·bine (tėr′bən), a machine with turning, fanlike blades that runs a generator. *n.*, *pl.* **tur·bines.**

tornado
Tornadoes come from storm clouds.

turbine
power plant with **turbine**

a	hat	**ī**	ice	** u̇**	put	**ə** stands for
ā	age	**o**	not	**ü**	rule	**a** in about
ä	far, calm	**ō**	open	**ch**	child	**e** in taken
âr	care	**ȯ**	saw	**ng**	long	**i** in pencil
e	let	**ô**	order	**sh**	she	**o** in lemon
ē	equal	**oi**	oil	**th**	thin	**u** in circus
ėr	term	**ou**	out	**ᴛʜ**	then	
i	it	**u**	cup	**zh**	measure	

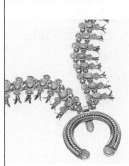

turquoise (def. 1-2)

necklace with **turquoise**

stones

tur·moil (tėr′moil), state of agitation or commotion; disturbance; tumult: *Unexpected guests put us in a turmoil.* *n.*

tur·quoise (tėr′koiz or tėr′kwoiz), **1** a sky-blue or greenish-blue mineral often used as a gem. **2** sky-blue; greenish-blue. 1 *n.*, 2 *adj.* [*Turquoise* came into English about 600 years ago from French (*pierre*) *turquoise*, meaning "Turkish (stone)."]

tu·tor (tü′tər or tyü′tər), **1** a private teacher. **2** teach; instruct individually or privately: *If my math grade doesn't improve, I may need tutoring.* 1 *n.*, 2 *v.*, **tu·tored, tu·tor·ing.**

TV (tē′vē′), television.

type·writ·er (tīp′rī′tər), machine for writing which reproduces letters, figures, etc., similar to printed ones. *n.*

U

um·brel·la (um brel′ə), a light, folding frame covered with cloth or plastic, used as a protection against rain or sun. *n.*

un·a·ble (un ā′bəl), not able: *A newborn baby is unable to walk or talk.* *adj.*

un·a·fraid (un′ə frād′), not fearful, not frightened. *adj.*

un·be·liev·a·ble (un′bi lē′və bəl), not believable; incredible: *an unbelievable lie.* *adj.*

un·buck·le (un buk′əl), unfasten the buckle or buckles of. *v.*, **un·buck·led, un·buck·ling.**

un·cer·tain·ty (un sėrt′n tē), uncertain state or condition; doubt. *n.*, *pl.* **un·cer·tain·ties.**

un·cle (ung′kəl), **1** brother of one's father or mother. **2** husband of one's aunt: *I visited my uncle's business.* *n.*

un·clear (un klir′), not easily seen, heard, or understood; not plain; indistinct: *The meaning of the sentence was unclear.* *adj.*

un·der·stand·a·ble (un′dər stan′də bəl), able to be understood. *adj.*

un·ex·pect·ed (un′ek spek′tid), not expected: *an unexpected difficulty, an unexpected change in the weather.* *adj.*

un·for·tu·nate (un fôr′chə nit), **1** not lucky; having bad luck. **2** an unfortunate person. 1 *adj.*, 2 *n.* —**un·for′tu·nate·ly**, *adv.*

Un·ion (yü′nyən), **1** the United States of America. **2** those states that supported the federal government of the United States during the Civil War. *n.*

un·lim·it·ed (un lim′ə tid), without limits; boundless. *adj.*

un·nec·es·sar·y (un nes′ə ser′ē), not necessary; needless. *adj.*

un·spoiled (un spoild), undamaged; uninjured: *The beauty of that forest is completely unspoiled.* *adj.*

un·sure (un shùr), uncertain; having doubt; not positive: *I am unsure of their guilt.* *adj.*

un·til (un til′), **1** up to the time of: *It was cold from December until April.* **2** up to the time when: *We waited until the sun had set.* *prep.*

up·on (ə pòn′ or ə pon′), on. *prep.*

ur·gent (ėr′jənt), demanding immediate action or attention; pressing; important: *an urgent duty, an urgent message.* *adj.*

u·su·al·ly (yü′zhü ə lē), according to what is usual; commonly; ordinarily; customarily: *We usually eat dinner at 6.* *adv.*

U·tah (yü′tò or yü′tä), one of the western states of the United States. *Abbreviation:* Ut. or UT *Capital:* Salt Lake City. *n.*

V

va·ca·tion (vā kā′shən), freedom from school, business, or other duties: *There is a vacation from school every summer.* *n.* —**va·ca·tion·er**, *n.*

val·ley (val′ē), low land between hills or mountains: *Most large valleys have rivers running through them.* *n.*, *pl.* **val·leys.**

val·u·a·ble (val′yü ə bəl or val′yə bəl), having value; being worth something: *valuable information, a valuable friend.* *adj.*

ven·tri·cle (ven′trə kəl), one of the two chambers of the heart that receive the blood from the auricles and force it into the arteries. *n.*

ver·te·brate (vėr′tə brit *or* vėr′tə brāt), animal that has a backbone. Fishes, amphibians, reptiles, birds, and mammals are vertebrates. *n., pl.* **ver·te·brates.**

ver·tex (vėr′teks), **1** point opposite the base of a triangle, pyramid, etc. **2** the point where the two sides of an angle meet. *n., pl.* **ver·tex·es, ver·ti·ces** (vėr′tə sēz).

vet·er·i·nar·i·an (vet′ər ə ner′ē ən), doctor or surgeon who treats animals. *n.*

ve·to (vē′tō), the right of the president, governor, etc., to reject bills passed by a lawmaking body: *The President has the power of veto over most bills passed in Congress. n., pl.* **ve·toes.**

vid·e·o (vid′ē ō), a musical or other show which can be transmitted by tape through a television set. *n., pl.* **vid·e·os.**

vil·lain (vil′ən), a very wicked person: *The villain stole the money and cast the blame on a friend. n.*

Vir·gin·ia (vər jin′yə), one of the southeastern states of the United States. *Abbreviation:* Va. *or* VA *Capital:* Richmond. *n.*

vol·ley·ball (vol′ē bol′), a ball used in a game of the same name, in which two teams hit the ball back and forth over a net with their hands or forearms without letting it touch the ground. *n.*

vol·un·teer (vol′ən tir′), **1** offer one's services: *She volunteered for the Peace Corps.* **2** to offer of one's own free will: *He volunteered to help.* **3** someone who offers his or her services. 1,2 *v.,* **vol·un·teered, vol·un·teer·ing;** 3 *n.*

vow (vou), **1** a solemn promise: *a vow of secrecy, marriage vows.* **2** make a vow: *I vowed never to leave home again.* 1 *n.,* 2 *v.,* **vowed, vow·ing.**

voy·age (voi′ij), a journey by water; cruise: *We had a pleasant voyage to England. n.*

W

wage (wāj), amount paid for work: *wages of $400 a week. n., pl.* **wag·es.**

waltz (wȯlts), a smooth, even, gliding dance with three beats to a measure. *n.*

want (wănt *or* wȯnt), wish for; wish: *We want a new car. I want to become an engineer. v.*

war (wôr), **1** any fighting or struggle; strife; conflict: *Doctors carry on war against disease.* **2** make war; fight: *to war with an aggressor, to war against poverty.* 1 *n.,* 2 *v.,* **warred, war·ring.**

war·ri·or (wôr′ē ər *or* wor′ē ər), person experienced in fighting battles. *n.* [*Warrior* came into English about 700 years ago from French *werreieor,* and can be traced back to *werre,* meaning "war."]

wash·a·ble (wȧsh′ə bəl *or* wȯ′shə bəl), able to be washed without damage: *washable silk. adj.*

wasp (wȧsp *or* wȯsp), insect related to the ants and the bees, having a slender body, two pairs of wings, and a powerful sting. Hornets and yellow jackets are kinds of wasps. *n.*

watt (wȧt), a unit for measuring power. *n., pl.* **watts.**

wealth·y (wel′thē), having wealth; rich: *She's the wealthiest person in town. adj.,* **wealth·i·er, wealth·i·est.**

weap·on (wep′ən), any object or instrument used in fighting. Swords, spears, arrows, clubs, guns, cannons, and shields are weapons. Animals use claws, horns, teeth, and stings as weapons. *n.*

wear·y (wir′ē), worn out; tired: *weary feet, a weary brain. adj.*

weath·er (weŦH′ər), condition of the atmosphere with respect to temperature, moisture, wind, cloudiness, etc.: *hot weather. The weather is very windy today in Chicago. n.*

veterinarian

volunteer (def. 3)
A **volunteer** helps pass the day.

a	hat	ī	ice	u̇	put	ə stands for	
ā	age	o	not	ü	rule	a	in about
ä	far, calm	ō	open	ch	child	e	in taken
âr	care	ȯ	saw	ng	long	i	in pencil
e	let	ô	order	sh	she	o	in lemon
ē	equal	oi	oil	th	thin	u	in circus
ėr	term	ou	out	ŦH	then		
i	it	u	cup	zh	measure		

went (went), past tense of **go**. *I went home promptly after school. v.*

were (wėr), form of the verb **be** used with *you, we, they* or any plural noun to indicate the past tense. *The officer's orders were obeyed. v.*

we're (wir), we are.

weren't (wėrnt), were not.

we've (wēv), we have.

whal·ing (hwā′ling), the hunting and catching of whales. *n.*

what'll (hwotl or hwutl), what will.

what's (hwots or hwuts), what is: *What's the latest news?*

when (hwen), at the time that: *Stand up when your name is called. adv.*

where (hwâr), **1** in what place; at what place: *Where do you live? Where is he?* **2** in which; at which: *That is the house where I was born.* 1 *adv.,* 2 *conj.*

wheth·er (hweTH′ər), Whether is used in expressing a choice or an alternative. *It matters little whether we go or stay. conj.*

which (hwich), **1** *Which* is used in connecting a group of words with some word in the sentence. *Read the book which you have (pron.). Be careful which way you turn (adj.).* **2** the one that; any that: *Here are three boxes. Which do you like best?* 1,2 *pron.,* 1 *adj.*

whis·tle (hwis′əl), make a clear, shrill sound by forcing breath through one's teeth or pursing one's lips: *He was whistling a tune. v.,* **whis·tled, whis·tling.**

who'd (hüd), **1** who would. **2** who had.

whole (hōl), full; entire: *We worked the whole day. adj.*

who's (hüz), **1** who is. **2** who has.

who've (hüv), who have.

width (width), how wide a thing is; distance across; breadth: *The room is 12 feet in width. n.*

wind·mill (wind′mil), a mill or machine worked by the action of the wind upon a wheel of vanes or sails mounted on a tower. Windmills are mostly used to pump water. *n., pl.* **wind·mills.**

wind·pipe (wind′pīp′), the passage by which air is carried from the throat to the lungs; trachea. *n.*

wind·shield (wind′shēld′), sheet of glass, etc., to keep off the wind. *n.*

witch (wich), woman supposed to be under the influence of supernatural spirits and to have magic powers in order to do evil. *n.*

windmill

wrestling
students in a **wrestling** match

with·out (wiTH out′ or with out′), with no; not having; free from; lacking: *A cat walks without noise. prep.*

wom·an (wum′ən), an adult female. When a girl grows up she becomes a woman: *a woman's size 8 shoe, the women's tennis finals. n., pl.* **wom·en** (wim′ən).

worm (wėrm), **1** a small, slender, crawling or creeping animal. Most worms have soft bodies and no legs. **2** move like a worm; crawl or creep like a worm. 1 *n.,* 2 *v.*

would·n't (wud′nt), would not.

wran·gler (rang′glər), (in the western United States and Canada) person in charge of herding horses or cattle. *n., pl.* **wran·glers.**

wrap (rap), cover with paper and tie up or fasten: *Have you wrapped your presents yet? v.,* **wrapped, wrap·ping.**

wreck (rek), destruction of a motor vehicle, ship, building, train, or aircraft: *The hurricane caused many wrecks. Reckless driving causes many wrecks. n.*

wres·tling (res′ling), sport or contest in which two opponents try to throw or force each other to the ground. The rules for wrestling do not allow using the fists or certain holds on the body. *n.*

wrist·watch (rist′wăch′ or rist′wŏch′), a small watch worn on the wrist. *n., pl.* **wrist·watch·es.**

write (rīt), make letters or words with pen, pencil, or chalk. *v.,* **wrote, writ·ten** (rit′n), **writ·ing.**

Y

yard (yärd), unit of length equal to 36 inches; 3 feet. *n.*

you're (yur; *unstressed* yər), you are.

you've (yüv; *unstressed* yuv), you have.

Z

zo·ol·o·gist (zō ol′ə jist), an expert in the study of animals. *n.*

Writer's Thesaurus

Introduction

Many of your spelling words have synonyms, words with similar meanings. This thesaurus lists those spelling words alphabetically, defines them, and provides synonyms. For many words, you can also look up antonyms, words with opposite meanings. This thesaurus can even introduce you to new words.

Understand a Thesaurus Entry

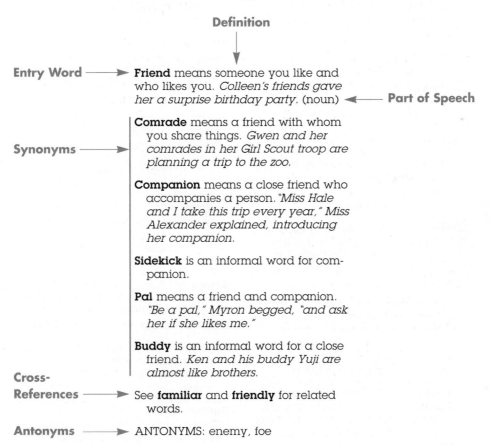

Definition

Entry Word → **Friend** means someone you like and who likes you. *Colleen's friends gave her a surprise birthday party.* (noun) ← **Part of Speech**

Synonyms → **Comrade** means a friend with whom you share things. *Gwen and her comrades in her Girl Scout troop are planning a trip to the zoo.*

Companion means a close friend who accompanies a person. *"Miss Hale and I take this trip every year," Miss Alexander explained, introducing her companion.*

Sidekick is an informal word for companion.

Pal means a friend and companion. *"Be a pal," Myron begged, "and ask her if she likes me."*

Buddy is an informal word for a close friend. *Ken and his buddy Yuji are almost like brothers.*

Cross-References → See **familiar** and **friendly** for related words.

Antonyms → ANTONYMS: enemy, foe

A a

Accompany means to go along with someone or something. *Lightning and thunder often accompany heavy rain.* (verb)

Attend can mean to go along with someone in order to assist. *Attended by two secretaries, the head of the company arrived at the meeting.*

Escort means to go along with someone on official business, or as someone's date. *The President is escorted by Secret Service agents.*

Chaperon means to go along with and supervise young people. *Four parents and two teachers will chaperon the seventh-grade dance.*

Adapt means to change something or someone so as to suit a need. *Bill had to adapt to sharing his room when baby Albert was born.* (verb)

Adjust means to change something to a better position or fit. *You can adjust the seat of the car if you are cramped.*

Accommodate can mean to adapt. *The Chens accommodated to their new country quite quickly.*

Conform means to act so as to suit rules or standards. *I don't want to be friends with Becky if that means conforming to her ideas of how to dress.*

Admit means to make something known or say that something is true, especially when you don't really want to. *I have to admit your costume is funnier than mine.* (verb)

Acknowledge means almost the same as admit, but is used especially about information that has been kept back until then. *Tiffany acknowledges that she borrowed your book and forgot to tell you.*

Confess means to admit something bad that you have done. *Larry confessed to his aunt that he fell asleep when he should have been cleaning the basement.*

Own up to is an idiom meaning to confess. *Blair owned up to having started the argument.*

Get something off your chest is an idiom meaning to confess completely. *Let me get the whole story off my chest.*

Make a clean breast of is an idiom meaning to confess completely. *Rod made a clean breast of his part in the practical joke.*

ANTONYM: deny

Amount means the figure you get when you add up all the things that you are measuring or counting. *Sherry was surprised at the amount of the grocery bill.* (noun)

Quantity means an amount. *The fruit punch contains only a small quantity of sugar.*

Number means the figure you get when you count a group of people or things. *The number of goats in Saada's father's herd grew by twelve that spring.*

Answer means to say or write something in response to a question or request. *Ernesto is the only one who answered the fourth question correctly.* (verb)

Reply means to answer. It is a somewhat more formal word and may suggest thoroughness and thoughtfulness. *The store manager replied to Aunt Delva's complaint with a careful and detailed explanation.*

Respond means to answer by words or by actions. *The students responded to the news of the hurricane by collecting money for the victims.*

Argue means to disagree strongly and give reasons for your opinion. *Sandy argued with the umpire who called her out at second base.* (verb)

Dispute can mean to argue loudly or at length. *The neighbors are disputing about how late it's OK to play music.*

Quarrel means to dispute angrily. *We heard Dave and Chuck quarrel and then saw them wrestle on the ground.*

ANTONYM: agree

WATCH IT !

Amount can mean how many or how much. **Number** means only how many. You can speak of an amount of milk or an amount of beans, but you wouldn't speak of a number of milk.

Less means how much. **Fewer** means how many. How much milk? Less. How many beans? Fewer.

People are often careless in the way they use *less* and *fewer.* If you see an advertisement for a food with less calories, the writer was careless. Think how strange it would sound the other way— if the ad said, "Fewer Fat!"

B b

Beautiful means very pleasing to the senses or the mind. *These beautiful rugs were made by hand in Turkey 100 years ago, but they still look almost like new.* (adjective)

Pretty means pleasing to see or hear. It is often used to describe girls and women. *Mariko looks really pretty in that hat.*

Handsome means pleasing to see. It is often used instead of beautiful or pretty to describe a man or boy. *Candace thinks Mr. Walking Bear, the science teacher, is awfully handsome.*

Good-looking means handsome or pretty. *My mother always tells my father how good-looking he is because she knows it makes him feel good.*

ANTONYMS: ugly, unattractive

Because means for the reason mentioned. *Lyle is late tonight, because he missed the bus.* (conjunction)

Since can mean because. It is used when the cause is explained before the effect. *Since Lyle missed the bus, he is late tonight.*

For means because. This meaning is used mostly in writing. *The people rejoice tonight, for the long war has ended.*

So means with the effect mentioned, or for the purpose mentioned. *Tawana washed the dishes, so you don't have to.*

As a result means with the effect mentioned. *Mickey went around the corner too fast, and as a result the bike skidded.*

Belief means an idea that someone holds to be true. *It is Joanna's belief that Willard sent her that valentine.* (noun)

Trust means belief that someone or something will do what is expected. It suggests expecting good things. *"And this be our motto," wrote Francis Scott Key, "'In God is our trust.'"*

Confidence means trust. It suggests sureness based on experience. *Mr. Anagnos has such confidence in Peter that he lets him help the mechanics work on cars.*

Faith means a very strong, unquestioning belief. *Rev. Martin Luther King, Jr., spoke of his faith in freedom and justice.*

ANTONYMS: disbelief, doubt, mistrust

Big means more than the usual size, number, or amount. *Since Ramona is big for her age, she can wear her mother's old coat.* (adjective)

Large means big. It often describes the extent or amount of something. *Will the auditorium be large enough for the championship rally?*

Great means large and out of the ordinary. *Great crowds came out for the parade welcoming the soldiers home.*

Sizable means fairly big. It is a somewhat formal word, often used for understatement. *This fossil shark had sizable jaws.*

ANTONYMS: little, small, tiny

This fossil shark had **sizable** jaws.

C c

Careful means paying close attention to what you say and do. *I feel safe in the car with Mrs. Gomez, who is a very careful driver.* (adjective)

Cautious means careful to avoid danger. *Pia has been very cautious about riding her bike in the street after seeing the bike safety movie.*

Wary means very careful and expecting danger. *Mice have to be wary of cats and owls.*

ANTONYMS: careless, negligent, thoughtless

Celebrate means to note a special day with proper activities. *Mexicans proudly celebrate their independence with two days of colorful fiestas.* (verb)

Commemorate means to show respect for a memory, often on a special day. *In January, the United States commemorates the birth of Rev. Martin Luther King, Jr.*

Honor can mean to show respect, often at a particular time. *At this morning's ceremony, the city will honor those firefighters who have died in the line of duty.*

ANTONYM: ignore

Choose means to decide to do or take something. *Nestor chose to give his report on the life of Manuel Quezon y Molina, first president of the Philippine Commonwealth.* (verb)

Pick means to choose from many things just what you want. *Robin picked the gray kitten because it was the liveliest of the four.*

Select means to choose from many things after thinking carefully. *"We're only going to rent one movie, Deke, so be sure about the one you select," his mother advised.*

SEE **decide** for related words.

ANTONYM: reject

Clothes means covering for a person's body. *Miguel has grown so much he needs new clothes.* (noun)

Clothing means clothes. It is a slightly more formal word. *That store sells both women's and men's clothing.*

Outfit can mean clothes that go together. *Mom has a plaid skirt and a red blouse that she wears as an outfit with her velvet blazer.*

Uniform means the clothes worn by some special group while at work. *When Aunt Phyllis goes to her Army Reserve training, she looks strong and proud in her uniform.*

Comfortable means giving or feeling comfort and pleasure. *Andrew wants to keep his old sneakers because they're so comfortable.* (adjective)

Comfy is an informal word meaning comfortable. *Doesn't Buster look comfy, curled up in the sunlight?*

Relaxing means giving peace and comfort. *After driving her bus all day, Mom likes to spend a relaxing half hour with the paper before starting dinner.*

Cozy means comfortable, warm, and giving or feeling friendly happiness. *Half asleep in the cozy tepee, Two Baskets listened to the prairie wind howling.*

Complain means to say that something is not the way it should be, and that you are unhappy about it. *Mrs. Baylor complained to the landlord about the lack of heat in the apartment.* (verb)

Grumble means to complain in a growling, angry way. *The sailors grumbled about the food until the captain threatened not to give them any.*

Whine means to complain in a sad voice, especially about unimportant things. *My brother often whines about having to go to bed.*

Gripe is an informal word that can mean to complain in a continuous, annoying way. *Rob gripes about the hard work on his paper route, but he likes the money.*

Squawk is a slang word that means to complain loudly about something. *The umpire tried to calm the squawking manager.*

Kvetch is a Yiddish word meaning to complain steadily. *If Rasia found money, she'd kvetch about having to pick it up.*

Moan and groan means to complain bitterly. It suggests too much complaining. *Coach says no more moaning and groaning about early practice.*

Control means the ability to direct or guide people or events. *The governor announced that the forest fires are now under control.* (noun)

Power can mean control. *Marilynn has the power to make my day with one smile.*

Authority means control, often of a particular sort. *A police officer has the authority to arrest people.*

Command can mean a position of control. *The pilot is in command of the airplane during a flight.*

AROUND THE WORLD: CLOTHING

burnoose (North Africa and the Middle East)

caftan (Turkey and Egypt)

cheongsam (China)

dashiki (Africa)

kilt (Scotland)

kimono (Japan)

muu-muu (Hawaii)

parka (Alaska, NE Asia)

poncho (South America)

sari (India)

sarong (Malaysia)

serape (Mexico)

Create means to bring something into being. *The Johnsons created a study area for their children by putting a large table and some bookshelves in one corner of the dining room.* (verb)

Invent means to think up something completely new and bring it into being. *Thomas Edison invented the phonograph in 1877.*

Originate means to start new ideas or methods. *The ancient Greeks originated the concept of democracy.*

Think up means to have an idea. *Tom thought up a great way to raise money for our school club.*

Crime means an act that breaks a law. *Why are television shows so full of crimes?* (noun)

Offense means an act that breaks a law, or an act that many people think is bad. *Driving a car with a broken rear light is a minor offense, so the police officer wrote a warning ticket.*

Wrong can mean an offense. *I think Peter has done me a wrong, but he refuses to apologize.*

Sin means an act that breaks a religious law. *The Ten Commandments forbid sins such as killing, stealing, and lying.*

Cute means pleasing or good-looking. It is a general word used to show liking and approval. *The kittens were all so cute I had a hard time deciding which one I wanted.* (adjective)

Attractive means interesting and pleasing to look at. *Benito's apartment is very attractive.*

Amusing means pleasantly entertaining and interesting. *I like spending time with Chantal because she is amusing.*

Adorable can mean very attractive. This meaning is informal. *Wet, my terrier looks like a drowned rat; dry, she's adorable.*

SEE **beautiful** for related words.

D d

Dangerous means likely to cause injury or harm. *Yelling insults at a superhero is a dangerous thing for a movie villain to do.* (adjective)

Unsafe means dangerous. *Bilal could see that the leaky boat was unsafe.*

Risky means involving a chance of injury or harm. *Sarah doesn't ride her bike after dark because it's risky.*

Precarious means with a chance of danger at any time. *The mountain goat stands in a precarious position at the edge of a cliff.*

ANTONYMS: harmless, safe

The mountain goat stands in a **precarious** position at the edge of a cliff.

Decide means to make up your mind. *It was such a hot day that we decided to go to the city swimming pool.* (verb)

Determine means to decide firmly, often from several choices. *Jolene is still trying to determine which hairdo looks best on her.*

Settle means to decide finally. *Bella thinks Sally should settle on a ponytail.*

SEE **choose** for related words.

The buffalo stampede **destroyed** the cornfield.

Destroy means to put an end to something, often by breaking or pulling it to pieces. *The buffalo stampede destroyed the cornfield.* (verb)

Demolish means to smash to pieces. *An earthquake can demolish buildings.*

Wreck means to break something so completely that it cannot be fixed. *During last night's storm, lightning wrecked the gas station sign.*

Ruin means to make something worthless or useless. *If Paul doesn't stop sliding around in the dirt like that, he's going to ruin his jeans.*

ANTONYMS: create, make

Different means not alike. *Edgar and Edwin try hard to be different, because they don't want to be known as "the twins."* (adjective)

Various means different. It is used when there are many different things. *Every morning, Babur opens his family's shop and sets out the thirty baskets of various spices.*

Diverse means varied. *Sue reads books on many diverse subjects.*

Assorted means mixed. *I always choose assorted jellybean flavors because I can never decide on just one flavor.*

ANTONYMS: alike, identical, same, similar

Disappoint means not to keep a promise to someone. *Curtis promised to play with his sisters and won't disappoint them.* (verb)

Fail can mean to be of no use when needed. *The flashlight failed because the batteries were too old.*

Betray can mean to hurt someone who trusts you, on purpose. *When Babette heard what Alyx had said about her, she felt betrayed.*

Let down can mean to disappoint or hurt the feelings of someone who trusts you. *We were very hopeful that this drug would stop the fungus, but it has let us down.*

E e

Embarrassed means uneasy, self-conscious, and insecure. *Midge was terribly embarrassed when Jeff told everyone at the party that she didn't want to be there.* (adjective)

Flustered means confused and nervous. *Boos from the fans got the pitcher flustered, and he walked the next two batters.*

Disconcerted means flustered. It is a formal word. *Disconcerted by criticism in the newspapers, the opera singer canceled the rest of his performances.*

Discombobulated is an informal word that means completely confused, nervous, and upset. *When the famous movie star winked at the coatroom attendant, the attendant got so discombobulated that she gave him the wrong coat.*

Especially means more than others or in a special way. *Luis likes to eat fruit, especially papaya. Mary Ann was especially glad to see Philip, since he had been away all summer.* (adverb)

Particularly means especially. *"I hate getting out of bed," Minh yawned, "particularly on dark, rainy days like this."*

Specifically means with attention to a single item or detail. *Isabel wants to be a nurse, specifically to help old people.*

Examine means to look at something carefully in order to find out about it. *The dentist will examine Sari's teeth for cavities.* (verb)

Inspect means to examine something, especially officially. *The immigration officer inspected the Miklos family's papers, and then welcomed them to the United States of America.*

Study can mean to examine thoroughly. *Gregory studied the bus schedule again, wondering if his grandmother had missed a connection somewhere.*

Check can mean to look at something in order to see if it is all right. *Kay needs a ride tomorrow because her mom has to have their car's brakes checked.*

F f

Famous means well-known and interesting to many people. *Marlene likes to read biographies of famous entertainers.* (adjective)

Noted means well-known, especially for a particular skill or accomplishment. *Marie Curie was a noted scientist who won two Nobel prizes.*

Celebrated means well-known and popular. *Jamal's mother is the dentist of celebrated TV star Lance Dawson.*

Notorious means famous for doing something bad. *Lake Silverset is notorious for its mosquitoes.*

ANTONYMS: obscure, unknown

Flexible means bending easily without breaking. *Why is toast so much less flexible than bread?* (adjective)

Elastic means able to bend or stretch easily and then return to its original shape. *These casual slacks feature roomy pleats and a comfortable elastic waistband.*

Resilient means springy. *The Nortons want to buy a firm, resilient mattress for Carol's bed.*

ANTONYMS: inflexible, rigid, stiff

Follow means to move in the same direction as someone or something. *The wolves follow the caribou, hoping to catch one.* (verb)

Chase means to follow fast and try to catch. *The Shermans' dog is locked in their yard because otherwise she chases cars.*

Pursue means to chase. It is a formal word. *Detective Garcia is now pursuing the car used in the robbery.*

Shadow can mean to follow closely and secretly. *The crooks shadowed the bank messenger, but he noticed them and got away.*

Tail means to follow closely and secretly. *If we tail the spy to her hideout, we may learn how she gets information.*

Tag along means to follow closely and constantly. It suggests that the follower is unwanted. *My sister has her own friends now, and she doesn't tag along after me anymore.*

Free means to let out of prison, slavery, or any kind of burden. *Three students helped Ms. Wyandotte free her car after the snowplow covered it with snow.* (verb)

Release can mean to free. *The net opened to release the dolphins.*

Liberate means to free. It is often used about public events. *In 1991, Kuwait was liberated from Iraqi rule after months of war.*

Emancipate is a formal word that means to free. *In 1861, millions of people in Russia became free when Czar Alexander II emancipated the serfs.*

Turn loose means to free. It suggests letting go from a leash, a cage, or something like them. *"Play time,"* Hilda said, pushing open the gate and turning loose the excited colt.

ANTONYM: imprison

Friend means someone you like and who likes you. *Colleen's friends gave her a surprise birthday party.* (noun)

Companion means a close friend who accompanies a person. *"Miss Hale and I take this trip every year,"* Miss Alexander explained, introducing her companion.

Pal means a friend and companion. *"Be a pal,"* Myron begged, *"and ask her if she likes me."*

Buddy is an informal word that means a close friend. *Ken and his buddy Yuji are almost like brothers.*

Amigo means a close friend who understands you well. *"Let's go, amigo,"* said David, grabbing his skateboard and Damian's arm.

ANTONYMS: enemy, foe

AROUND THE WORLD: FRIENDSHIP

A friend in need is a friend indeed.
— **English proverb**

A good friend is revealed on a bad day.
— **Turkish proverb**

On the day of poverty you know who is a true friend.
— **Ghanaian proverb**

He who helps you in need is a true friend.
— **Swahili proverb** (East Africa)

Know a friend when you are in trouble.
— **Tamil proverb** (India)

G g

General means for everyone or everything. *A G-rated movie is suitable for a general audience.* (adjective)

Universal means general. It emphasizes how widely something exists or happens. *There was universal relief when the Civil War finally ended.*

Global can mean universal. *The astronauts' plight was a matter of global concern.*

Public means for all the people. *The public schools get their money from taxes.*

Widespread can mean existing in many places, among many people. *In our neighborhood there is widespread interest in lowering taxes.*

Get means to have something that you did not have before. *Linc gets a letter every week from his father, who works overseas.* (verb)

Obtain means to get something by an effort. *After weeks of practice, Rita obtained her driver's license on the first try.*

Acquire means to get and own, usually after much effort. *After years of hard work and saving, the Loneros were finally able to acquire their own home.*

Receive means to get something that has been given or sent or handed to you. *Harold received a black eye in the fight.*

Earn means to get something by working for it. *Wendy earns her allowance by taking out the garbage every day.*

Gain can mean to get something worth having. *"Now Jackson gains control of the basketball and races down the court!" the sportscaster cried.*

Guard means to keep someone or something safe. *Secret Service agents guard the President at all times.* (verb)

Defend means to guard, especially from an attack. *Ute warriors gathered to defend their village against the Navajo.*

Protect means to guard, especially from danger. *Jorge wears goggles while welding in order to protect his eyes.*

H h

Happen means to take place. *"What happened at school today?" asked Sam's mother.* (verb)

Chance means to happen for no clear reason. *Janos chanced to run into an old friend at the mall.*

Occur means to happen. It is used mostly about specific events. *The 1989 San Francisco earthquake occurred during the World Series.*

Healthy means in good condition of body and mind and free of disease. *Children who don't get enough to eat are never really healthy.* (adjective)

Well can mean healthy, especially when someone has been sick or might be. *Mom goes to work even if she doesn't feel well.*

Fit can mean healthy and strong. *After his operation, Jarel exercised carefully until he was fit again.*

Robust means healthy, strong, and full of energy. *Only someone as robust as Maria could be both in dance club and on the track team.*

Sound means perfectly healthy. *Since Mr. Carberry quit smoking twenty-five years ago, his lungs are now completely sound.*

In the pink is an idiom that means sound. *Rover had worms last month, but he's in the pink now.*

SEE **strong** for related words.

ANTONYMS: ill, sick, unhealthy

Humor means the quality of being funny. *"I fail to see the humor in your silly pranks, George," said Mr. Johnson.* (noun)

Wit can mean humor that is clever and full of ideas. *"Your paper is full of wit, Rosalie, but the organization still needs work," said Ms. Rivera.*

Comedy can mean the humor of something that happens. *We laughed when Ted dropped his jacket in a puddle, but he just couldn't see the comedy in it.*

Sarcasm can mean unfriendly humor that comes from saying or writing the opposite of what is really meant. *You know, Bryce's sarcasm isn't really funny.*

AROUND THE WORLD: HEALTH

To a healthy person, everything seems healthy.
— **Russian proverb**

Health is better than wealth.
— **English proverb**

He who has health has hope, and he who has hope has everything.
— **Arabic proverb**

I i

Imagine means to form a mental picture of something. *Lying on her bunk, Corporal D'Annunzio imagined the parade she'd get for coming home a hero.* (verb)

Visualize means to imagine. *"Visualize a cabin in the woods," said Dr. Wright to his audience, "a gathering darkness, heavy rain."*

Envision means to imagine. *Louise envisioned herself wearing high heels and falling flat on her face.*

Picture can mean to imagine. *Here in the cold, it is hard to picture Grandma and Uncle Tomás in the hot sunshine.*

SEE **pretend** for related words.

Information means things that are known. *"I need more information," Alfred said to the salesman, "about your replacement parts and the guarantee."* (noun)

Data means recorded facts, often technical or scientific. *For her report on regional weather over the past year, Julia got data from the National Weather Service.*

News means information about recent events. *Cordelia has been homesick for a week, and she's eager for news from school.*

Word can mean news, usually of one event. *We received word this morning that Mrs. Czerny had her baby.*

Innocent means not guilty. *"Why do I get blamed for everything when I'm perfectly innocent?" Rona sighed to herself.* (adjective)

Blameless means not deserving any blame. *"James was nowhere near the fight," Adam defended his friend. "He's blameless, I assure you."*

Guiltless means innocent. It suggests feeling no guilt. *The bus driver insists she is guiltless of the accident.*

ANTONYM: guilty

J j

Joy means great happiness. *Let's all wish the newly married couple years of joy.* (noun)

Glee means lively joy. *Imagine Sasha's glee when he learned that the saddle was his to keep.*

Bliss means complete joy and satisfaction. *"This is bliss," Emma said, munching on a freshly picked peach.*

K k

Know means to have knowledge of something or someone. *Marina knows a beautiful spot in the state park.* (verb)

Realize means to understand that something is true. *Watching Mr. Brigano work in his garden, we never realized he was almost 90.*

Recognize can mean to realize. *Matt recognizes now that he was wrong to break up with Lewsha.*

Understand means to get the meaning of something. *After years of work, scientists are beginning to understand the writing carved on this stone by an ancient people.*

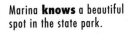

Marina **knows** a beautiful spot in the state park.

L l

Live means to have a home in a certain place. *After the fire, the Mendez family had to find a new house to live in.* (verb)

Dwell is a formal word that means to live. *People first began to dwell in cities more than 5,000 years ago.*

Reside is a formal word that means to live in one place over a period of time. *Only people who have resided in the city for at least six months may vote in local elections.*

Stay can mean to live somewhere for a while as a guest. *Marvella's cousins are staying with her right now.*

Lonely means feeling sad because of a need for company. *Dorothy was lonely in the new neighborhood until she met Patty.* (adjective)

Lonesome means feeling sad because of being alone. *When I get lonesome, I go to the playground.*

Forlorn means lonely and sad, usually because of being left behind. *Sampson the cat looked terribly forlorn when Faith left him behind.*

Loyal means always having the same good feelings for someone or something and always on the same side. *Ed isn't the best debater, but he's a loyal member of the team.* (adjective)

True can mean loyal. *Kwa-Mei promised her grandmother to be true to the ways of her ancestors.*

Faithful means loyal and always acting from loyalty. *Grandma Rose has been a faithful fan of the Dover Skylarks for forty years.*

Devoted means very loyal and faithful and giving all your time and strength to someone or something. *Rosemary and Blaine are really devoted to each other.*

ANTONYMS: disloyal, unfaithful

M m

Main means most important. *According to Mr. Boykin, the main problem with the car is the transmission.* (adjective)

Central can mean main. *The central library sends books to a branch library near our house.*

Major means more important than most others. *Houston is one of the major cities of the United States.*

ANTONYM: minor, subordinate

Measure means to find the size or amount of something. *When Yin measured her room, she found it was nine feet wide and ten feet long.*

Weigh means to find out how heavy something is. *Since Herb went on a diet, he weighs himself every morning.*

Survey can mean to measure land for its area, boundaries, and shape. *The Wilcox farm must be surveyed before it can be sold.*

Gauge means to measure. It is mostly used in discussing science. *We gauged the amount of rain that fell yesterday as half an inch.*

Mystery means something that has not been explained or cannot be completely understood. *Faith's absence was a mystery to her classmates until Jerrold called her house. The reason for the disappearance of the dinosaurs is still something of a mystery.* (noun)

Problem means a difficult question or a mystery. *On tonight's show, Lt. Singletary catches a killer dentist in "The Problem of the Poisoned Toothbrush."*

Puzzle means a challenging problem. *Many people find it a real puzzle to set their VCR timers.*

WORDS AT PLAY

Alone in the house late at night
I had only a candle for light
But was doing my best to ignore
Shadows creeping like mice on the floor
And the wind outside howling like doom.
The clock struck; as its chime pierced the gloom,
I beheld, with a sway of the drape,
A most dreadful, mysterious shape!

"Ah, great heavens," I cried, "what a fright!
My hands shake, and my hair's turning white!
Tell me how did you get here, and where
Did you come from, and must I beware?

Is this mystery meant just for me?
Who—or what—is this shape that I see?"

N n

Naughty means not behaving well or not being nice. *Christine charges extra to baby-sit with those naughty O'Toole kids.* (adjective)

Bad can mean not behaving well. *"Bad dog!" shouted Mr. Ortiz, but the puppy paid no attention.*

Mischievous means taking pleasure from behaving badly. *Some mischievous person put Rob's bicycle in a tree.*

Disorderly can mean making trouble. *The disorderly group was put out of the concert hall by the security guards.*

Rowdy means disorderly or quarrelsome. *The rowdy class quieted down fast when the principal walked through the door.*

ANTONYMS: good, obedient, well-behaved

Necessary means needed. *Iron, coal, and limestone are necessary to make steel.* (adjective)

Essential means completely necessary. *The keyboard is an essential part of a computer.*

Vital can mean essential. *Lt. Privac returned from her mission with the vital supplies.*

Required means necessary. It suggests that the need is a result of a decision or rule. *Lindsay did the four required book reports and one more for extra credit.*

ANTONYM: unnecessary

Noise means an unpleasant sound. *The noise of the jet engine made Gina cover her ears.* (noun)

Racket means a banging noise. *The plumber banging on the pipes downstairs made a terrible racket.*

Clatter means a loud noise of things knocking or banging together. *From the kitchen came a loud clatter of plates being put away quickly and carelessly.*

Commotion means a noisy, excited disturbance. It suggests disorderly sounds and movement. *"What's all the commotion about?" asked Officer Jimson, as he walked up to the people clustered on the sidewalk.*

ANTONYMS: quiet, silence

O o

Obstacle means something that stands in the way and prevents or delays action. *"Not knowing how to read," confessed Mr. Fitzroy, "has been the greatest obstacle of my life."* (noun)

Obstruction means an obstacle. *An obstruction in the pipe caused the sink to overflow.*

Barrier means an obstacle. It suggests something like a long high wall. *The new treaty removes most barriers to free trade between the two countries.*

Hindrance means something that prevents or delays action. It suggests holding back or standing in the way. *Experts fear that environmental problems may be a hindrance to the country's economic progress.*

SEE **prevent** and **stop** for related words.

Opponent means a person on the opposite side in a game, argument, or fight. *Pablo is my favorite opponent, because he's so good at the game.* (noun)

Antagonist means an opponent, especially an unfriendly one. *Captain Corcoran's antagonist in the struggle for control of the starship was a creature from Planet Omicron.*

Rival means an opponent who wants the same things as another person. *Kelly and Iona are rivals for a single opening on the softball team.*

Competitor means a rival. *The Kleen Again dry-cleaning store has survived three competitors on that block.*

ANTONYM: ally

Pablo is my favorite **opponent,** because he's so good at the game.

P p

Part means some piece or amount that is less than the whole. *Andrea gave me part of her doughnut.* (noun)

Portion means a part. It is often used about parts that are shared among several people. *Lori gave everyone a big portion of the tuna casserole.*

Section means a part, especially one that can be considered or handled by itself. *Chandu is reading the sports section of the newspaper.*

Share means the part that belongs to each person. *Charlotte has already eaten her share of the blueberries.*

Division can mean one of the parts into which a thing is divided. *Mark's mother works in the repairs division of the bus company.*

SEE **piece** for related words.

ANTONYM: whole

Person means a human being. *"I'm my own person; I don't have to do what you do," Samantha said to her twin sister.* (noun)

Human means a person. It is used when other living things are also being mentioned. *Kara, a chimpanzee, can speak in sign language to the humans in the lab.*

Individual means a person. *Our laws protect the rights of every individual.*

Fellow can mean a person. *"Poor fellow. He must not have known the forecast called for rain," said Mrs. Tilson sympathetically.*

Guy is an informal word that means fellow. *"Dad, tell that guy to move his car from our driveway," Mark whined.*

Piece means a small part of something larger, or one thing among others like it. *Della swept the pieces of the broken glass into a pile. The platter was the largest piece of china on the Serra's dinner table.* (noun)

Bit means a small piece of something larger. *Caroline tore the letter into bits.*

Particle means a very little bit. *Dust particles from the volcano make the sunsets very colorful.*

Pollute means to make something filthy and unfit for human use. It is used mostly about the environment. (verb) *The engines of buses, trucks, and cars pollute the air.*

Contaminate means to pollute, especially by contact with something unclean. *"Once a needle has been used, it's contaminated, so we use a new needle for every shot," the nurse explained.*

Poison can mean to put something dangerous to life into something else. *The chemical factory is poisoning the river with toxic wastes.*

ANTONYMS: cleanse, purify

Practice means doing something over and over in order to increase skill. *You can tell from Boris's juggling act how much practice he's had.* (noun)

Drill can mean training by doing something over and over in the same ways. *There will be fire drills every week until we get them right.*

Review means studying something again in order to be sure of knowing it. *The class will spend all next week on a review of decimals.*

Aunt Alma says the city air is so **polluted** that the birds should wear gas masks.

Rehearsal means practice of something that will be performed in public. *"Remember, tomorrow's rehearsal is at 4:30 in the concert hall!" said Mr. Umiker.*

Pretend means to make yourself seem to be doing something that you are not really doing. *Gerry knew that Grandpa was only pretending to be asleep.* (verb)

Make believe means to pretend to be someone or something else. *"OK, now we'll make believe I'm the movie star and you're the TV reporter," said Stephen.*

Act can mean to pretend you are feeling something when you really are not. *Jody is really stuck-up, even though she tries to act nice and friendly.*

Bluff means to try to fool someone by pretending you are confident. *Glinda is just bluffing when she claims that she's sure to make the team.*

SEE **imagine** for related words.

Prevent means to stop something from happening. *Brushing and flossing help to prevent cavities.* (verb)

Block means to stop the progress of someone or something. *Tina leaned out the car window, trying to see what was blocking traffic.*

Avert means to prevent something bad from happening. *By making a backup copy, Jo averted a disaster when her computer crashed.*

SEE **obstacle** and **stop** for related words.

ANTONYMS: allow, permit

Proud means pleased with yourself and with what you have done. *Congresswoman Martinez ended her victory speech by telling her election workers that they should all be proud of themselves.* (adjective)

Arrogant means haughty. *The arrogant general gave his soldiers no credit for the victory.*

Vain means conceited, especially about good looks. *"Well, if Miguel is vain, he's sure got good reasons," said Tom wistfully.*

Stuck-up is an informal word that means conceited and haughty. *Patricia is so stuck-up that she has no friends at all.*

ANTONYMS: humble, modest

R r

Repair means to put something that is broken or that doesn't work back into good condition. *"I've got to get this thing repaired," thought Colleen, when another tape jammed in her player.* (verb)

Fix can mean to repair. *"Lester, will you help me fix my bike seat?" asked his younger brother.*

Mend means to make something whole again that was torn, broken, or worn out. It is often used about things that have holes in them. *"There's a hole that needs mending in the west pasture fence," Joe reported to the ranch foreman.*

Rise means to get up or go up. *"All rise," said the court officer as the judge entered.* (verb)

Ascend means to go upward steadily. *"We are now ascending to an altitude of twenty thousand feet," the airplane captain announced.*

Lift can mean to go up slowly. *As the hot-air balloons lifted into the sky, their colors were beautiful against the clouds.*

ANTONYMS: descend, fall

S s

Share means to divide something into parts and give part to each person. *Ricardo and his brothers shared the peanut brittle.* (verb)

Portion means to share. *The counties agreed to portion water from the reservoir for their irrigation projects.*

Divide can mean to share. *After selling all the cans they had collected, Roy and Shirley divided the money.*

HAVE YOU HEARD...?

You may have heard people say, "If it's not broken, don't fix it." But you may also have heard people say, "A stitch in time saves nine." You can see that these proverbs say opposite things. There are many other contradictory sayings:

"Absence makes the heart grow fonder," but "Out of sight, out of mind."

"Haste makes waste," but "He who hesitates is lost."

"Many hands make light work," but "Too many cooks spoil the broth."

Can you think of any others?

Shrink means to become smaller or make smaller. *Luke's shirt shrank in the wash, but it still fits him.* (verb)

Miniaturize means to make something very much smaller. *A miniaturized radio in the wolf's collar tells naturalists where it is.*

Compress means to make something smaller by pressure. *A hay baler compresses alfalfa into bales and binds them with twine.*

ANTONYM: expand

Sign means an indication of something that will happen. *The first red and yellow leaves are a sign that summer is over.* (noun)

Indicator can mean a sign. *A sudden drop in air pressure may be an indicator of an approaching storm.*

Symptom means a sign, especially of illness or suffering. *Symptoms of neighborhood poverty include closed stores and empty buildings.*

Warning means something that tells of possible trouble or danger to come. *"Let that be a warning to you," Alejandro told the sobbing bully.*

Slide means to move along smoothly and easily on a surface. *Dad fixed my dresser, and now the drawers slide in and out properly.* (verb)

Skid means to slide sideways, out of control of where you are going. *The dog raced onto the wet floor and skidded helplessly across the room.*

Skate means to slide on wheels or blades. *Meera wears a helmet and kneepads whenever she goes skating.*

Slither means to slide along a surface with a twisting, wavelike motion. *The boa constrictor slithered down the tree limb.*

Stop means to keep from doing or happening. *Uncle Henry patched the roof to stop the rain from leaking in.* (verb)

Halt means to force to stop for a time. *The police halted traffic until the fallen tree was removed from the road.*

Cease means to stop something that has been going on for a while. *The two countries have ceased fighting, and peace is near.*

ANTONYMS: begin, continue, start

Strong means having great power or strength. *The strong man lifted a huge weight over his head.* (adjective)

Powerful means full of power and force. *The school's program to send books to Mozambique is the result of Ms. Masire's powerful speech about her country's needs.*

Sturdy means strong and solidly built. *This sturdy table will not wobble.*

ANTONYM: weak

The **strong** man lifted a huge weight over his head.

Subject means what something is about, as in a book, a picture, a talk, or a movie. *"The American Revolution will be the subject of today's discussion," announced Mr. Leffer.* (noun)

Theme means a subject. *"Fighting Pollution" was the theme of the science fair.*

Topic means the subject of a speech or piece of writing. It is often used when the subject is happening now. *The main topics of conversation at Gregg's party were music videos and the new gym teacher.*

Succeed means to do what you planned and hoped, with a good result. *The doctors succeeded in finding a cure for the disease.* (verb)

Prosper is a formal word that means to succeed for some time. It often suggests a gain in wealth. *Some computer manufacturers have prospered, but some have gone out of business.*

Thrive means to flourish, often for a particular reason. It may suggest overcoming difficulty. *Once he makes some friends, Ernie should thrive in his new school.*

Win means to gain victory in competition. *Derek Walcott of the West Indies won the Nobel prize for literature in 1992.*

ANTONYM: fail

Suggest means to offer an idea to someone. *"I suggest we vote on what movie to rent," said Margaret.* (verb)

Propose means to suggest an idea for someone to consider and then decide about. *Mr. Ortiz has proposed we take a lunch break and meet back here in an hour.*

Advise means to suggest an idea and say that it should be used. *It was supposed to rain that afternoon, so Aunt Lovella advised Tim to take an umbrella.*

Put forward can mean to propose an idea, usually publicly. *Hundreds of people have put forward names for the zoo's new baby hippopotamus.*

Sure means having no doubt. *Are you sure you turned out the lights?* (adjective)

Positive means sure, without any second thoughts. *Eric is positive that he had ten dollars when he started.*

Certain means sure, based on the facts. *After looking at the map, Donna was certain that she was heading in the wrong direction.*

Confident means sure, with a hopeful feeling. *Joaquín studied hard for the social studies test and is confident he did well on it.*

ANTONYMS: unsure, uncertain

T t

Terrible means very bad. *Cathy had a terrible scrape on her knee.* (adjective)

Awful can mean very bad or unpleasant. *There was an awful crash on the highway last night.*

Nasty can mean very unpleasant. *Sammy fell on the ice and got a nasty cut on his forehead.*

Horrible can mean very bad or foul. *The rotten fish left a horrible odor in the kitchen.*

ANTONYMS: excellent, great, wonderful

Then means following in time or place. *To get to the concert, Miles and Tyrone had to ride the subway first and then transfer to a bus.* (adverb)

Next means immediately following. *First Aunt Julia arrived; next Uncle Bill came; and finally Grandpa and Grandma showed up.*

Later means at a following time. It suggests that time has passed. *Later the detective realized that the suspects had been telling the truth all along.*

Afterwards means later. *Miguel and Luisa went to a movie, and afterwards they stopped for ice cream.*

Hundreds of people have **put forward** names for the zoo's new baby hippopotamus.

Blackbeard the **pirate** was a terror to sailors.

Thief means a person who steals, especially in secret. *Some thief got the radio out of Mr. Manilow's car.* (noun)

Robber means a person who steals by force. *Unlike most robbers, Robin Hood stole from the rich to give to the poor.*

Mugger means a person who assaults people in order to rob them. *A policewoman will speak at assembly on how to avoid muggers.*

Burglar means a person who breaks into a building in order to steal. *Mr. Gaston chased off the burglar who had broken into his house.*

Shoplifter means a person who steals from stores while pretending to be a customer. *"Shoplifters will be prosecuted," said the sign in the hobby shop.*

Pirate means a person who attacks ships at sea and steals from them. *Blackbeard the pirate was a terror to sailors.*

Thoughtful means careful of other people's feelings. *"How thoughtful!" said Angelique. "You brought my favorite flowers!"* (adjective)

Considerate means thoughtful. It suggests thinking of people's feelings without having to be told. *They tried to be considerate of the downstairs neighbors by walking quietly in the hallway.*

Sympathetic means thoughtful, kind, and able to understand how someone else feels. *When he saw my braces, Emilio showed his own in a sympathetic smile.*

Concerned can mean thoughtful and interested. It suggests some worry. *A concerned neighbor spotted the smoke and called the fire department in time.*

ANTONYMS: inconsiderate, thoughtless

V v

Valuable means worth very much. Something may be valuable because it costs a lot, or because people care a lot about it. *Even more valuable than the silver prize cup is the pride in his talent that Darnell has gained.* (adjective)

Precious means specially valuable. It is often used about things that people care about. *"These pictures are precious to me," Mr. Spencer told his class, "because I never saw my grandfather's face except in them."*

Priceless means too valuable for any price. *The little plane battled fierce storms to bring priceless medicine to the Arctic town.*

ANTONYMS: worthless

W w

Want means to feel an urge to have or do something. *Peter wants a pair of in-line skates for his birthday.* (verb)

Wish means to want or hope for something. *"If you wish to become a ballerina," Madame Claire told Ramona, "you must work as hard as you can."*

Have your heart set on means to want something and not be able to imagine not getting it. *Wanda has her heart set on playing in the marching band.*

Wealth means a very large amount of money or things. *Charmayne likes novels about people of wealth and power.* (noun)

Riches means wealth. *The lonely millionaire died and left his riches to his six cats.*

Money can mean wealth. *The da Silvas made their money in the pineapple business.*

ANTONYM: poverty

Whole means with all its parts and with nothing left out. *Adam watched the whole movie, but Bert left when it got scary.* (adjective)

Complete means whole. *Consuela gave complete instructions for making a piñata.*

Entire means whole. *Did Lucy and Calvin eat the entire batch of cookies?*

Full can mean whole. *Jimmy can't do the full set of exercises because of his sore elbow.*

Total means all added together. *The total bill was $81.16.*

The Word List in English and Spanish

A

abolish (CC)	abolir
accept (34)	aceptar
accident (9)	accidente
accidents (CC)	accidentes
accurate (14)	preciso
accuse (14)	acusar
acre (19)	acre
actually (13)	en realidad
acute triangle (CC)	triángulo acutángulo
adjust (1)	ajustar
admiration (28)	admiración
admit (CC)	admitir
adventure (9, CC)	aventura
adventurous (CC)	aventurero, aventurera
again (8)	otra vez
against (8)	contra
aghast (3)	horrizado, horrizada
agreeable (27)	agradable
agriculture (CC)	agricultura
ahead (8)	adelante
air pollution (CC)	contaminación del aire
Alabama (33)	Alabama
Alaska (33)	Alaska
aliens (10)	de otro planeta
all right (35)	bien
alligator (CC)	caimán
allowed (23)	permitirse (pasado)
a lot (7)	mucho
aloud (23)	en voz alta
already (8)	ya
always (7)	siempre
among (2)	entre
amount (20)	cantidad
amused (5)	entretener (pasado)
amusing (5)	entretenido, entretenida
Anasazi (CC)	Anasazi
and (9)	y
animals (CC)	animales
annoy (20)	molestar
another (32)	otro, otra
answer (13)	respuesta
antelope (10)	antílope
anything (16)	algo, alguna cosa
apartment (21)	apartamento
appear (22)	aparecer
appreciation (CC)	apreciación
approximate (CC)	aproximado, aproximada
argue (21)	discutir
Arizona (33)	Arizona
Arkansas (21)	Arkansas
army (21)	ejército
arrest (1)	arrestar
arrow (10)	flecha
assignment (CC)	tarea
athlete (7)	atleta
atom (CC)	átomo
atrium (CC)	atrio
attendance (CC)	asistencia
attraction (28)	atracción
audience (CC)	público
available (CC)	disponible
aware (22)	consciente

B

baby-sit (CC)	cuidar niños
backbone (CC)	columna vertebral
balance (31)	equilibrio
Baltimore (33)	Baltimore
banjos (17)	banjos
bar graph (CC)	gráfica de barras
bargain (32)	pacto; ganga
batteries (4, CC)	pilas
beard (22)	barba
beautiful (19)	bello, bella
because (9)	porque
before (9)	antes
beliefs (17)	creencias
believe (8)	creer
belong (9)	pertenecer
benches (4)	bancos
beware (22)	tener cuidado con
bigger (5)	más grande
biggest (5)	el más grande, la más grande
blank (2)	en blanco
blindfold (35)	venda
blood (9)	sangre
board (23)	tabla

boast | contestant

boast (1)	jactarse
bomb (3)	bomba
bookshelf (35)	estante
booth (11)	puesto
bored (19, 23)	aburrido, aburrida
bounce (34)	saltar; hacer rebotar
bounds (34)	límites
bowling (10)	bolos
brain (10)	cerebro
brainstorm (CC)	tener un torrente de ideas
brakes (CC)	frenos
breath (25)	respiración
breathe (25)	respirar
breeze (8)	brisa
brisk (1)	fresco, fresca
broom (11)	escoba
buffalo (CC)	búfalo
built (19)	construir (pasado)
burglar (7)	ladrón
bushes (4)	arbustos
buy (23)	comprar
by (23)	por; al lado de

C

Cabinet (CC)	Consejo de ministros
cafeteria (CC)	cafetería
calendar (32)	calendario
California (31)	California
can't (15)	no poder
cancel (32)	cancelar
captain (32, CC)	capitán
car pools (CC)	grupo de personas viajando en un solo coche
car washing (CC)	lavando coches
caramel (13)	caramelo
career (22)	carrera
careful (CC)	cuidadoso, cuidadosa
carefully (CC)	cuidadosamente
caught (19)	atrapar (pasado)
celebrate (31)	celebrar
centimeter (CC)	centímetro
centuries (4)	siglos
cerebellum (CC)	cerebelo
cerebrum (CC)	cerebro
channel (32)	canal
character (14)	personaje
characters (CC)	personajes
cheery (22)	alegre

cheese (8)	queso
Cherokee (CC)	Cherokee
chief (8)	jefe
child's (29)	del niño
childish (CC)	infantil
children's (29)	de los niños
chimney (7)	chimenea
chipmunk (2)	ardilla listada
choice (20)	selección
choking (CC)	estrangulando
choose (11)	escoger
chord (14)	acorde
chorus (14)	coro
Christmas (3)	Navidad
circle graph (CC)	gráfica circular
circuit (CC)	circuito
civil (32)	civil
claim (10)	reclamar
classify (CC)	clasificar
cliffs (17)	precipicios
climate (CC)	clima
climber (3)	alpinista
cloth (25, CC)	tela
clothes (25)	ropa
clothing (2)	ropa
collect (CC)	juntar
comedians (CC)	comediantes
comedy (CC)	comedia
comfortable (27, CC)	cómodo, cómoda
common name (CC)	nombre común
commotion (CC)	disturbio
companies (4)	compañías
compare (CC)	comparar
comparing (CC)	comparando
complain (10)	quejarse
compromise (CC)	llegar a un acuerdo
computer (32)	computadora
conclusion (CC)	conclusión
conductor (CC)	conductor, conductora
Confederacy (CC)	Confederación
conferences (CC)	conferencias
confident (27)	seguro, segura
confidently (CC)	con confianza
conflict (CC)	conflicto
Congress (CC)	Congreso
conservation (CC)	conservación
constant (31)	constante
contestant (27)	concursante

control (CC)	control	destructive (CC)	destructivo, destructiva
conversation (28)	conversación	Detroit (33)	Detroit
convertible (27)	convertible	diaphragm (CC)	diafragma
corn (CC)	maíz	didn't (7)	no (pasado)
costumes (4)	disfraces	different (31)	diferente
couch (20)	sofá	diner (34)	comensal; restaurante barato
could've (15)	podía haber		
courage (21, CC)	valor	dinner (34)	cena
courageous (CC)	valiente	disability (CC)	desabilidad
course (CC)	curso	disappoint (26)	desilusionar
courtesy (21)	cortesía	disapprove (26)	desaprobar
cousin's (29)	del primo, de la prima	discover (CC)	descubrir
cousins' (29)	de los primos	discovered (26)	descubrir (pasado)
cowboys (4)	vaqueros	dismay (CC)	consternación
crawl (CC)	gatear	disobey (26)	desobedecer
create (25)	crear	disorder (26)	desorden
creature (25)	criatura	doctor's (29)	del doctor, de la doctora
crew (11, CC)	tripulación; equipo	doctors' (29)	de los doctores
crime (10)	crimen	doesn't (7)	no
crisp (1)	crujiente	don't (15)	no
crosswalk (CC)	cruce	donkeys (4)	burros
cuffs (17)	puños; vueltas	downtown (20)	centro
cupcake (35)	pastelillo	dream (25)	sueño
curl (21)	rizo	dreamt (25)	soñar (pasado)
current (CC)	corriente	dresses (4)	vestidos
curtain (32)	cortina	drew (11)	dibujar (pasado)
customary units (CC)	unidades de costumbre	droughts (CC)	sequías
cuter (5)	más lindo, más linda	drown (20)	ahogar
cutest (5)	el más lindo, la más linda	Duluth (33)	Duluth

D

Dad's (29)	de Papá
dairy (22)	lácteos; lechería
dam (CC)	dique
dangerous (28)	peligroso, peligrosa
data (CC)	datos
daughter (11)	hija
daylight (16)	luz del día
dear (22)	querido, querida
decided (9)	decidir (pasado)
declare (22)	declarar
decoration (28)	decoración
defiant (27)	desafiante
degree (8)	título; grado
dentist (13)	dentista
desert (34)	desierto
dessert (34)	postre
destroy (20)	destruir

E

each other (35)	uno a otro, una a otra
earlier (5)	más temprano
earliest (5)	lo más temprano
earthquake (16)	terremoto
easier (5)	más fácil
easiest (5)	lo más fácil
eaten (32)	comido
echoes (17)	ecos
education (28)	educación
either (32)	o
elect (25)	elegir
election (25)	elección
electricity (CC)	electricidad
electron (CC)	electrón
elements (CC)	elementos
elevation (CC)	elevación
elevator (31)	ascensor

English	Spanish
Emancipation Proclamation (CC)	Proclamación de emancipación
emergency (CC)	emergencia
emotional (CC)	emocional
endangered species (CC)	especies en peligro de extinción
energy (CC)	energía
enough (7)	suficiente
equipment (7)	equipo
escape plan (CC)	plan de escape
esophagus (CC)	esófago
especially (31)	especialmente
estimating (CC)	estimar
everybody (35)	todo el mundo
everyone (35)	todos, todas
everything (2)	todo
evil (32)	malo, mala
exact (7, CC)	exacto, exacta
examine (7)	examinar
except (34)	excepto
exceptional (CC)	excepcional
excited (5)	emocionado, emocionada
exciting (5)	emocionante
executive branch (CC)	rama ejecutiva
exhale (CC)	exhalar
exist (7)	existir
expedition (CC)	expedición
experience (CC)	experiencia
experiment (CC)	experimento
exploration (CC)	exploración

F

factories (CC)	fábricas
faithful (CC)	leal
famous (28)	famoso, famosa
fantasy (CC)	fantasía
fasten (3)	sujetar
favorite (10)	preferido, preferida
feet (CC)	pies
finally (31)	finalmente
finished (13)	terminar (pasado)
fireplace (16)	hogar
first aid (35)	primeros auxilios
fish (CC)	pez, peces
flexible (27)	flexible
flood (9)	inundación
followed (5)	seguir (pasado)
following (5)	siguiendo; después de

English	Spanish
fossil (32)	fósil
fossil fuels (CC)	combustibles fósiles
fountain (32)	fuente
freedom (CC)	libertad
frequency table (CC)	tabla de frecuencia
friend (19)	amigo, amiga
friend's (29)	del amigo, de la amiga
friends (4)	amigos
frightening (13)	espantoso, espantosa
front-end digits (CC)	dígitos delanteros
frontier (CC)	frontera
frozen (32)	congelado, congelada
furniture (21, CC)	muebles
fuses (CC)	fusibles
future (11)	futuro

G

garbage (21)	basura
general (14)	general
generator (CC)	generador
genus (CC)	género
geography (CC)	geografía
Georgia (14)	Georgia
getting (13)	recibiendo; tomando
ghost (3)	fantasma
gills (CC)	agallas
glassware (CC)	cristalería
gliding (CC)	deslizándose
globe (10)	globo
goalie (8)	portero
grabbed (13)	agarrar (pasado)
grades (4)	notas
grading (CC)	anotar
grains (CC)	granos
grandfather's (29)	del abuelo
grandmother's (29)	de la abuela
grandparent (35)	abuelo
grasp (1)	agarrar (pasado)
grocery (31)	comestibles
growl (20)	gruñir
guard (19)	guardia
guitar (21)	guitarra

H

habitat (CC)	hábitat
haircut (16)	corte de pelo
Halloween (8)	Halloween
halves (17)	mitades
hamburger (21)	hamburguesa

handwriting (16)	escritura	**inflation** (28)	inflación
hanger (2)	gancho	**information** (28)	información
happened (13)	pasar (*pasado*)	**inhale** (CC)	inhalar
harmony (CC)	armonía	**innocent** (31)	inocente
Hawaii (33)	Hawaii	**instruction** (28)	instrucción
health (CC)	salud	**instruments** (CC)	instrumentos
heard (19)	oír (*pasado*)	**insulators** (CC)	insuladores
heavy (8)	pesado, pesada	**into** (16)	dentro de
helmet (CC)	casco	**invention** (CC)	invento
heritage (CC)	herencia	**invertebrates** (CC)	invertebrados, invertebradas
heroes (17)	héroes	**Iroquois** (CC)	iroquois
hexagon (CC)	hexágono	**it's** (23)	es
hideout (16)	escondite	**its** (23)	su, sus
high school (35)	secundaria		
hilariously (CC)	divertidísimamente	**J**	
hire (CC)	alquilar; contratar; emplear	**jealous** (8)	celoso, celosa
home run (35)	jonrón	**jellyfish** (CC)	medusa
homespun (CC)	casero, casera	**jewel** (11)	joya
hoofs (17)	pezuñas	**jewelry** (19)	joyas
horrible (19)	horrible	**journal** (21)	diario
horseback (16)	a caballo	**journey** (21)	jornada
hot dog (35)	perro caliente	**joyous** (28)	alegre
House of Representatives (CC)	Cámara de Representantes	**judge** (14)	juez
housework (16, CC)	quehaceres domésticos	**judicial branch** (CC)	rama judicial
Houston (33)	Houston	**jungle** (9)	selva
humor (11)	humor	**junior** (14)	estudiante en el tercer año del instituto de bachillerato
humorous (28, CC)	gracioso, graciosa		
hundred (19)	cien	**justices** (CC)	magistrados
hustle (3)	apresurar	**K**	
hydroelectric power (CC)	fuerza hidroeléctrica	**Kentucky** (33)	Kentucky
hypothesis (CC)	hipótesis	**kickstand** (16)	soporte
		kilometers (CC)	kilómetros
I		**kingdom** (CC)	reino
I'll (15)	yo + (*futuro*)	**kisses** (4)	besos
I'm (15)	soy, estoy	**knapsack** (3)	mochila
I've (15)	he	**knead** (3, 23)	amasar
Illinois (20)	Illinois	**knew** (3)	saber (*pasado*)
illustrations (CC)	ilustraciones	**knitting** (3)	tejiendo de punto
illustrator (CC)	ilustrador	**knock-knock-joke** (CC)	chiste de tan-tan
imagination (28)	imaginación	**know** (3)	saber
imagine (CC)	imaginar	**knowledge** (3)	conocimiento
in-line skates (CC)	patines de ruedas en línea	**L**	
inches (CC)	pulgadas	**label** (32)	etiqueta
incinerators (CC)	incineradores	**labor unions** (CC)	sindicatos
Indiana (33)	Indiana	**landfills** (CC)	basureros
indigo (CC)	índigo	**landforms** (CC)	accidentes geográficos
industries (CC)	industrias	**lariat** (CC)	lazo

ENGLISH/SPANISH WORD LIST

laughter | nourish

laughter (CC) — risa
launch (11) — lanzar
laundry (11) — ropa sucia
lawn mowing (CC) — cortando césped
leaves (17) — hojas
ledge (14) — antepecho
legend (14) — leyenda
legislative branch (CC) — rama legislativa
length (13) — largo
let's (15) — vamos a
library (13) — biblioteca
life span (CC) — duración de la vida
lighter (5) — más claro, más clara; más lijero, más lijera
lightest (5) — el más claro, la más clara; el más lijero, la más lijera
lightning (2) — relámpago
listening (3) — escuchar
Little Rock (33) — Little Rock
lives (17) — vidas
living room (35) — sala de estar
loaves (17) — barras
lobster (9) — langosta
lodge (14) — posada
lonely (19) — solo, sola
longhorn (CC) — ganado de longhorn
longhouse (CC) — casa comunal
Los Angeles (33) — Los Ángeles
loyal (20) — leal

M

machine (CC) — máquina
mailbox (16) — buzón
main (10, 23) — principal
majestic (CC) — majestuoso, majestuosa
major (14) — mayor
manager (31) — gerente
mane (23) — melena
mapmakers (CC) — cartógrafos, cartógrafas
marvelous (28) — maravilloso, maravillosa
mass production (CC) — producción en masa
matches (4) — fósforos
maybe (13) — quizás
meadow (8) — prado
measure (8) — medir
mechanic (14) — mecánico, mecánica
memories (CC) — recuerdos
Memphis (33) — Memphis
metals (CC) — metales

meter (CC) — metro
metric units (CC) — unidades métricas
Miami (33) — Miami
midnight (26) — medianoche
midstream (26) — medio del río
midway (26) — a medio camino
midweek (26) — a mitad de la semana
midyear (26) — a mitad del año
mileage (CC) — distancia en millas
miles (CC) — millas
millimeter (CC) — milímetro
minute (13) — minuto
miserable (CC) — desgraciado, desgraciada
missiles (4) — proyectiles
mistletoe (3) — muérdago
moist (25) — húmedo
moisten (25) — humedecer
molecule (CC) — molécula
mollusks (CC) — moluscos
Mom's (29) — de Mamá
months (4) — meses
mornings (4) — mañanas
museum (19) — museo
music (11) — música
mysterious (28) — misterioso, misteriosa
mystery (13) — misterio

N

natural resources (CC) — recursos naturales
naughty (11) — travieso, traviesa
navigation (CC) — navegación
nearby (16) — cerca
nearest (CC) — el más cerca, la más cerca
necklace (7) — collar
need (23) — necesitar
nervous (28) — nervioso, nerviosa
neutron (CC) — neutrón
no one (35) — nadie
noisy (20) — ruidoso, ruidosa
nomads (CC) — nómadas
nonmetals (CC) — no metales
nonrenewable resources (CC) — recursos no renovables
north (2) — norte
northern (19) — del norte
notebook (16) — cuaderno
nothing (2) — nada
nourish (21) — nutrir

316

English	Spanish
nowhere (35)	en ninguna parte
nuclear energy (CC)	energía nuclear
nucleus (CC)	núcleo
numb (3)	entumecido, entumecida
nurture (CC)	nutrir

O

obediently (CC)	obedientemente
observant (27)	observador, observadora
observations (CC)	observaciones
obtuse triangle (CC)	triángulo obtusángulo
occasion (14)	ocasión
occupant (27)	ocupante
occur (14)	ocurrir
octagon (CC)	octágono
of (34)	de
off (34)	de
one (7)	uno
opened (13)	abrir (pasado)
opponent (27)	adversario, adversaria
opportunities (CC)	oportunidades
opportunity (31)	oportunidad
orchestra (14)	orquesta
Oregon (33)	Oregon
organization (28)	organización
organize (CC)	organizar
our (20)	nuestro, nuestra
outside (20)	afuera
owner (10)	dueño, dueña
oxygen (CC)	oxígeno
oyster (20)	ostra

P

pads (CC)	rodilleras, codilleras
part (25)	parte
partial (25)	parcial
particular (32)	particular
passed (23)	pasar (pasado)
passes (4)	pasa; pases
past (9, 23)	pasado
patios (17)	patios
pavement (CC)	pavimento
peanut butter (35)	mantequilla de maní
pedestrian (CC)	peatón
pen pal (35)	corresponsal
pentagon (CC)	pentágono
people's (29)	de la gente
percentage (CC)	porcentaje
perhaps (9)	quizá
person's (29)	de una persona

English	Spanish
pet-sitter (CC)	persona que cuida mascotas
pianos (17)	pianos
pictures (4)	fotos
piece (8)	pieza
pierce (19)	perforar
pioneer (22)	pionero
Pittsburgh (33)	Pittsburgh
planet (34)	planeta
plant (34)	planta
pleasant (25)	agradable
please (25)	complacer
plumbing (3)	plomería
poison (20)	veneno
pollute (31)	contaminar
population (CC)	población
portfolios (CC)	portafolios
possession (CC)	posesión
possible (9)	posible
potatoes (17)	papas
powder (20)	polvo
practical (25)	práctico, práctica
practice (25)	práctica
prairie (22)	pradera
precipitation (CC)	precipitación
precook (26)	cocinar de antemano
prepaid (26)	pagado por adelantado
preparation (28)	preparación
prepare (22)	preparar
prerecorded (26)	grabado de antemano
preschool (26)	preescolar
president (31)	presidente
President (CC)	Presidente
pretend (9)	aparentar
pretest (26)	evaluación de antemano
prevent (CC)	prevenir
prisoner (31)	prisionero, prisionera
probably (31)	probablemente
problem (9, CC)	problema
project (CC)	proyecto
protection (CC)	protección
proton (CC)	protón
proud (CC)	orgulloso, orgullosa
provide (CC)	proveer
pueblo (CC)	pueblo
pumping (CC)	bombear
pumpkin (13)	calabaza
pun (CC)	juego de palabras

punch line | skinny

punch line (CC)	gracia		**roundups** (CC)	rodeos
purpose (21)	intención; propósito		**rumbling** (7)	ruido
purse (21)	bolsa			
python (9)	pitón		**S**	

Q

quadrilateral (CC)	cuadrilátero		**sacrifice** (CC)	sacrificar
quarrel (32)	riña		**saddle** (CC)	estribo
quarter (13)	moneda de 25 centavos		**said** (8)	decir *(pasado)*

R

raccoon (14)	mapache		**sailor** (CC)	marinero
radio (19)	radio		**sample** (CC)	muestra
radios (17)	radios		**sandwich** (13)	emparedado
railroads (CC)	vías de tren		**sausage** (11)	salchicha
raise (34)	alzar		**scar** (21)	cicatriz
rattlesnake (16)	serpiente de cascabel		**school** (11)	escuela
realize (31)	darse cuenta de		**scientific method** (CC)	método científico
really (31)	en realidad		**scientific name** (CC)	nombre científico
reasonable (27, CC)	razonable		**scoop** (11)	sacar; cucharón
reassuring (CC)	tranquilizador, tranquilizadora		**scrubbers** (CC)	depuradores
receive (19)	recibir		**secede** (CC)	separarse
record (CC)	registrar		**sectionalism** (CC)	seccionalismo
recycling (CC)	reciclar		**segment** (CC)	segmento
reference point (CC)	punto de referencia		**selection** (28)	selección
reindeer (22)	reno		**Senate** (CC)	Senado
rejection (28)	rechazo		**senses** (CC)	sentidos
renewable resources (CC)	recursos renovables		**sensible** (27)	sensato, sensata
repair (22)	reparar		**servant** (27)	sirviente, sirvienta
representatives (CC)	representantes		**setting** (CC)	escena
research (CC)	investigación		**settled** (CC)	colonizar *(pasado)*
resident (27)	residente		**sewage** (CC)	aguas cloacales
resource (CC)	recurso		**share** (22, CC)	compartir
responsible (27)	responsable		**she's** (15)	ella es, ella está
return (21)	regresar		**shipbuilding** (CC)	construcción de buque
reversible (27)	reversible		**should've** (15)	debía haber
rhythm (CC)	ritmo		**shriek** (19)	chillido
rice (CC)	arroz		**shrink** (2)	encoger
riddle (CC)	acertijo		**shuttle** (9)	servicio regular entre dos puntos
ridge (14)	cordillera			
right (23)	correcto, correcta		**sidewalk** (10)	pavimento
right triangle (CC)	triángulo rectángulo		**sign** (25)	letrero
rise (34)	levantarse; elevarse		**signature** (25)	firma
risk (1)	riesgo		**silverware** (CC)	vajilla de plata
road maps (CC)	mapas de carretera		**Sioux** (CC)	Sioux
roller skates (CC)	patines de ruedas		**siren** (32)	sirena
roofs (17)	techos		**sister's** (29)	de la hermana
rounding (CC)	redondear		**sisters'** (29)	de las hermanas
			skateboard (CC)	patineta
			skeleton (1)	esqueleto
			skillful (CC)	hábil
			skinny (1)	flaco, flaca

skunk (1)	zorrillo	survive (10)	sobrevivir
slavery (CC)	esclavitud	swung (9)	balancearse (*pasado*)
slide (10)	deslizarse; tobogán	symbol (CC)	símbolo
slope (10)	cuesta		
smear (22)	mancha	**T**	
smoke detectors (CC)	detectores de humo	talent (CC)	talento
snowball (10)	bola de nieve	task (1)	tarea
solar (32)	solar	taught (11)	enseñar (*pasado*)
solar energy (CC)	energía solar	temperature (CC)	temperatura
solid waste (CC)	desperdicios sólidos	tentacles (CC)	tentáculos
solve (9)	resolver	tepee (CC)	carpa de los indios norteamericanos
someone (35)	alguien		
something (16)	algo	terrible (31)	terrible
sometimes (16)	a veces	textbook (16, CC)	libro de texto
South Carolina (33)	Carolina del Sur	Thanksgiving (2)	Día de Acción de Gracias
spaghetti (3)	espaguettis		
spare (22)	prescindir de; de sobra	that's (15)	eso es, eso está
species (CC)	especies	their (19)	su, sus
speeches (4)	discursos	themselves (17)	ellos mismos, ellas mismas
spider (1)	araña		
spilled (1)	derramar (*pasado*)	then (2)	luego
spinach (1)	espinacas	theory (CC)	teoría
spoil (20)	echar a perder	there (2)	ahí, allí, allá
sponge (CC)	esponja	there's (15)	hay
stairway (22)	escalera	they (2)	ellos, ellas
starve (21)	morir de hambre	they're (15)	ellos son, ellos están
statue (1)	estatua	thief (8)	ladrón, ladrona
sting (2)	picadura	though (2)	aunque
stopped (1)	detenerse; parar (*pasado*)	thought (2)	pensar (*pasado*)
		threw (11, 23)	echar (*pasado*)
stranger (10)	desconocido, desconocida	through (23)	por; entre; a través de
		to (23)	a
strategy (CC)	estrategia	tobacco (CC)	tabaco
strike (CC)	hacer una huelga	today's (29)	de hoy
strong (2)	fuerte	tomatoes (17)	tomates
student (27)	estudiante	tomb (3)	tumba
students (CC)	estudiantes	too (23)	demasiado; también
stumble (1)	dar traspiés	tornadoes (17)	tornados
style (1)	estilo	towel (20)	toalla
subject (14)	tema	trachea (CC)	tráquea
succeed (8)	tener éxito	traditions (CC)	tradiciones
suggest (1)	sugerir	traits (CC)	rasgos, características
sunset (16)	puesta del sol	treasure (CC)	tesoro
supposed (31)	deber (*pasado*)	treatment plant (CC)	planta de tratamiento
Supreme Court (CC)	Corte Suprema	tried (5)	intentar (*pasado*)
surface (21)	superficie	trunk (2)	cajuela, baúl
surrender (CC)	rendirse	trying (5)	intentando
surround (20)	cercar	tumble (19)	dar volteretas; caerse
survey (CC)	encuesta	turbines (CC)	turbinas
		tutoring (CC)	dar clases privadas

TV | you've

TV (7)	televisión
typewriter (35)	máquina de escribir

U

unable (26)	incapaz
unbuckle (26)	desabrocharse
unclear (26)	poco claro
uncle's (29)	del tío
uncles' (29)	de los tíos
Union (CC)	Unión (sinónimo de Estados Unidos de América)
unlimited (26)	ilimitado, ilimitada
unsure (26)	inseguro, insegura
until (7)	hasta
upon (7)	sobre
urgent (27)	urgente
usually (11)	usualmente
Utah (11)	Utah

V

vacation (10)	vacación
valleys (4)	valles
valuable (27)	valioso, valiosa
ventricle (CC)	ventrículo
vertebrates (CC)	vertebrados
vertex (CC)	vértice
vertices (CC)	vértices
videos (17)	videos
Virginia (33)	Virginia
volleyball (16)	voleibol
volunteer (22)	ofrecer; voluntario, voluntaria
vow (CC)	promesa
voyage (20, CC)	viaje por mar

W

wages (CC)	salario
want (7)	querer
washable (27)	lavable

wasp (1)	avispa
watts (CC)	vatios
we're (15)	somos, estamos
we've (15)	hemos
weapon (8)	arma
weary (22)	agotado, agotada
weather (34)	tiempo
went (7)	ir (pasado)
were (34)	ser, estar (pasado)
weren't (15)	no ser, no estar (pasado)
whaling (CC)	caza de ballenas
what's (15)	qué es
when (13)	cuando
where (34)	dónde, donde
whether (34)	si
which (34)	cuál, que
whistling (3)	silbando
who's (15)	quien es, quien está
whole (10)	entero, entera
width (13)	anchura
windmills (CC)	molinos de viento
windpipe (CC)	tráquea
witch (34)	bruja
without (2)	sin
woman's (29)	de mujer
women's (29)	de mujeres
wouldn't (15)	no + (condicional)
wranglers (CC)	vaqueros
wrapped (5)	envolver (pasado)
wrapping (5)	envolviendo
wristwatch (35)	reloj de pulsera
write (23)	escribir

Y

yards (CC)	yardas
you're (15)	tú eres, tú estás; usted es, usted está
you've (15)	tú has, usted ha